DATE DUE

APR 0 7 2009			
FEB 2 0 2012			
			JN 1 0 2004

DEMCO 38-297

CALIFORNIA POETRY

FROM THE GOLD RUSH TO THE PRESENT

Edited by Dana Gioia,
Chryss Yost & Jack Hicks

SANTA CLARA UNIVERSITY, SANTA CLARA, CALIFORNIA
HEYDAY BOOKS, BERKELEY, CALIFORNIA

For more, visit www.californiapoetry.org.
This project is supported in part by an award from The James Irvine Foundation.

© 2004 by Dana Gioia, Chryss Yost, and Jack Hicks
Introduction © 2004 by Dana Gioia

Library of Congress Cataloging-in-Publication Data

California poetry : from the Gold Rush to the present / edited by Dana Gioia, Chryss Yost, and Jack Hicks.
    p. cm. – (A California legacy book)
Includes index.
  ISBN 1-890771-72-4 (pbk. : alk. paper)
  1. American poetry–California. 2. California–Poetry. I. Gioia, Dana. II. Yost, Chryss. III. Hicks, Jack, 1942- IV. Series.
  PS571.C2C236 2003
  811.008'09794–dc22
                                        2003018826

Cover and Interior Design: Philip Krayna Design, Berkeley, CA
Printing and Binding: McNaughton and Gunn, Saline, MI

Orders, inquiries, and correspondence should be addressed to:
    Heyday Books
    P.O. Box 9145, Berkeley, CA 94709
    (510) 549-3564, Fax (510) 549-1889
    www.heydaybooks.com

Printed in the United States of America

10 9 8 7 6 5 4 3 2 1

Contents

Acknowledgments

Creating the biographical and critical notes for *California Poetry* involved substantial original research. The editors could not have written the book's extensive critical apparatus without the assistance of the following people.

Richard Hughey was enormously generous in sharing his own extensive research on George Sterling and Nora May French. He also provided personal reminiscences of the late Lew Welch. John Hart gave us information and documentation on the Activists, a movement in which his father played a central role. David Mason wrote several of the biographies and critical notes, including the entries on Robert Hass, Gary Snyder, and Dana Gioia. Meg Schoerke provided essential parts of the notes on George Oppen, Robert Duncan, and Josephine Miles. Jan Goggans provided invaluable assistance in drafting more than twenty biographies in the last stages of this book.

Samuel Maio, Michael Dylan Welch, Christopher Buckley, Tara Penry, Jack Foley, Walter Martin, Suzanne Lummis, Jenny Factor, Sara Hodson, Terry Beers, Glenna Luschei, Marty Williams, Jackson Wheeler, Tony Magagna, Christian Kiefer, Leslie Liberato, and Jon Peede provided helpful research on various writers. Dan Stone assiduously fact-checked entries.

Chryss Yost would like to extend special personal thanks to Susan and Bill Glanz, Roger and Judy Anderson, Kristin Anderson, Joelle Dohrman, Dave Prine, and, most importantly, her daughter, Cassidy Yost.

Introduction
by Dana Gioia

I.

California Poetry is the first comprehensive historical anthology of the state's poetry from the Gold Rush to the present. Featuring 101 poets spanning over 150 years, this book attempts to present the finest poetry by California authors of all schools. Although longer poems have been omitted because of the limitations of space, the volume covers the full range of shorter forms—from lyric and satiric to narrative and prophetic—in every style from traditional to experimental. The book also tries to present the complex and often neglected history of California poetry by introducing each author with a biographical note, sometimes of substantial length.

Although there have been numerous anthologies of California poetry published over the last century, there has—rather astonishingly—never been a book that presented the full historical range of the state's enduring poetic achievement. The major California anthologies from *Continent's End* (1925) to *The Geography of Home* (1999) have instead tried mostly to provide a snapshot of the contemporary poets active and visible at the moment. With the exception of *The Geography of Home*, these anthologies have also rarely made distinctions between poets genuinely rooted in California and those merely passing through. In *19 New American Poets of the Golden Gate* (1984), for example, only five of the nineteen featured writers were actually born in California. While that fact did not affect the anthology's value as a collection of new American poets, it did limit its authority in describing the particular qualities of specifically Californian poetry. There have also been numerous general anthologies of California literature across all genres, such as *Many Californias: Literature from the Golden State* (1992) and the two-volume *Literature of California* (volume one, 2000), but their mandate of including fiction, memoir, nature writing, drama, and history, in addition to verse, has prevented them from providing an adequate representation of the development of poetry in the state.

Some earlier California poetry anthologies have also expressed a specific aesthetic vision, often presenting one school of poetry to the exclusion of all others. *Twelve Poets of the Pacific* (1937), for example, contained almost exclusively formal poets whereas *19 New American Poets of the Golden Gate* offered almost entirely poets working in free verse. There have been other books that represented the state's poetic affinities solely as Beat poetry, Language poetry, "Stand Up" poetry, political verse, or other specific schools. There have also been numerous collections featuring poets associated with a single city or region, such as Los Angeles, San Francisco, Fresno, Palo Alto, or the Central Valley. While each of these anthologies made interesting work available, they provided only a partial view of California's literary heritage and identity.

The primary criteria for inclusion in *California Poetry* have been literary excellence, historical importance, and representative range. Literary excellence may currently be an imperiled concept in some academic circles, but it remains an inescapable notion for any literary anthology that seeks to present poetry as an expressive art rather than a didactic medium. The editors of this book espouse no narrow definition of poetic excellence, but we do subscribe to the principle that every poem in the anthology should demonstrate imaginative force, vividly concise writing, and memorable language. We have worked to exclude dull poems on representative themes along with lifeless works that merely exemplify a particular school or style. While attempting to be broad and inclusive in our taste, the editors have also been determined to include no poem that at least one of us did not genuinely admire.

Many recent anthologies have been guided by a numbingly abstract sense of editorial obligation to include numerous selections with which the editors seem to have no authentic personal connection. Although such collections advertise their intellectual modernity, openness, and probity, such an editorial approach tends to have a dehumanizing effect, and the reader often feels that he or she is dealing with a faceless committee rather than actual people. Poetry must make a human connection, or else it loses its *raison d'etre*. "Reader, this is no book. Who touches this touches a man," wrote Walt Whitman, articulating the central impulse of the poet's art. Nowhere is this creative mandate more relevant than in the history of California poetry. To have compiled a volume based on received opinion or abstract theory would have undermined the very nature of our enterprise. Unless *California Poetry* presents real poetry, no other aspect of its mission matters.

Historical importance is also a meaningful concept because this anthology hopes to demonstrate the chronological development and imaginative interrelation of the diverse and often seemingly contradictory styles of English-language poetry practiced in California. This objective required an enormous amount of reading and research into the works of now little-known or forgotten writers. Which of their poems, if any, deserved revival? Some of the earlier poets had major reputations. Edwin Markham's "The Man with the Hoe" and Bret Harte's "The Society upon the Stanislaus," for example, once exercised considerable literary influence and enjoyed international popularity. There have been significant shifts in literary taste over the past 150 years that require an open and historically informed reading of pre-modernist California verse. However unfashionable by current standards, some of the old anthology favorites may remain vital and interesting. While this anthology includes no poem because it was once popular, it also excludes no good poem because it was famous. An informed, chronological survey of California poetry is in itself such a novel enterprise that there is no need to seek revisionism at the cost of historic insight and continuity.

Although *California Poetry* strives to represent the full variety of enduring work across all short verse forms and genres, it limits itself only to poetry in English written since California achieved statehood in 1850. This decision does not mean to diminish the importance of poetry by Californians written in other languages, but the editors lacked both the expertise and space to examine, evaluate, and present the best work from the state's rich American Indian literatures or the substantial Spanish, Japanese, Chinese, and other traditions. Several bilingual poets have been included, but only with work they have written in English. The monolingual focus of this volume, however, was not merely a result of the insufficient editorial expertise and publisher's proposed page-count; it was also an intellectual necessity for two central purposes of the anthology—to establish California's rightful place in the history of American poetry and to insist on the state's position as a significant and distinct region in English-language literature.

In pursuing these goals, *California Poetry* has not declined to make the many editorial judgments, large and small, necessary to a useful anthology. Major poets have been represented in greater depth than lesser figures, and authors have been showcased by what the editors considered their best work, even if that emphasis omitted other aspects of their careers. It would have been a silly and misplaced egalitarianism to feature as many poems by Charles Warren Stoddard as by Robinson Jeffers, though both writers deserve a place in the rolls of California literary history. Similarly, posterity has no compelling need to explore the serious verse of humorist Gelett Burgess. Our goal has been to provide the reader with an informed, balanced, and useful book. We also wanted to create a survey that was ample but not overwhelming.

Has some deserving poet been unjustly—if also unintentionally—omitted from his or her proper place in this book? Undoubtedly. Almost by definition, an anthology is a book that omits one's favorite poem. (And also a volume that canonizes poems one abhors.) Time will surely reveal worthy authors whom we have ignorantly excluded. In the meantime we encourage outraged readers to compile competing anthologies of their own. We welcome all serious rivals. California poetry deserves multiple studies. No one book will ever exhaust the richness of the subject.

While the anthology has no stylistic prerequisites for inclusion—except expressive power, verbal felicity, and poetic memorability—it does have a declared bias toward native Californians and long-standing residents versus literary tourists and temporary inhabitants. A good anthology could be compiled of poems about California written by visitors from other regions and countries, but *California Poetry* is not that book. Instead, it seeks to present the effect the state's unique geography, history, and culture have had on the poetic imagination of its natives and permanent inhabitants. For this reason, *California Poetry* includes only the work of poets who are either native-born and raised here or writers who have spent at least half their lives in the state. A few exceptions were made among the earliest authors, but otherwise the residency requirement has been rigorously applied. This criterion excludes many distinguished poets, like Mary Austin, Ernest Lawrence Thayer, Robert Frost, Randall Jarrell, Kenneth Patchen, Allen Ginsberg, Weldon Kees, Jack Gilbert, Barry Spacks, Adrienne Rich, Carolyn Kizer, Quincy Troupe, B. H. Fairchild, Mark Jarman, Carol Muske-Dukes, and Charles Harper Webb, all of whom have spent only portions of their lives in California. The editors have also excluded California-born poets who have left the state, like Michael Harper and Ron Silliman. The only exceptions have been made for two significant California-born poets, Lawson Fusao Inada and Robert McDowell, who currently live in Oregon's southernmost county, which was historically part of California and, in fact, has never formally seceded. This one bit of casuistry has allowed the inclusion of two influential figures in the state's recent literary history. Much good work has, therefore, been excluded, but our residency requirement helps focus the anthology on its main mission—to examine and present the achievements of poets with a lifelong relation to the state, its culture, climate, people, and landscape.

The editors fully understand how controversial their residency require-
ment will be, especially among the many living poets and their partisans.
The curatorial decision did not originate from any notion of literary qual-
ity. No alert and observant reader would consider Weldon Kees or
Carolyn Kizer inferior writers to their contemporaries included in the
book. Likewise the decision did not arise from thematic relevance. Allen
Ginsberg and Mark Jarman have both written brilliantly about California.
Rather the decision to limit the anthology to poets who had spent the
majority of their lives in California came from an experimental impulse
to investigate the nature of the state's impact on the artistic imagination.
How does the physical and cultural reality of California shape the poet's
mind and work differently from other regions of the English-speaking
world? There is no way to answer this question reliably except through a
rigorous appraisal of the work of the Golden State's best native writers.

II.

Over half a century ago poet Hildegarde Flanner complained that "tourist
fancy" colored the literature of California. "Aliens in a land toward which
it is impossible to remain indifferent," these poets either treated
California as a novelty or misconstrued their experience to fit familiar cat-
egories. Such intellectual tourism has not been limited to verse but has
also shaped much fiction, drama, and even criticism. One important rea-
son that the state's distinctive literary identity has not been well under-
stood is surely that critics and anthologists have too rarely distinguished
writing *about* California from writings *by* Californians. Such critical dis-
crimination has been no easy undertaking in a state famous for its immi-
grant population booms from the Gold Rush to the dot-com bubble.
Even as late as 1930 only one in five inhabitants of California was native
born. In such a fluent society what truly constitutes a native perspective?

Great books about California have been written by outsiders—full of
insight and imagination, though often mixed with fantasy and invective.
What reader would want American literature to lack *The Day of the
Locust, The Last Tycoon,* or *The Crying of Lot 49*? And who would wish
modern Anglo-Irish fiction without *The Loved One, After Many a
Summer Dies the Swan,* or *The Great Victorian Collection*? Yet despite
their indisputable brilliance, these books offer foreign views of the state.
Compare them to the novels of Jack London, John Steinbeck, or John
Fante—or Raymond Chandler, Ross Macdonald, or Ray Bradbury—and

one finds a radically different sense of both human society and the natural world. *The Galton Case* may not be a better novel than *The Loved One*, but, to a Californian, it seems a truer book about the Southland.

To their credit, some fiction critics have intelligently explored the discrepancies of treatment between outsiders like Waugh and West versus natives like Steinbeck and Fante. Books and essays on California writing by Joan Didion, David Fine, Gerald Haslam, Paul Skenazy, Scott Timberg, David Ulin, Walter Wells, and others have carefully documented the novelistic depictions of the state. California poetry, however, has never received the same careful and sustained scholarly attention, at least on this particular topic. Instead it has generally received bland oversight and uncritical boosterism. But to the informed and careful observer, the difficulty of imaginative assimilation has been a constant issue.

Even in 1925 the problem of creative integration was apparent to some western writers. In their trio of introductions to *Continent's End: An Anthology of Contemporary California Poets*, editors George Sterling, Genevieve Taggard, and James Rorty each puzzled over the singularity and elusiveness of their subject. "With the landscape before his eyes," declared Taggard, "the old formula declares the poet unable to function." The natural beauty and cultural dynamism of California, they asserted, overwhelmed the newly arrived poet, leaving what Rorty termed "a phase of bewilderment." In his classic study, *Southern California: An Island on the Land* (1946), Carey McWilliams also surveyed the reams of contemporary touristic verse and prophesied that it is "only after the new and strange have become an integral part of the poet's experience that he can express his feelings toward the land." A period of imaginative adjustment was required—at least until a native generation of poets emerged—though no one seemed quite sure how long that period would be. At the risk of seeming hasty, we suggest—eight decades later—that the waiting period is now over.

III.

This anthology rests on the simple but significant assumption that a distinct and memorable poetic tradition has emerged over the past 150 years in California as writers have struggled to assimilate the literary traditions of English with the "new and strange" reality of the Golden State. Encountering a natural world and cultural reality unlike anything in the traditions of English or American literature, poets had to adapt the language, imagery, modes, and methods of poetry to describe the experiences adequately. The book makes the further and perhaps more controversial assumption that California itself now constitutes a separate and distinct literary region—one that can only be genuinely understood by reading works written by authors whose imaginations have been shaped by the state's unique geography, history, and culture. These circumstances distinguish its writings not only from the traditional regions of American literature (New England, New York, the South, and the Midwest) but also from other parts of the West and Southwest.

What distinguishes the Californian literary sensibility from those of other regions in the English-speaking world? Perhaps the easiest way to establish the state's defining characteristics is to compare it to New England. The differences are both clear and profound. California's religious roots are Mediterranean Catholic, not Puritan Protestant. The old towns here are named Sacramento, Los Angeles, and San Diego, not New Haven, Canaan, and Concord. Asia lies across the ocean, not Europe—a geographic fact reflected in the different ethnic mixes of each region. For California, Latin America is the major neighboring foreign presence, not French Canada. The presence of Spanish is a constant transformative element in California poetry, which colors the regional language not only in place names like El Segundo, Sierra Nevada, La Mirada, and Palo Alto but in the vocabulary needed to describe the local world, like canyon, rancho, arroyo, mesa, and adobe. Not only is California's mostly arid landscape and weather distinct from New England but also the manners in which the states have been cultivated. From the compulsory collective utopias of the early Franciscans to the current agribusiness corporations, California has never been a place characterized by the small family farm. Dominated by large-scale agriculture and its harsh class distinctions between owners and laborers, it has never resembled the land of the Yankee freeholder.

The similarities between California and other areas of the West and Southwest are strong, but there remain enormous differences that have shaped the state in unique and ineradicable ways. As Theodore Roosevelt once remarked, "When I am in California, I am not in the west, I am west of the west." California was not settled by families moving overland from the East in orderly progression. It was originally populated in explosive bursts by young men of various races and nationalities arriving from the sea. The social, economic, and moral norms of small farm settlements enforced by pastor, wife, and mother did not prevail in thriving new seaports and mining towns. The rapid creation of colossal wealth in the Gold

Rush era and its aftermath created a population mix and social upheaval unprecedented in history—with adventurers, entrepreneurs, and opportunists, initially almost all male, arriving from Asia, Latin America, Europe, and the eastern United States. Out of the boisterous and anarchistic Forty-niner period came a culture enamored with sudden riches and risk-taking that later nourished industries like oil, motion pictures, rock music, aeronautics, electronics, biotechnology, water trading, venture capital, and the Internet. The social dynamism of the Gold Rush days and the economic inequities of the subsequent Robber Baron era (and the legal backlash) also fostered the radical, antiestablishmentarian populism that has characterized the state's political history. Innovation and experimentation, not stability and continuity, became California's governing traditions.

Despite its reputation for quick wealth and upward mobility, California has not been content with changing only social and economic systems. From the early Franciscans to present-day Buddhists, the state has also been obsessed with transforming humanity itself through various religious, political, and behavioral creeds. Los Angeles is not merely the mecca of popular entertainment. It was also the base for Aimee Semple McPherson, the first radio evangelist, and the Scientology movement of science fiction novelist L. Ron Hubbard. From anarchism, communism, and pacifism to nudism, vegetarianism, psychedelic drugs, and transcendental meditation, California has been at the center of modern social and spiritual experimentation. It has not only been modern America's cultural laboratory but the world's leading test market for utopian individualism.

California's regional character has also from the beginning been conspicuously international. Originally populated by diverse Indian tribes who spoke more than a hundred languages from many different families, the state was successfully colonized by the Spanish (and unsuccessfully by the Russians) before being annexed by the United States and repopulated by Yankees, South Americans, Germans, French, Irish, Italians, Basques, Poles, Finns, Chinese, Japanese, Pacific Islanders, African Americans, and—above all—Mexicans. Multiculturalism is not a late twentieth-century ideal in California. Since well before 1900, social diversity has been a constant, troublesome, explosive, enlivening, and transformative reality. Facing Asia and not Europe, adjacent to Mexico (which still governs Baja California), the state has never defined itself so much in comparison to the eastern United States as it has to the rest of the world. Multiculturalism has shaped the state's literary history. California's first significant English-language poet was John Rollin Ridge, also known as Yellow Bird, a Choctaw refugee from the Trail of Tears. California also welcomed Yone Noguchi, the first significant Asian American author. Such unorthodox literary careers were unlikely to have occurred in Boston or New York during the same era.

Significantly, California's internationalism has co-existed with a seemingly contradictory sense of isolationism. Cut off from the eastern United States by mountains and deserts, California has habitually seen its destiny as distinct in some mysterious way from the rest of America. This "curious combination of isolation and internationalism," to borrow a phrase from Carol Muske-Dukes, is deeply reflected in the sensibility of its major poets like Robinson Jeffers, Yvor Winters, Kenneth Rexroth, Robert Duncan, Josephine Miles, William Everson, and Thom Gunn. However radically they differ in style or aesthetic, they share a broad worldview, a common loyalty to the state, and a profound suspicion of nationalism in all of its forms.

The two cardinal mistakes literary critics habitually make about California literature are to define it as some monolithic entity (usually unified by a theme of cultural rebellion) and to discuss it with the Northeast, especially New York City, as its only frame of reference. No single quality characterizes all, or even most California writing, and there is more to the state's literary identity than its ongoing rivalry with Manhattan. Such simplistic analysis reduces California poetry to a mere regional response to some putative "mainstream" American poetry rather than seeing it as its own distinct imaginative enterprise. Although these critical clichés contain an element of truth, they omit essential elements needed to understand the nature of West Coast literary imagination. Half-truths do not provide an adequate intellectual foundation to analyze a distinct and original phenomenon.

There are many unifying features that characterize English-language California poetry, but none of them are stylistic or aesthetic. The defining elements depend more on an underlying worldview than any specifically literary allegiance. In general terms, California poets tend to have a genuine reverence for the natural landscape along with an anxiety, not always consciously articulated, about its Indian and Spanish past as well as its current human despoliation. California writers also tend to see themselves outside history and frequently look toward myth, religion, and philosophy to clarify their circumstances. Historically rooted poets like Robert Lowell, Robert Penn Warren, and Allen Tate are inconceivable in

California terms, just as mythic visionaries like Jeffers, Everson, or Duncan would be impossible figures in Boston, New York, or Nashville. In some sense California poets also see themselves in opposition — aesthetically or ideologically—to some imaginary official literary norm. This defiantly contrarian stance is what unifies the divergent styles of Jeffers, Winters, and Rexroth. Each deliberately wrote differently from his eastern contemporaries, and often in implicit or explicit opposition to the East's presumed social, cultural, or political codes.

Critics who try to simplify California poetry into a solely free verse tradition not only exclude major figures like Winters, Gunn, Edgar Bowers, Timothy Steele, and Kay Ryan, they also miss the odd originality of these writers. Winters reinvented English prosody to create a poetic idiom separate and opposed to the lush neo-romanticism of Edna St. Vincent Millay as well as the dense modernist lyricism of Hart Crane. Winters's minimalist "plain style" was as radical an innovation as Marianne Moore's complex syllabics or Jeffers's magisterial long lines, which mix elements of free verse and classical meters. Likewise Kay Ryan's idiosyncratic use of rhyme and intermittent meter is distinguished mostly by its lack of similarity to any other current poetry in form or free verse.

If there is no way to describe California poetry adequately without accounting for its persistent reinventions of formalism, it is equally impossible to present it without celebrating its restless explorations of free verse. In a culture that sees itself existing largely outside history, any stylistic choice has less to do with aesthetic continuity than individual self-creation. Californian metrical verse, from Winters's "plain style" to the more vernacular New Formalism, has characteristically been conceived in contrarian terms to the prevalent mainstream models. That oppositional quality unifies much of the innovation originating among California literary movements, from the Beats to the Activists, through the Language Poets and New Formalists. Nowhere is this oppositionalist radicalism currently more pronounced than in the Spoken Word movement, in which the post-Renaissance primacy of the printed word in literature is itself rejected. Independence and opposition are the most enduring impulses in the state's poetic history.

Independence and opposition have also characterized the ideological loyalties of California poets. Rebellious individualism has not only produced writers inspired by anarchist and radical politics, like Rexroth, Duncan, Lawrence Ferlinghetti, Philip Levine, and George Oppen. This oppositional idealism also typifies the labor activism of Edwin Markham, the radical isolationism and antihumanism of Jeffers, the passionate rejection of the traditional poetic canon by Winters (a diehard leftist despite his formal prosody), the religious mysticism and pacifism of Everson, the calm courage to conquer physical disability in an unaccommodating age by Josephine Miles, the environmentalism of Gary Snyder, the pioneering homosexual declarations of Duncan, the defiantly exuberant squalor of Charles Bukowski, the multicultural affirmations of Ishmael Reed, the bilingual aesthetic of Francisco X. Alarcón, the polyphonic experiments of Jack Foley, and the post-feminist sexuality of Jenny Factor. Only in California does such radical individualism appear quite traditional.

If *California Poetry* is a historical anthology, it is only in an incomplete and retrospective sense. The literary tradition it attempts to survey is still a vital and dynamic enterprise. There have never been more poets in California than at present. (Perhaps there have never been more poets anywhere.) This anthology is merely one attempt to sketch out the complex and diverse traditions that have created a distinct but varied regional poetry. There will be others. As California continues to grow in population, wealth, and influence, its literature will also develop, often in unexpected ways. Lew Welch wrote about California's terminal position in the American West, "This is the last place. There is nowhere else to go." True Californians refuse to be alarmed by this apocalyptic vision. Living in this astonishing state, who needs an elsewhere?

PART I

EARLY POETS

John Rollin Ridge (Yellow Bird)
(1827–1867)

John Rollin Ridge (Yellow Bird) has been rediscovered as a mid-nineteenth-century novelist of significance, as the author of *The Life and Adventures of Joaquín Murieta, the Celebrated California Bandit* (1854)—the first novel to be written in California and the first novel to be published by an American Indian. Born in 1827 in the Eastern Cherokee Nation (near what is now Rome, Georgia), Ridge was the son and grandson of tribal leaders, both of whom were murdered on the same day in 1839 as acts of political revenge for having ceded traditional Cherokee territory to the U.S. government.

The surviving members of Ridge's family fled to Arkansas, where Ridge settled and married. A young man with a literary penchant, he was intent on rebuilding the lost family reputation and fortune. But Cherokee infighting shaped his life again in 1849 when Ridge fought over a horse with an enemy from a faction still hostile to his family, shooting and killing his opponent. He fled and in 1850 joined a wagon train bound for the California gold country. He never returned to the Cherokee Nation.

Like Mark Twain, Ridge tried mining and other schemes promising sudden wealth, but he found the work hard and unprofitable. He soon turned to newspaper reporting, and later, editing. He was simultaneously contributing poetry to San Francisco newspapers and literary magazines, and by the time *The Life and Adventures of Joaquín Murieta* was published, his was a familiar name.

Avenging brutal treatment at the hands of renegade whites, Joaquín Murieta had formed an outlaw gang and become a legendary figure—equal parts avenging Robin Hood and bandit killer—until he was tracked, shot, and beheaded by bounty hunters in 1853. Outraged at the treatment of the first peoples of California (Indians and Mexicans), Ridge identified with Murieta and embroidered on the historical legend in writing his only published prose narrative, which found small financial success but considerable authority as a historical source. His "nonfiction novel" was taken as fact for many years—by historians as eminent as Hubert H. Bancroft—until it was finally recognized as having been invented and diligently recorded in equal parts.

John Rollin Ridge published work in magazines early and late in his life. *Poems* (1868), his only collection, was issued a year after his death in Grass Valley. "Mount Shasta," an imitation after Shelley's "Mont Blanc," was his best-known work, following the model in lofty natural description, language, and metrical scheme. Ridge's early subjects were the majestic California landscape and the siren calls of unidentified female temptresses, some of whom he described as "wild half-breeds." His early models were romantic, often Shelley and Byron, and only later (in "California," for example) did he rise above the imitative and derivative. In his later work, he outlined a vision of history that suggested social classes, races, and nations were in the midst of evolving to higher planes of consciousness.

Ridge was an enigmatic figure in his time and remains so now. His prose sketches a strong familiarity and personal identification with the way Indians and Mexicans were treated as California was developed, but his poetry gives little sense of either his Cherokee heritage or his concern with racial injustice. Contemporary scholars, notably Louis Owens in his landmark study of American Indian fiction, *Other Destinies*, are reexamining Ridge's work and significance as a seminal Native American and California writer.

Mount Shasta

Behold the dread Mt. Shasta, where it stands

Imperial midst the lesser heights, and, like
Some mighty unimpassioned mind, companionless
And cold. The storms of Heaven may beat in wrath
Against it, but it stands in unpolluted
Grandeur still; and from the rolling mists upheaves
Its tower of pride e'en purer than before.
The wintry showers and white-winged tempests leave
Their frozen tributes on its brow, and it
Doth make of them an everlasting crown.
Thus doth it, day by day and age by age,
Defy each stroke of time: still rising highest
Into Heaven!
Aspiring to the eagle's cloudless height,
No human foot has stained its snowy side;
No human breath has dimmed the icy mirror which
It holds unto the moon and stars and sov'reign sun.

We may not grow familiar with the secrets
Of its hoary top, whereon the Genius
Of that mountain builds his glorious throne!
Far lifted in the boundless blue, he doth
Encircle, with his gaze supreme, the broad
Dominions of the West, which lie beneath
His feet, in pictures of sublime repose
No artist ever drew. He sees the tall
Gigantic hills arise in silentness
And peace, and in the long review of distance
Range themselves in order grand. He sees the sunlight
Play upon the golden streams which through the valleys
Glide. He hears the music of the great and solemn sea,
And overlooks the huge old western wall
To view the birth-place of undying Melody!

    Itself all light, save when some loftiest cloud
Doth for a while embrace its cold forbidding
Form, that monarch mountain casts its mighty
Shadow down upon the crownless peaks below,
That, like inferior minds to some great
Spirit, stand in strong contrasted littleness!
All through the long and Summery months of our
Most tranquil year, it points its icy shaft
On high, to catch the dazzling beams that fall
In showers of splendor round that crystal cone,
And roll in floods of far magnificence
Away from that lone, vast Reflector in
The dome of Heaven.
Still watchful of the fertile
Vale and undulating plains below, the grass
Grows greener in its shade, and sweeter bloom
The flowers. Strong purifier! From its snowy
Side the breezes cool are wafted to the "peaceful
Homes of men," who shelter at its feet, and love
To gaze upon its honored form, aye standing
There the guarantee of health and happiness.
Well might it win communities so blest
To loftier feelings and to nobler thoughts—

The great material symbol of eternal
Things! And well I ween, in after years, how
In the middle of his furrowed track the plowman
In some sultry hour will pause, and wiping
From his brow the dusty sweat, with reverence
Gaze upon that hoary peak. The herdsman
Oft will rein his charger in the plain, and drink
Into his inmost soul the calm sublimity;
And little children, playing on the green, shall
Cease their sport, and, turning to that mountain
Old, shall of their mother ask: "Who made it?"
And she shall answer, — "GOD!"

And well this Golden State shall thrive, if like
Its own Mt. Shasta, Sovereign Law shall lift
Itself in purer atmosphere — so high
That human feeling, human passion at its base
Shall lie subdued; e'en pity's tears shall on
Its summit freeze; to warm it e'en the sunlight
Of deep sympathy shall fail:
Its pure administration shall be like
The snow immaculate upon that mountain's brow!

from *California*

And shall we view these miracles and more
Which mind and muscle never wrought before,
Without remembrance in these latter years,
Of those brave men, those hardy Pioneers,
Who led the way for Science, Art, and Law,
'Mid dangers their successors never saw,
And countless hardships that they never knew?
The famed and unfamed heroes tried and true,
Who crowded into months or days the deeds
Of years, and of young empire sowed the seeds?
Amid the mass there here and there appears
Some reverend head, majestic as a seer's —
Arising from the rest like snow-crowned peak,

Around whose brow the whitening tempests break!
These are the Pioneers of Pioneers,
Those elder heroes in the fight, who, years
And years agone, did drive the wild beast back
To plant their homes where late he left the track.
They're sinking, one by one, like pines that long
Have braved, erect, the howling winters strong,
To fall at last midst stillest peace profound,
And wake the woods with wonder at the sound.
Shall these old heroes be forgot? Not so,
For, while they yet survive Time's downward flow,
I see a rescuing hand stretched forth to save
The good, the true, from dark Oblivion's grave.
'T is woman's hand that thus would snatch from night
Those honored names far worthier of the light,
And them transmit to shine on History's scroll
When that gray sage his records shall unroll.
And yet some whom the weeping muse laments,
Have their unwrit but lasting monuments.
Such is that Peak which bears brave Lassen's name —
A fit memorial of the grandest fame;
For it shall stand while crowns and laurels fail,
And Time strews men like leaves upon the gale.

Bret Harte

(1836–1902)

Born Francis Bret Hart in Albany, New York, Bret Harte was of
Dutch and English stock. His father changed the spelling of the family
name to Harte and died shortly thereafter. Young Bret took a variety
of odd jobs to contribute to family finances, and by age fifteen he was
self-supporting and already taken with poetry fever. His brother
Henry wrote him exciting letters about military service in the Mexican-
American War in the exotic new state of California. A published poet in
local newspapers from age eleven, Harte was inflamed by his brother's
accounts and began to write in earnest.

Harte's mother moved to California to remarry in 1853, and Harte
joined her in 1854. He bounced from one odd job to another as he
continued to write doggerel, and when he was offered a post as a printer's
helper at the *Northern Californian*, he seized it. He took advantage of
the position, often publishing his own poems, and rose to the rank of
managing editor before he was run out of town by a mob enraged over
an article he wrote about locals attacking an Indian settlement. A fund
of colorful tales collected since childhood, a taste for the raw energy of
his adopted state, and a canny understanding of what his audiences
wanted soon contributed to commercial literary success.

Harte was already a recognized young talent by the time he became
the editor of *The Overland Monthly* in 1868. In 1865 he had published
Outcroppings, the first anthology of California poetry, and he was a
recognized figure on the San Francisco literary scene. He was seen as
an imaginative poet and editor, and when he published "The Luck of
Roaring Camp" and "The Outcasts of Poker Flat" in early issues of *The
Overland Monthly*, he became an instant national sensation. Harte cast
society's lessers—gamblers, prospectors, whores, shiftless cowboys, and
local bumpkins—in a series of raucous gold country melodramas that
captured national attention and helped spotlight frontier California in
the national literary imagination, and they made him famous.

As a poet, Harte was lofty, formulaic, and melodramatic—precisely
what his readers wished him to be—but he was not unaware of the social
tragedies that had mounted in California as gold-seekers rushed in. He
had been dispatched from Arcata in 1859 for publishing a story many
locals saw as pro-Indian, and he was sensitive to Chinese victims of racism

in San Francisco, treating them in stories, essays, and poems, including his most popular work of low poetry, "Plain Language from Truthful James." The real nature of Harte's attitude toward Chinese and Chinatown continues to be a matter of debate; he protested his innocence and later called the poem "the worst I ever wrote," but it helped launch a tide of anti-Asian sentiment, a nadir in California history.

Harte's fame was solidified by the publication of *The Luck of Roaring Camp and Other Sketches* (1870), and when the owners of the *Atlantic Monthly* offered him the astonishing annual salary of ten thousand dollars to come back East and write for them, he took it. However isolated he had always felt in California, he was certainly no happier in New York. His work was seen as repetitive and dated, and he soon fell out of fashion. In 1878 he was rescued by a U.S. consular appointment to Germany. Bret Harte spent the last twenty years of his life in literary anonymity in Europe before dying of throat cancer in 1902.

The Society upon the Stanislaus

I reside at Table Mountain, and my name is Truthful James;
I am not up to small deceit, or any sinful games;
And I'll tell in simple language what I know about the row
That broke up our Society upon the Stanislow.

But first I would remark, that it is not a proper plan
For any scientific gent to whale his fellow-man,
And, if a member don't agree with his peculiar whim,
To lay for that same member for to "put a head" on him.

Now nothing could be finer or more beautiful to see
Than the first six months' proceedings of that same Society,
Till Brown of Calaveras brought a lot of fossil bones
That he found within a tunnel near the tenement of Jones.

Then Brown he read a paper, and he reconstructed there,
From those same bones, an animal that was extremely rare;
And Jones then asked the Chair for a suspension of the rules,
Till he could prove that those same bones was one of his lost mules.

Then Brown he smiled a bitter smile, and said he was at fault—
It seemed he had been trespassing on Jones' family vault.
He was a most sarcastic man, this quiet Mr. Brown,
And on several occasions he had cleaned out the town.

Now I hold it is not decent for a scientific gent
To say another is an ass—at least, to all intent;
Nor should the individual who happens to be meant
Reply by heaving rocks at him, to any great extent.

Then Abner Dean of Angel's raised a point of order—when
A chunk of old red sandstone took him in the abdomen,
And he smiled a kind of sickly smile, and curled up on the floor,
And the subsequent proceedings interested him no more.

For, in less time than I write it, every member did engage
In a warfare with the remnants of a palæozoic age;
And the way they heaved those fossils in their anger was a sin,
Till the skull of an old mammoth caved the head of Thompson in.

And this is all I have to say of these improper games,
For I live at Table Mountain, and my name is Truthful James;
And I've told in simple language what I know about the row
That broke up our Society upon the Stanislow.

Plain Language from Truthful James

Table Mountain, 1870

Which I wish to remark,
    And my language is plain,
That for ways that are dark
    And for tricks that are vain,
The heathen Chinee is peculiar,
    Which the same I would rise to explain.

Ah Sin was his name;
    And I shall not deny,
In regard to the same,

What that name might imply;
But his smile it was pensive and childlike,
　　As I frequent remarked to Bill Nye.

It was August the third,
　　And quite soft was the skies;
Which it might be inferred
　　That Ah Sin was likewise;
Yet he played it that day upon William
　　And me in a way I despise.

Which we had a small game,
　　And Ah Sin took a hand:
It was Euchre. The same
　　He did not understand;
But he smiled as he sat by the table,
　　With the smile that was childlike and bland.

Yet the cards they were stocked
　　In a way that I grieve,
And my feelings were shocked
　　At the state of Nye's sleeve,
Which was stuffed full of aces and bowers,
　　And the same with intent to deceive.

But the hands that were played
　　By that heathen Chinee,
And the points that he made,
　　Were quite frightful to see,—
Till at last he put down a right bower,
　　Which the same Nye had dealt unto me.

Then I looked up at Nye,
　　And he gazed upon me;
And he rose with a sigh,
　　And said, "Can this be?
We are ruined by Chinese cheap labor,—"
　　And he went for that heathen Chinee.

In the scene that ensued
    I did not take a hand,
But the floor it was strewed
    Like the leaves on the strand
With the cards that Ah Sin had been hiding,
    In the game "he did not understand."

In his sleeves, which were long,
    He had twenty-four jacks—
Which was coming it strong,
    Yet I state but the facts;
And we found on his nails, which were taper,
    What is frequent in tapers,—that's wax.

Which is why I remark,
    And my language is plain,
That for ways that are dark
    And for tricks that are vain,
The heathen Chinee is peculiar,—
    Which the same I am free to maintain.

What the Bullet Sang

O joy of creation
                To be!
O rapture to fly
                And be free!
Be the battle lost or won,
    Though its smoke shall hide the sun,
I shall find my love—The one
                Born for me!

I shall know him where he stands,
                All alone,
With the power in his hands
                Not o'erthrown;
I shall know him by his face,
    By his god-like front and grace;

I shall hold him for a space,
    All my own!

It is he—O my love!
    So bold!
It is I—All thy love
    Foretold!
It is I. O love what bliss!
 Dost thou answer to my kiss?
Oh! sweetheart, what is this!
    Lieth there so cold!

Joaquin Miller
(1841–1913)

With his typical flair for embellishment, Joaquin Miller claimed to have been born in 1841 "in a covered wagon, pointed West." In fact, Cincinnatus Hiner Miller was probably born on a farm in central Indiana in 1837, a bland beginning for one of the most flamboyant figures of the American West, one who inspired Buffalo Bill Cody and others with his long hair, buckskin coats, and colorful fabrications. Miller's embellishments on his colorful life have made the biographer's task difficult: Ambrose Bierce called him "the greatest liar this country has ever produced."

Miller's Quaker family moved to the Oregon Territory in 1852 and established a home in the Willamette Valley. When the nineteen-year-old Miller broke the leg of a neighbor's cow while carelessly rolling boulders down a hill, he and a friend made a dash for the California goldfields, beginning a series of adventures that would transform him into Joaquin Miller, the self-styled "Byron of the Sierras." Within a year of his arrival in California in 1855, Miller and an Indian scout tracked and attacked a band of Indian marauders; his relationship with the Indians of California was always ambivalent. He lived among them and fought battles with them, and his relationships provided the core for his prose account *Life Among the Modocs* (1883). He took up housekeeping with a Modoc wife, Paquita, with whom he had a daughter, Cali-Shasta, and yet while he lived with her, he was part of a vigilante expedition that massacred an entire village of Indians—men, women, and children—near Mount Shasta. Three years later, he claimed that Paquita was killed fleeing a posse, but it is more likely that he simply abandoned the family, at least temporarily.

Miller's other misadventures included stealing a mule, breaking out of jail, shooting a constable sent to arrest him, and practicing law without a license. His claim to have joined an expedition to Nicaragua has proven false, and he may or may not have found gold in Idaho. He did indeed eventually become a partner in the Pony Express Company, and when it was sold to Wells, Fargo and Company, he invested his profits in the *Democratic Register*, a pro-South, pro-slavery newspaper in Eugene, Oregon, where he published strident editorials and florid verse.

Having offended the local citizenry almost at once, and after a tumultuous eleven months as a journalist, Miller resigned on Valentine's Day, 1863, and headed to San Francisco. Bret Harte had published some of Miller's poems in *The Golden Era* a literary magazine he was editing, and Miller now began writing for the journal. It was a short-lived relationship. Harte could not pay Miller (or his wife, who also wrote for the *Era*), and they moved on. Miller established an ersatz legal practice in Canyon City, Oregon, and continued to scribble poems every chance he had.

Miller's first book, *Specimens*, was published in Portland in 1868; *Joaquin, et al.* was published a year later, and neither received any attention save a mention from Harte in *The Golden Era*. Beset by domestic problems, Miller returned to the Bay Area, where Ina Coolbrith, prominent poet and woman of letters, took him under her wing. She oversaw his transformation to Joaquin Miller and urged him to start his career anew in Europe. He rewarded Coolbrith by leaving Cali-Shasta for her to raise.

In buckskins and shoulder-length hair, Miller was immediately celebrated in London. *Pacific Poems* came out in a tiny edition in 1871, and it was soon followed by *Song of the Sierras*, published simultaneously to appreciative audiences in London and Boston. Miller evoked a mythic California and West in Byronic couplets, and people flocked to his evening readings. A flood of publications followed—poetry, memoirs, plays, and novels—capitalizing on his fame as "the singer of the Sierras." Miller now had financial means and respectability, marrying hotel heiress Abigail Leland in New York City in 1879.

In 1887, he returned to California to purchase the seventy-five acres near Oakland where he built his estate, "The Hights," complete with waterfall. It became a mecca for almost any literary personage who came through. Denounced by some as a literary fraud and "Poet Lothario" for his poor treatment of his various wives and families, Joaquin Miller ruled his Oakland empire like the last of the forty-niners and welcomed the parade of literary visitors. Thirsty for a few last adventures, he traveled to the Klondike goldfields and China before his death in 1913.

Columbus

Behind him lay the gray Azores,
  Behind the Gates of Hercules;
Before him not the ghost of shores,
  Before him only shoreless seas.
The good mate said: "Now must we pray,
  For lo! the very stars are gone.
Brave Admiral, speak, what shall I say?"
  "Why, say, 'Sail on! sail on! and on!'"

"My men grow mutinous day by day;
  My men grow ghastly wan and weak."
The stout mate thought of home; a spray
  Of salt wave washed his swarthy cheek.
"What shall I say, brave Admiral, say,
  If we sight naught but seas at dawn?"
"Why, you shall say at break of day,
  'Sail on! sail on! sail on! and on!'"

They sailed and sailed, as winds might blow,
  Until at last the blanched mate said:
"Why, now not even God would know
  Should I and all my men fall dead.
These very winds forget their way,
  For God from these dread seas is gone.
Now speak, brave Admiral, speak and say" —
  He said: "Sail on! sail on! and on!"

They sailed. They sailed. Then spake the mate:
  "This mad sea shows his teeth to-night.
He curls his lip, he lies in wait,
  With lifted teeth, as if to bite!
Brave Admiral, say but one good word:
  What shall we do when hope is gone?"
The words leapt like a leaping sword:
  "Sail on! sail on! sail on! and on!"

Then, pale and worn, he kept his deck,
  And peered through darkness. Ah, that night

Of all dark nights! And then a speck—
    A light! A light! A light! A light!
It grew, a starlit flag unfurled!
    It grew to be Time's burst of dawn.
He gained a world; he gave that world
    Its grandest lesson: "On! sail on!"

A California Christmas

Behold where Beauty walks with Peace!
Behold where Plenty pours her horn
Of fruits, of flowers, fat increase,
As generous as light of morn.

Green Shasta, San Diego, seas
Of bloom and green between them rolled.
Great herds in grasses to their knees,
And green earth garmented in gold.

White peaks that prop the sapphire blue
Look down on Edens, such as when
That fair first spot perfection knew,
And God walked perfect earth with men.

I say God's kingdom is at hand
Right here, if we but lift our eyes;
I say there lies no line or land
Between this land and Paradise.

By the Pacific Ocean

Here room and kingly silence keep
Companionship in state austere;
The dignity of death is here,
The large, lone vastness of the deep;
Here toil has pitched his camp to rest:
The west is banked against the west.

Above yon gleaming skies of gold
One lone imperial peak is seen;
While gathered at his feet in green
Ten thousand foresters are told:
And all so still! so still the air
That duty drops the web of care.

Beneath the sunset's golden sheaves
The awful deep walks with the deep,
Where silent sea doves slip and sweep,
And commerce keeps her loom and weaves.
The dead red men refuse to rest;
Their ghosts illume my lurid West.

Dead in the Sierras

His footprints have failed us,
Where berries are red,
And madroños are rankest—
The hunter is dead!

The grizzly may pass
By his half-open door;
May pass and repass
On his path, as of yore.

The panther may crouch
In the leaves on his limb;
May scream and may scream—
It is nothing to him.

Prone, bearded, and breasted
Like columns of stone;
And tall as a pine—
As a pine overthrown!

His camp-fires gone,
What else can be done

Than let him sleep on
Till the light of the sun?

Ay, tombless! What of it?
Marble is dust,
Cold and repellent;
And iron is rust.

Ina Coolbrith
(1841–1928)

Poet, publisher, and muse, Ina Coolbrith was a central figure in California's Golden Era and the state's first true woman of letters. A niece of Mormon prophet Joseph Smith, Coolbrith was born Josephine Donna Smith and came to California at the age of ten with her mother, who was fleeing the polygamy of the Mormon church. At seventeen, Coolbrith married a flamboyant and jealous actor, Robert Carsley, and the disastrous union was dissolved in 1861 (Carsley was later shot to death in a duel). Meanwhile, Coolbrith had published lyrics in the *Los Angeles Star* and the *California Home Journal*, establishing her literary reputation by the time she was twenty.

After a deep depression following her failed marriage and the death of her infant son, Coolbrith moved to San Francisco in 1862, adopting her mother's maiden surname. Arriving with a reputation as a poet, she soon began writing for *The Golden Era* and *The Californian*, forming intimate friendships with Bret Harte, Charles Warren Stoddard, and Mark Twain, among others. With Harte and Stoddard, Coolbrith formed the group dubbed the "Golden Gate Trinity," which edited the influential *Overland Monthly*. Early on, she proved a constant mentor to writers and artists from Joaquin Miller to Jack London and Isadora Duncan. It was Coolbrith who suggested to Cincinnatus Hiner Miller that he adopt the name of an infamous California outlaw, outfit himself in buckskin, and move to Europe to recreate himself as the "Bard of California"; when Miller returned, he was one of the most recognized literary figures of the West.

Saddled by obligations to support her mother, her sister's orphaned children, and Miller's half-Indian daughter, Cali-Shasta (whom the infamous "Poet Lothario" had all but abandoned on Coolbrith's doorstep as he left to travel the world), she took a job at the Oakland Free Library. As a librarian, she had an enormous influence on generations of readers and writers. In 1906, at the height of his fame, Jack London wrote to her: "No woman has affected me to the extent you did…in all the years that have passed, I have met no woman so 'noble' as you."

When her home and substantial notes were destroyed in the great San Francisco fire of 1906, Coolbrith abandoned hopes of writing her autobiography and focused her energy on nurturing literary culture, holding salons at her San Francisco home. In 1915, the president of the University of California and the Board of Regents presented her with the title "California's loved, laurel-wreathed poet," and the California state legislature confirmed her position as poet laureate—the first in the United States—in 1918. She bore the honor until her death in 1928, but she was quickly forgotten; her grave was unmarked until 1986, when the Ina Coolbrith Circle donated a headstone in her honor, and she is now acknowledged as a significant literary figure.

Coolbrith published three collections: *A Perfect Day* (1881), *The Singer of the Sea* (1894), and *Songs from the Golden Gate* (1895). A traditional poet comfortable with formal sonnets, abstract diction, and lofty topics, she remains primarily significant as California's first woman of letters, an influential editor, and an inspiring and tireless teacher and mentor. Her name is now almost as widespread as that of the state's first internationally famous poet, Robinson Jeffers, gracing numerous libraries, parks, and literary contests as well as a mountain peak in Sierra County.

The Years

What do I owe the years, that I should bring
    Green leaves to crown them king?
Blown, barren sands, the thistle, and the brier,
    Dead hope, and mocked desire,
And sorrow, vast and pitiless as the sea:
    These are their gifts to me.

What do I owe the years, that I should love
    And sing the praise thereof?
Perhaps, the lark's clear carol wakes with morn,
    And winds amid the corn
Clash fairy cymbals; but I miss the joys,
    Missing the tender voice—
Sweet as a throstle's after April rain—
    That may not sing again.

What do I owe the years, that I should greet
    Their bitter, and not sweet,
With wine, and wit, and laughter? Rather thrust
    The wine-cup to the dust!
What have they brought to me, these many years?
    Silence and bitter tears.

Retrospect

(In Los Angeles)

A breath of balm—of orange bloom!
    By what strange fancy wafted me,
Through the lone starlight of the room?
    And suddenly I seem to see

The long, low vale, with tawny edge
    Of bills, within the sunset glow;
Cool vine-rows through the cactus hedge,
    And fluttering gleams of orchard snow.

Far off, the slender line of white
    Against the blue of ocean's crest;
The slow sun sinking into night,
    A quivering opal in the west.

Somewhere a stream sings, far away;
    Somewhere from out the hidden groves,
And dreamy as the dying day,
    Comes the soft coo of mourning doves.

One moment all the world is peace!
    The years like clouds are rolled away,
And I am on those sunny leas,
    A child, amid the flowers at play.

Ambrose Bierce
(1842–1914?)

Ambrose Bierce was born on a farm in Horse Cave Creek, Ohio, and raised in northern Indiana. After finishing high school, the idealistic young Bierce worked as a printer's devil for an abolitionist newspaper. When the Civil War erupted in 1861, he enlisted in the Union Army. A brave soldier, he fought in several of the bloodiest battles in American history, including Shiloh and Chickamauga, and was seriously wounded in 1864. (He eventually received a merit promotion to major in 1867.) After leaving the Army, Bierce headed west to San Francisco, where he quickly became a popular journalist, publishing articles, poems, and stories. In 1871 he married a local heiress and the couple moved to London. Bierce spent three happy years in England, where he published his first three books and saw the birth of his two sons.

Homesick for California, Bierce's wife convinced him to return to San Francisco in 1875. He gradually became the West Coast's leading literary journalist. In 1887 newspaper magnate William Randolph Hearst hired him for the *San Francisco Examiner* and gave him complete freedom to write what he wished. This string of good fortune ended the next year when the Bierces' marriage dissolved, and soon thereafter one of their sons was killed in a duel. In 1896 Bierce moved to Washington. In 1909 he left journalism to prepare his twelve-volume *Collected Works* (1909–1912) for publication. Disillusioned with American life, he left Washington in 1913 to travel through Mexico, where he planned to join the revolutionary army of Pancho Villa as an observer. He disappeared in Mexico in January 1914. No body was ever found, and no reliable account of his death has ever been provided.

A brilliantly talented and prolific writer, "Bitter Bierce" was best known as a sardonic satirist. His newspaper columns frequently featured the cynical definitions that eventually formed *The Devil's Dictionary* (1911), an imaginative enterprise reminiscent of Flaubert's *Dictionary of Received Ideas*. Bierce's beautifully phrased and savagely funny definitions still ring true: "*bore, n.* a person who talks when you wish him to listen"; or "*misfortune, n.* the kind of fortune that never misses"; or "*consult, v.t.* to seek another's approval on a course already decided on." Bierce's short stories and fables were often ingeniously plotted—none more so than "An Occurrence at Owl Creek Bridge," whose narrative structure prefigures modernist fiction. The story was first collected in *Tales of Soldiers and Civilians* (1891), a volume that reflects the influence of Edgar Allan Poe and draws on Bierce's own experiences in the Civil War.

A Rational Anthem

My country, 'tis of thee,
Sweet land of felony,
　　Of thee I sing—
Land where my fathers fried
Young witches and applied
Whips to the Quaker's hide
　　And made him spring.

My knavish country, thee,
Land where the thief is free,
　　Thy laws I love;
I love thy thieving bills
That tap the people's tills;
I love thy mob whose will's
　　All laws above.

Let Federal employees
And rings rob all they please,
　　The whole year long.
Let office-holders make
Their piles and judges rake
Our coin. For Jesus' sake,
　　Let's *all* go wrong!

Orthography

A spelling reformer indicted
For fudge was before the court cicted.
　　The judge said: "Enough—
　　His candle we'll snough,
And his sepulchre shall not be whicted."

Two epigrams

For those this mausoleum is erected
Who Stanford to the Upper House elected.
Their luck is less or their promotion slower,
For, dead, they were elected to the Lower.

Here Stanford lies, who thought it odd
That he should go to meet his God.
He looked, until his eyes grew dim,
For God to hasten to meet him.

Charles Warren Stoddard
(1843–1909)

Publishing his earliest poems under the name "Pip Pepperpod," Charles Warren Stoddard became best known as a chronicler of the South Sea Islands and an editor of *The Overland Monthly*. Born in New York, Stoddard came to San Francisco with his strict Protestant family in 1855. He began submitting his poems anonymously to *The Golden Era* and was hailed as a "boy prodigy." Bret Harte edited and published Stoddard's *Collected Poems* in 1867, and the poet quickly became a model for poetic decadence. Haunted by poor health, he briefly tried the stage but abandoned it for travel to the South Sea Islands, where he wrote his *South-Sea Idyls*, a series of letters published in book form in 1873. He made several visits to Molokai, where he met Father Damien, the Catholic priest who ministered to the leper colony there. Soon after his first trip to the Islands, Stoddard became an ascetic Catholic. His religious books include the story of his conversion, *A Troubled Heart and How it Was Comforted at Last* (1885), of which he said, "Here you have my inner life laid bare," and *The Lepers of Molokai* (1886).

Troubled throughout his life by illness, Stoddard nonetheless traveled frequently. He taught briefly at the University of Notre Dame and at Catholic University in Washington, D.C. Close companion of Robert Louis Stevenson, with whom he shared a love of the South Seas, Stoddard was also Mark Twain's secretary in London and a friend to Joaquin Miller, George Sterling, Ina Coolbrith, and many other writers of his time. Stoddard was a gentle, sensitive, and repressed man, a lover of exotic moods and dreamy climes (both Old California and the Sandwich Islands), and his poetry reflects a sensibility tuned for mood and hazy romance. The subtle but unmistakable homoeroticism that suffuses his poetry has attracted recent scholarship on gay issues in his work.

Ina Coolbrith agreed to edit a final book of poems after his death, and while Stoddard claimed to have assembled a manuscript, none was ever found. As she wrote in the foreword to *Poems of Charles Warren Stoddard* (1917), "From the fact that the files of local magazines and papers had nearly all been destroyed, in the San Francisco fire of 1906, and in the absence of any clue to non-local publications in which they might have appeared, it became, veritably, a *labor* of love, which many times seemed as hopeless as it was long, to gather [these] poems." With additional introductions by Miller, Thomas Walsh, and Sterling, this is the most complete record of Stoddard's poems. Sterling's introductory poem, "Charles Warren Stoddard," concludes, "From all he wrote (not for his day), / A sense of marvel drifts to me — / of morning on a purple sea, / and fragrant islands far away."

Old Monterey

Sleep on in thy sunny sand-dunes and slumber in thy byways;
    In the hollow of thy drowsy hills, lo! sleep and the shadow of death.
Dream on, O dear enchantress, of the babel that filled thy highways,
    When passionate throngs sang thy song of songs and a war-cry was
        thy breath.

Now in thy listless languor, lo! the encircling sea-mew —
    Gulls in the wild sea-gardens; and the curve of the lateen sail
As it cleaves like a silver scimitar the mist of the sea; and dream you
    Of the treasure vast and the glory past—the visions of no avail.

Dream of the splendid trappings of the troops that met and mingled—
    Mexican cavaleros and hidalgos of old Castile:
Hark to the music of the spurs of silver that jolted and jingled;
    And loudly laugh, as the wine you quaff, at the past beyond appeal.

Where are they now, O dreamer? thy treasures have vanished whither?
    Thou who wast first to the headland-front and Queen of the western sea:
Long have I watched and have waited and have wandered hither and
        thither
    Asking a word with a voice unheard and now I would ask it of thee.

The bitter tang of the sea is ours and the winds forever roaming;
    The fleecy crest of the breaking wave and the ribbons of streaming kelp;
The fishers mending their nets in the sun, and the crickets in the
        gloaming,
    And the seal's gruff bark, in the dew and the dark, and the whine of
        her hungry whelp.

The wind and the wave pour over the rocks that are barren and bony;
　　Like ghosts of avalanches the fog sweeps down from the heights:
The star-fish sprawl in the briny meadows; the abalone
　　Hides, where it lies, its rainbow dyes in a dome of dim delights.

There is spice of the pine in plenty and oak and the cypress tangle;
　　And the bleaching bones of the strand whale, and sea-shells near
　　　　and far—
No soft refrain of old, old Spain, or voices in musical wrangle;
　　Nor the click of the clashing castanets nor the throb of the hushed
　　　　guitar.

There is never a day in the year but tells of thy glory gone forever,
　　And never a dusk that hovers near in the sea-shell pink of the sky,
But we sit in the chill adobe shade with hearts that are past endeavor—
　　While the mists unfurl like the gates of pearl, as we watch the
　　　　daylight die.

Edwin Markham
(1852–1940)

Edwin Markham was born in Oregon City, in the Oregon Territory. His pioneer parents had already separated by the time of his birth, and his mother soon took Markham and the other two youngest of her six children to an isolated California ranch near Sacramento. Markham was raised by the strict Disciples of Christ sect, which took a dim view of literature and the other arts. His domineering and miserly mother demanded that he quit school to work at fifteen, which prompted the young poet to run away from home for two months until she relented. He earned a teacher's certificate at California College in Vacaville and California State Normal School (now California State University) in San Jose—always moving with his mother, who lived with him until her death in 1891. He married for the first of three times in 1875 and taught at various northern California high schools while drifting in and out of spiritualist sects and numerous love affairs. In 1878 he became a disciple of Thomas Lake Harris, who headed a religious cult in Santa Rosa called the Brotherhood of the New Life. Harris's credo of Christian Socialism and mystical sexuality became Markham's lifelong philosophy.

While supporting himself as a teacher, Markham gradually discovered himself as a writer and developed influential friendships with the naturalist fiction writers then working in San Francisco, including Jack London, Frank Norris, and Ambrose Bierce. (Norris used Markham as the model for Presley, the protagonist of his classic 1901 novel *The Octopus.*)

The critical moment in Markham's life came unexpectedly in 1898 at a New Year's Eve party. The forty-six-year-old author read his new poem, which was inspired by the French artist Jean-François Millet's painting *The Man with the Hoe,* which depicts a bent and brutish peasant in a field. Half naturalistic and half visionary, Markham's poem dramatized the oppression of labor and predicted the violent consequences of its liberation. The editor of the *San Francisco Examiner* heard Markham's recitation, and on January 18, 1899, he published the poem on the front page of William Randolph Hearst's influential newspaper. "The Man with the Hoe" created an immediate public sensation. It was eventually reprinted in over ten thousand journals. Its reception made Markham world-famous as "the bard of labor." It also made him rich—he eventually made a quarter million dollars from the poem, an enormous sum by the standards of the time. The poem, he later remarked, was "a chance stroke: I caught the eye and ear of the world."

Moving to New York, Markham helped found the Poetry Society of America in 1910. Hailed as America's "greatest living poet," he traveled the country in a four-month celebrity speaking tour. In 1922, at the invitation of former President William Howard Taft, the tall, bearded Markham read his poem "Lincoln, the Man of the People" at the dedication of the Lincoln Memorial in Washington. In 1930 Staten Island declared his birthday a public holiday; schools were closed annually so that children could parade through the streets in Markham's honor. His eightieth birthday was celebrated at Carnegie Hall, and thirty-five nations sent representatives to salute the poetic patriarch of the international labor movement. Crippled by a stroke in 1938, he died two years later on Staten Island.

Markham's work marks the end of the nineteenth-century tradition of the poet as a public figure. His work also shows the close connection that once existed in America between poetry and journalism. Newspapers were the primary publishers of poetry, which still commanded a large readership eager to discover new talent. Markham directly addressed the political issues of time—from the Russian Revolution to drug addiction—and mastered an elevated but accessible style. He also wrote important articles and books on political issues, most notably *Children in Bondage* (1914), which helped foster child-labor reform legislation. Markham represented the new democratic spirit of the American West.

At the height of his fame, his friend Ambrose Bierce, San Francisco's most mordant literary critic, speculated that "The Man with the Hoe" would eventually kill him as a poet. Bierce's warning proved sadly true. Markham never developed into a major poet, but his signature poem still ranks as the high point of American naturalism in verse.

The Man with the Hoe

Written after seeing Millet's World-Famous Painting

God made man in His own image,
in the image of God made He him.
                        —Genesis

Bowed by the weight of centuries he leans
Upon his hoe and gazes on the ground,
The emptiness of ages in his face,
And on his back the burden of the world.
Who made him dead to rapture and despair,
A thing that grieves not and that never hopes,
Stolid and stunned, a brother to the ox?
Who loosened and let down this brutal jaw?
Whose was the hand that slanted back this brow?
Whose breath blew out the light within this brain?

Is this the Thing the Lord God made and gave
To have dominion over sea and land;
To trace the stars and search the heavens for power;
To feel the passion of Eternity?
Is this the Dream He dreamed who shaped the suns
And pillared the blue firmament with light?
Down all the stretch of Hell to its last gulf
There is no shape more terrible than this—
More tongued with censure of the world's blind greed—
More filled with signs and portents for the soul—
More fraught with menace to the universe.

What gulfs between him and the seraphim!
Slave of the wheel of labor, what to him
Are Plato and the swing of Pleiades?
What the long reaches of the peaks of song,
The rift of dawn, the reddening of the rose?
Through this dread shape the suffering ages look;
Time's tragedy is in that aching stoop;
Through this dread shape humanity betrayed,
Plundered, profaned and disinherited,

Cries protest to the Judges of the World,
A protest that is also prophecy.

O masters, lords and rulers in all lands,
Is this the handiwork you give to God,
This monstrous thing distorted and soul-quenched?
How will you ever straighten up this shape;
Touch it again with immortality;
Give back the upward looking and the light;
Rebuild in it the music and the dream;
Make right the immemorial infamies,
Perfidious wrongs, immedicable woes?

O masters, lords and rulers in all lands,
How will the Future reckon with this Man?
How answer his brute question in that hour
When whirlwinds of rebellion shake the world?
How will it be with kingdoms and with kings—
With those who shaped him to the thing he is—
When this dumb Terror shall reply to God,
After the silence of the centuries?

Outwitted

He drew a circle that shut me out—
Heretic, rebel, a thing to flout.
But Love and I had the wit to win:
We drew a circle that took him in!

Charlotte Perkins Gilman
(1860–1935)

Charlotte Perkins Gilman was born in Hartford, Connecticut. Her father was the writer Frederick Beecher Perkins (a nephew of reformer-novelist Harriet Beecher Stowe and abolitionist minister Henry Ward Beecher), but he abandoned the family shortly after his daughter's birth. Raised in meager surroundings, the young Gilman adopted her intellectual Beecher aunts as role models. As her mother moved from one relation to another, Gilman's early education was neglected, and at fifteen she had had only four years of schooling. In 1878 she studied commercial art at the Rhode Island School of Design. In 1884 she married Charles Walter Stetson, an artist. After the birth of their daughter, Katherine, in 1885, she experienced severe depression. The rest cure her doctor prescribed became the basis of her famous novella, *The Yellow Wallpaper,* which powerfully combined elements of Gothic fiction with a subversive feminist perspective.

In 1888 Gilman left Stetson and moved with her daughter to Pasadena, California, and her first marriage eventually ended in an amicable divorce. She then began a literary career in earnest, becoming a celebrated essayist and public speaker and an important early figure in American feminism. In 1891 she moved to Oakland to become more closely involved with the reform movements emerging in the Bay Area, especially the Nationalist Party, a xenophobic socialist group. She helped organize the California Women's Congress in 1894 and 1895. Her constant travel, however, made it difficult to care for her daughter, and in 1894 she reluctantly relinquished custody of Katherine to Stetson.

Gilman's study *Women and Economics* (1898) stressed the importance of both sexes having a place in the working world. Her feminist-Utopian novel, *Herland* (1915), described a thriving nation of women without men. In 1900 Gilman married a second time—more happily—to her cousin George Houghton Gilman. Soon after his sudden death in 1934, Gilman discovered she had inoperable breast cancer. After finishing her autobiography, she killed herself with chloroform.

Although Gilman's work had been praised by influential critics like William Dean Howells, her writing had already fallen into obscurity by the time of her death. By mid-century, her critical reputation was so marginal that her name did not even appear in most literary reference

works. In 1973, however, a new edition of *The Yellow Wallpaper*
appeared with an afterword by Elaine Hedges that claimed Gilman's
tale was a feminist masterpiece—an assertion subsequent critics have
endorsed.

Gilman is now best remembered for her short stories, but in her own
lifetime she was better known for poetry than fiction. Her first book, *In
This Our World* (1893), was a collection of verse, and she eventually
published over five hundred poems. Her verse usually had a strongly
didactic tone, and she frequently wrote on political subjects like
women's suffrage, world peace, labor reform, and even meatpacking
safety. Gilman's best poetry, however, was satiric, enlived by her keen
eye for social hypocrisy and her sharp sense of humor. Like Edwin
Markham, Gilman represents an older tradition of public and political
poetry that would slowly disappear as the twentieth century progressed.

Matriatism

Small is the thought of "Fatherland,"
With all its pride and worth;
With all its history of death;
Of fire and sword and wasted breath—
By the great new thought which quickeneth—
The thought of "Mother Earth."
Man fights for wealth and rule and pride,
For the "name" that is his alone;
Comes woman, wakening to her power,
Comes woman, opening the hour
That sees life as one growing flower,
All children as her own.

Fathers have fought for their Fatherland
With slaughter and death and dearth,
But mothers, in service and love's increase,
Will labor together for our release,
From a war-stained past to a world at peace,
Our fair, sweet Mother Earth.

California Colors

A Song

I came from Santa Barbara,
I went to San Jose,
Blue sky above—blue sea beside,
Wild gold along the way—
The lovely lavish blossom gold
Ran wild along the way.

The purple mountains loomed beyond,
The soft hills rolled between,
From crest to crest, like smoke at rest,
The eucalyptus screen
Its careless foliage drifting by
Against that all-enfolding sky
In dusky glimmering green;
With live-oak masses drowsing dark
On the slopes of April green;
More joy than any eye can hold,
Not only blue, not only gold,
But bronze and olive green.

Gelett Burgess

(1866–1951)

The man who became famous for never having seen a purple cow, noted humorist Gelett Burgess came to California as an engineering professor. Born in Boston, Frank Gelett Burgess had studied engineering at the Massachusetts Institute of Technology, and he came west to teach topographical drawing at the University of California, Berkeley. A believer in the occult and "sheer, premeditated absurdity," he was an enthusiast at San Francisco séances and bohemian parties.

Fired by the university after he toppled a statue of a noted temperance advocate, and impatient with genteel and pretentious writing, in 1895 Burgess started *The Lark*, a short-lived but celebrated little magazine devoted to silliness and absurdity. Patterned after the bohemian and aesthetic fin de siécle journals of Europe, *The Lark* embodied Burgess's motto, "It is the luxuries that are necessary." Elegantly printed, it attracted a circle self-termed Les Jeunes ("the youths") for their youthful spirit and zaniness. The first issue featured Burgess's now-famous quatrain, "The Purple Cow," which swept the nation. Before ceasing publication in 1897, the magazine had a circulation of three thousand. Burgess inherited the editorship of *The Wave*, another Bay Area journal, from Frank Norris. He left shortly for New York and Paris, but finally returned to California.

The irrepressible Burgess was a journalist and author of light verse, a prolific commercial writer who also wrote many books for juveniles. He is remembered for creating the "Goops"—fantastic three-eyed creatures with atrocious manners. In 1900, he collected his goop poems and illustrations in a decidedly untraditional book of etiquette, *The Goops and How to Be Them: A Manual of Manners for Polite Infants Inculcating Many Juvenile Virtues Both by Precept and Example, with Ninety Drawings*. Embraced by parents hoping to tease their children into good behavior, *Goops* is still in print today.

An indefatigable word player, Burgess coined two mainstays of our contemporary lexicon, the terms "blurb" and "bromide." He died in Carmel at age eighty-five, and two prose collections of his memories of early San Francisco were published posthumously.

The Purple Cow

Reflections on a Mythic Beast
Who's Quite Remarkable, at Least.

I never saw a Purple Cow,
I never hope to See One;
But I can Tell you, Anyhow,
I'd rather See than Be One!

The Purple Cow: Suite

Ah, yes, I wrote the "Purple Cow"—
I'm Sorry, now, I wrote it;
But I can tell you Anyhow
I'll Kill you if you Quote it!

On Digital Extremities

A Poem, and a Gem it Is!

I'd rather have Fingers than Toes;
I'd rather have Ears than a Nose;
    And as for my Hair,
      I'm Glad it's All There;
I'll be Awfully Sad when it Goes!

Table Manners

The Goops they lick their fingers,
And the Goops they lick their knives;
They spill their broth on the tablecloth—
Oh, they lead disgusting lives!
The Goops they talk while eating,
And loud and fast they chew;
And that is why I'm glad that I
Am not a Goop—are you?

George Sterling
(1869–1926)

George Sterling was a central figure in early twentieth-century Bay Area letters and in the establishment of Carmel as a bohemian enclave. Born in Long Island, he had been groomed to become a priest, but he renounced the calling and moved to California, where he worked halfheartedly in his uncle's Oakland real estate office, putting most of his energy into poetry.

In 1892, Sterling met Ambrose Bierce, a lifelong mentor who directed his reading, writing, and publication and introduced him to Bay Area *literati*. Bierce was a stern influence, disapproving of Sterling's idyll in Carmel and discouraging experimentation in the dawning American modernism, but he brought Sterling into the literary milieu of the times and prepared the way for extraordinary friendships. Besides Bierce, London, and Sinclair (closest to him), Sterling counted as friends Theodore Dreiser, Sinclair Lewis, H. L. Mencken, Edgar Lee Masters, Edwin Markham, James Marie Hopper, Mary Austin, Gertrude Atherton, Charles Warren Stoddard, and Robinson Jeffers, whose talent he discovered and praised first in a 1926 monograph. In particular, Sterling met Jack London, launching a lifelong friendship between "Greek" (Sterling) and "Wolf" (London). The writers were inseparable, and London seldom sent a manuscript to a publisher until Sterling had read and criticized it.

A self-published first book, *The Testimony of the Suns* (1903), made Sterling a local celebrity, and he moved to Carmel-by-the-Sea to live cheaply and write. Carmel grew as people sought refuge from earthquake-ravaged San Francisco, and Sterling became the "High Panjandrum"—inadvertently recreating the self-destructive bohemian atmosphere he had left behind. He ruled the enclave for a decade and helped establish its reputation as an artistic retreat. Heavy drinking and operatic love affairs overwhelmed the freedom and creativity that he had hoped for. When young poet Nora May French committed suicide in his home, people began drifting back to the rebuilt San Francisco. His wife left him, to commit suicide herself four years later. He returned to San Francisco in 1914, broke, divorced, and depressed.

Sterling was a gifted writer of occasional poems, and while he favored flashy images and stormy moods, he often lacked thematic substance.

He brought brilliant intellect and broad learning to the page and a technical talent for versifying. He mastered formal odes and the Italian sonnet perhaps better than anyone who had written in the form since its originator, Petrarch. He boasted that it rarely took longer than half an hour to compose a publishable sonnet and claimed the world-record time of eight minutes.

Sterling was key in the founding of San Francisco's Bohemian Club, his final home, and when he ingested cyanide there on November 17, 1926, it was not wholly unexpected. Club performances of verse dramas such as *The Triumph of Bohemia* and *Lilith* were wildly popular, but in many ways time had passed him by. He and Jack London once made a pact that they "would never sit up with the corpse" and that they would "exit laughing." On the recent successes of *Selected Poems* (1923) and *Lilith* (1919, 1926), Macmillan gave Sterling a contract for a last book. It was never completed, and he became the last of his circle to commit suicide, fulfilling his pact with London, who had died a decade earlier.

The Last Days

The russet leaves of the sycamore
Lie at last on the valley floor—
By the autumn wind swept to and fro
Like ghosts in a tale of long ago.
Shallow and clear the Carmel glides
Where the willows droop on its vine-walled sides.

The bracken-rust is red on the hill;
The pines stand brooding, somber and still;
Gray are the cliffs, and the waters gray,
Where the seagulls dip to the sea-born spray.
Sad November, lady of rain,
Sends the goose-wedge over again.

Wilder now, for the verdure's birth,
Falls the sunlight over the earth;
Kildees call from the fields where now
The banding blackbirds follow the plow;

Rustling poplar and brittle weed
Whisper low to the river-reed.

Days departing linger and sigh:
Stars come soon to the quiet sky;
Buried voices, intimate, strange,
Cry to body and soul of change;
Beauty, eternal fugitive,
Seeks the home that we cannot give.

Ballad of the Grapes

O Sadducees and Pharisees,
    Who harass the divine,
Now harken with reluctancy
    How Daphne made the wine!

(I drain a glass of bootleg Scotch,
    For fear my voice may tire.
I pause...I drain a larger one,
    Then whang the western lyre.)

It was in San Francisco town
    Once dedicate to joy,
Now given up to hypocrites
    And all reform's annoy.

Oh! Daphne was as brave a girl
    As ever wore a glove.
She made her prayer to Bacchus, Pan
    And all the gods of love.

Now Daphne bought a load of grapes
    With ocean-purple skin;
She bought some golden muscatel
    And called her lover in.

And thrice she scoured her bath-tub
    (A needless act, we know)
With Bon Ami, Dutch Cleanser
    And much Sapolio.

And thrice she washed her snowy legs,
    At which a faun might kneel,
With Ivory soap and Colgate soap
    And soap we call Castile.

Then in the tub they dumped the grapes
    And in the tub she stepped;
And oh! to see her nudity
    The men of God had wept!

Not as the grapes of wrath are trod
    Trod she the vintage there,
Up to her knees in scarlet foam, —
    Unhidden by her hair;

But rather as when dryads white
    Pace slowly in the dance,
She proved our old, delicious lies
    And certified romance.

O fumes of Bacchus that betrayed
    The spirit of the grape!
O unseen incense that arose
    Around that lyric shape!

A dream she was of pagan days
    Lost now to righteous man,
When through the vineyards of the Greek
    Rippled the rout of Pan.

Right gaily up and down she strode
    That treadmill of delight,
As on her breasts and on her thighs
    The drops lay pink and bright.

(O Sadducees and Pharisees,
    And had ye seen that dew
Ye would have longed to sip each drop—
    And no such luck for you!)

But tired she was as dear she was,
    Before the task was done;
So children with the close of day
    Weary of even fun.

Wherefore a little pause from toil
    They did not think amiss.
Perhaps they had a glass or two,
    And, it may be, a kiss.

But he had brought a goodly cask,
    Funnel and strainer too,
And so they filled that goodly cask
    With juice of ruddy hue.

And in a cool and darksome place
    They set that goodly cask
And had, perhaps, a glass or two,
    To celebrate the task.

Now months must come and months must go
    And men know joy and care,
But when that wine goes twelve per cent,
    May you and I be there!

The Black Vulture

Aloof within the day's enormous dome,
He holds unshared the silence of the sky.
Far down his bleak, relentless eyes descry
The eagle's empire and the falcon's home—
Far down, the galleons of sunset roam;
His hazards on the sea of morning lie;

Serene, he hears the broken tempest sigh
Where cold sierras gleam like scattered foam.

And least of all he holds the human swarm—
Unwitting now that envious men prepare
To make their dream and its fulfilment one,
When, poised above the caldrons of the storm,
Their hearts, contemptuous of death, shall dare
His roads between the thunder and the sun.

Yone Noguchi
(1875–1947)

Yone Noguchi, the first Asian American poet of significant influence, was born in Tsushima, a small town near Nagoya, Japan. He became interested in the English language and literature in public school. He later studied English at Keio University in Tokyo, but after two years he decided to immigrate to America. He arrived in San Francisco in December 1893, where he worked for a Japanese-language paper while studying American poetry. In 1896 he met the popular Western poet Joaquin Miller, who encouraged his literary ambitions. For three years Noguchi lived in a hut on Miller's hillside property above Oakland, and he associated with Les Jeunes, the group of young San Francisco writers that included Gelett Burgess. Noguchi soon published two books, *Seen and Unseen* (1897) and *The Voice of the Valley* (1897), which showed the influence of Miller and Walt Whitman. Although written in slightly odd English, these early books were praised for their freshness. His next two collections of poetry, *From the Eastern Sea* (1903) and *The Summer Cloud* (1906), not only display more confidence and originality, they also incorporate more traditional Japanese elements of style and structure. *The Summer Cloud*, which presented sixty-two prose poems, also demonstrated Noguchi's early interest in literary modernism.

In 1904 Noguchi returned to Japan, leaving behind his American lover, Leonie Gilmour, and their newborn son, Isamu Noguchi, who would become an internationally celebrated sculptor. Gilmour later followed the poet to Tokyo, where she remained with him although he soon married a Japanese woman.

Although he was back in Japan, Noguchi's role in English-language poetry was not yet finished. While teaching at Keio University, he published over ninety books, including four substantial volumes of English poetry. Noguchi corresponded with Ezra Pound and William Butler Yeats about Japanese literary aesthetics and thereby played an important but little-known role in the development of imagism. He also helped popularize haiku as an English-language form. His volume *Japanese Hokkus* (1920), which was dedicated to Yeats, stills stands as an early milestone in the American haiku tradition. Noguchi understood his unique role as a conduit between the Japanese and English-language literary traditions. "We must lose our insularity," he wrote of Japanese literature, but he could certainly have claimed to have helped broaden the perspective of American letters.

I Hear You Call, Pine Tree

I hear you call, pine tree, I hear you upon the hill, by the silent pond
    where the lotus flowers bloom, I hear you call, pine tree.
What is it you call, pine tree, when the rains fall, when the winds blow,
    and when the stars appear, what is it you call, pine tree?
I hear you call, pine tree, but I am blind, and do not know how to reach
    you, pine tree. Who will take me to you, pine tree?

from *Japanese Hokkus*

1
Suppose the stars
Fall and break?—Do they ever sound
Like my own love song?

12
Leaves blown,
Birds flown away,

I wander in and out the Hall of Autumn.

16
Are the fallen stars
Returning up the sky?—
The dews on the grass.

48
It is too late to hear a nightingale?
Tut, tut, tut,...some bird sings,—
That's quite enough, my friend.

61
Like a cobweb hung upon the tree,
A prey to wind and sunlight!
Who will say that we are safe and strong?

68
Oh, How cool—
The sound of the bell
That leaves the bell itself.

Nora May French
(1881–1907)

Nora May French is one of the neglected treasures of California poetry. A tragic and romantic figure, she committed suicide at twenty-nine while a guest at the Carmel home of the poet George Sterling. She had been writing poetry since she was twelve and left behind a small but distinguished body of work consisting of about seventy poems, including *The Spanish Girl*, a sequence of lyrics in three parts containing twenty-two separate poems. About a dozen of her poems were published before her death in the *Argonaut, Sunset, Current Literature*, and *The American Magazine.*

Nora May French was born in Aurora, New York. Her father, Edward French, was a professor at Wells College. Her mother, Mary Wells French, was the sister of Henry Wells of Wells, Fargo and Company. In 1888 her family moved to Los Angeles, where her prosperous father bought a ranch in what is now Glendale. A few years later a fire destroyed the French home and left the family impoverished.

French attended Otis Art Institute in Los Angeles, working for her room, board, and tuition. In 1905 the beautiful young poet was engaged to Alan Hiley, a wealthy timber farmer. Her apprehensions and fears of this union (the engagement was soon broken) provided the background for *The Spanish Girl*, her most ambitious work. While living in Los Angeles, French became a member of Charles Lummis's Arroyo Seco group of writers and poets, and Lummis published several of her poems in his *Out West* magazine. The feminist nature writer Mary Austin was a member of the group, and she came to regard French as a talent equal to George Sterling and Jack London.

French moved to San Francisco in 1906 not long after the great earthquake, and she quickly entered the bohemian subculture. She was involved in a love affair with Harry Lafler, a handsome editor and notorious womanizer. She broke off this affair only to begin another, while also reviving her earlier engagement with Hiley. French moved to Carmel in 1907 and lived with Sterling and his wife—growing more and more despondent in the lively bohemian atmosphere. She made plans to kill her former lover and herself. After a clumsy attempt to poison him failed, she took her own life with cyanide.

French's poems are often melancholy but never depressive, and there is a recurrent blend of whimsy and wonder at the beauty of nature. They also reveal the conflict in the poet's psyche over the desire to lead an independent and creative life and the social pressure to enter into a secure but passionless marriage. Her poems also reflect French's anguish at her rejection by other women. Tall and shapely, she had golden blond hair and bright blue eyes. A striking figure and dynamic conversationalist, she was conspicuously attractive to men. She claimed to have no female friends, inspiring nothing but envy from members of her own sex. In a short story published in the *Saturday Evening Post* a few weeks before her death, French expressed her frustration defensively, pointing out that anyone who deviated from social norms was judged "queer": "I *am* different," she said. "I don't see why I should pretend to deny that."

French did not publish a collection of poems in her lifetime. In 1910 three of the dead poet's friends brought out *Poems*, the only collection of her verse to be commercially published. Featuring a romantically beautiful portrait of the young poet by society photographer Arnold Genthe, the edition of five hundred sold out quickly. In 1936 the Book Club of California published a pamphlet of about twenty of her poems as part of a series on California poets for its members. Since then, French has remained almost completely unpublished and unread.

Ave Atque Vale

It gathers where the moody sky is bending,
    It stirs the air along familiar ways—
A sigh for strange things forever ending,
    For beauty shrinking in these alien days.

Now nothing is the same; old visions move me:
    I wander silent through the waning land,
And find for youth and little leaves to love me
    The old, old lichen crumbling in my hand.

What shifting films of distance fold you, blind you,
    The windy eve of dreams, I cannot tell.
I know they grope through some strange mist to find you,
    My hands that give you Greeting and Farewell.

The Mourner

Because my love has wave and foam for speech,
    And never words, and yearns as water grieves,
With white arms curving on a listless beach,
    And murmurs inarticulate as leaves—

I am become beloved of the night—
    Her huge sea-lands ineffable and far
Hold crouched and splendid Sorrow, eyed with light,
    And Pain who beads his forehead with a star.

PART II

CALIFORNIA MODERNISTS

Robinson Jeffers
(1887–1962)

John Robinson Jeffers, the great poet of the American West Coast, was born in the suburbs of Pittsburgh, Pennsylvania. His father, William Hamilton Jeffers, was a professor of Old Testament Biblical Theology and a Presbyterian minister. A strict disciplinarian and serious intellectual, the elder Jeffers determined that his son should be properly educated and gave him rigorous private lessons in Greek, Latin, and religion. By the time he was twelve, Jeffers was fluent in French, German, Greek, Latin, and English but awkward among other children. Not surprisingly, the boy developed complex feelings toward his deeply loving but authoritarian father.

Jeffers entered the University of Pittsburgh at fifteen and was awarded sophomore standing. When his father retired the next year, the family moved to Los Angeles and Jeffers transferred to Occidental College, from which he graduated in 1905 at seventeen. The precocious teenager did graduate work at several universities, including the University of Southern California, and he studied literature, medicine, and forestry before realizing that poetry was his calling.

At USC, Jeffers met Una Call Kuster, a beautiful woman who was not only three years older than he but married to a wealthy local attorney. Robin and Una fell irrevocably in love. After seven years of guilt-ridden romance with many renunciations, separations, reconciliations, and eventually a public scandal (reported by the *Los Angeles Times*), Una obtained a divorce on August 1, 1913. The next day she and Jeffers married.

By now Jeffers had dedicated himself fully to poetry. His first collection, *Flagons and Apples*, had appeared in 1912. He and Una traveled north on a horse-drawn mail coach to the wild Big Sur region of coastal California and rented a small cabin in the village of Carmel, which they recognized as their "inevitable place."

The twenty-seven-year-old poet knew that he had not yet written anything of enduring value. The death of both his father and his own newborn daughter in 1914 heightened his sense of mortality. After issuing a second collection, *Californians* (1916), Jeffers published nothing for eight years. He divided his time between writing and building a stone house—Tor House—for his family, which now included twin sons, on a promontory overlooking the Pacific. He carefully reconsidered his aims as a poet and underwent a slow but radical transformation. He rejected rhyme and traditional meter, which inhibited him from telling a story flexibly in verse. He also rejected the obscurity of modernist poetry. He determined to write a timeless and truthful poetry purged of ephemeral things.

In 1924 Jeffers published *Tamar and Other Poems* with a small vanity press in New York. It attracted no initial notice, but a year later it was suddenly taken up by several influential critics. Jeffers produced an expanded trade edition containing what would be his most famous narrative poem, "Roan Stallion." Both public and critical opinion were extraordinary. *Roan Stallion, Tamar and Other Poems* (1925) went into multiple reprintings. Praising his narrative energy, stylistic originality, and thematic profundity, critics compared him to Sophocles and Shakespeare.

Jeffers ignored his sudden celebrity and focused on his work. Over the next ten years he wrote the most remarkable, ambitious, and odd series of narratives poems in American literature. Published in eight major collections—*The Women at Point Sur* (1927), *Cawdor* (1928), *Dear Judas* (1929), *Descent to the Dead* (1931), *Thurso's Landing* (1932), *Give Your Heart to the Hawks* (1933), *Solstice* (1935), and *Such Counsels You Gave to Me* (1937)—these books appeared at the rate of almost one per year and add up to almost one thousand pages of verse in all. Nearly every volume centers on a long narrative usually set in or around Big Sur. Violent, sexual, philosophical, and subversive, these verse novels are alternately magnificent and hyperbolic, powerful and excessive, dramatic and overblown, and unlike anything else in modernist American poetry.

Almost immediately Jeffers's long narrative poems divided audiences. His explicit sexuality, violent plots, and overt anti-Christianity alienated conservative readers. Leftists were dismayed by his distrust of all political programs for human improvement. Meanwhile the New Critics perceived Jeffers's commitment to poetry of direct statement, expansive treatment, and linear narrative as a rejection of the compressed, indirect, and lyric high modernist mode they had all championed.

The controversy over Jeffers's narratives unfortunately overshadowed the shorter works tucked into the back pages of each new book. These lyric meditations, generally written in long rhythmic free verse lines, marked a new kind of nature poem which tried to understand the physical world not from a human perspective but on its own terms. Jeffers's phrase "Not man apart" became a famous rallying cry among environmentalists and conservationists, who consider him a seminal figure in the movement to protect natural habitat, wilderness, and coastal land. Jeffers's nature poetry is emotionally direct, magnificently musical, and philosophically profound.

By World War II Jeffers's critical reputation had collapsed and would not rise again until after his death. The Depression and the war had made his cosmic fatalism and distrust of all political systems less palatable to intellectuals caught up in international events. To the disgust of many Americans, he opposed America's entry into World War II, warning that the conflict would turn the United States into an imperial power. Jeffers still commanded a large group of serious readers, and his books sold well, but the literary establishment dominated by New Critics on the right and Marxists on the left had rejected him. Remote from the centers of literary power in London and New York, he seemed indifferent as his reputation slowly declined. In 1945, however, the noted actress Judith Anderson asked the poet to translate and adapt Euripides's classical tragedy for the modern stage. When Jeffers's *Medea* opened on Broadway in 1947, it stunned audiences and critics with its power and intensity. As its frequent revivals have demonstrated, it is one of the finest adaptations of classical drama in English.

Medea's success relieved Jeffers's financial worries, but the happiest days of his life were now behind him. After Una's slow death from cancer in 1950, he sank into a prolonged depression aggravated by heavy drinking. His eyesight failed. Jeffers published only one book during the last fourteen years of his life—*Hungerfield and Other Poems* (1954). The title poem is a violent and nightmarish narrative that ends unexpectedly with an authorial interruption, his heartbreaking invocation to his dead wife. A few days after his seventy-fifth birthday he died in his sleep at Tor House.

What saves Jeffers's poetry from unrelieved bitterness and nihilism is its joyful awe and indeed religious devotion to the natural world. Living on the edge of the Pacific, he found wisdom, strength, and perspective from observing the forces of nature around him. In "Rock and Hawk" he offers the image of a falcon perched on a tall coastal rock as a symbol of the proper human values: "bright power, dark peace; / Fierce consciousness joined with final / Disinterestedness, / Life with calm death." That unusual combination of sensual delight and resolve underlies much of Jeffers's best work. Magnificent, troubling, idiosyncratic, and uneven, Jeffers remains the great prophetic voice of American modernism.

Continent's End

At the equinox when the earth was veiled in a late rain, wreathed
    with wet poppies, waiting spring,
The ocean swelled for a far storm and beat its boundary, the
    ground-swell shook the beds of granite.

I gazing at the boundaries of granite and spray, the established
    sea-marks, felt behind me
Mountain and plain, the immense breadth of the continent, before
    me the mass and doubled stretch of water.

I said: You yoke the Aleutian seal-rocks with the lava and coral sowings
    that flower the south,
Over your flood the life that sought the sunrise faces ours that has
    followed the evening star.

The long migrations meet across you and it is nothing to you, you have
    forgotten us, mother.
You were much younger when we crawled out of the womb and lay in
    the sun's eye on the tideline.

It was long and long ago; we have grown proud since then and you have
    grown bitter; life retains
Your mobile soft unquiet strength; and envies hardness, the insolent
    quietness of stone.

The tides are in our veins, we still mirror the stars, life is your child,
    but there is in me
Older and harder than life and more impartial, the eye that watched
    before there was an ocean.

That watched you fill your beds out of the condensation of thin vapor
    and watched you change them,

That saw you soft and violent wear your boundaries down, eat rock,
  shift places with the continents.

Mother, though my song's measure is like your surf-beat's ancient
  rhythm I never learned it of you.
Before there was any water there were tides of fire, both our tones
  flow from the older fountain.

Shine, Perishing Republic

While this America settles in the mould of its vulgarity, heavily
  thickening to empire,
And protest, only a bubble in the molten mass, pops and sighs out,
  and the mass hardens,

I sadly smiling remember that the flower fades to make fruit, the fruit
  rots to make earth.
Out of the mother; and through the spring exultances, ripeness and
  decadence; and home to the mother.

You making haste haste on decay: not blameworthy; life is good, be it
  stubbornly long or suddenly
A mortal splendor: meteors are not needed less than mountains: shine,
  perishing republic.

But for my children, I would have them keep their distance from the
  thickening center; corruption
Never has been compulsory, when the cities lie at the monster's feet
  there are left the mountains.

And boys, be in nothing so moderate as in love of man, a clever servant,
  insufferable master.
There is the trap that catches noblest spirits, that caught—they say—
  God, when he walked on earth.

November Surf

Some lucky day each November great waves awake and are drawn
Like smoking mountains bright from the west
And come and cover the cliff with white violent cleanness: then suddenly
The old granite forgets half a year's filth:
The orange-peel, eggshells, papers, pieces of clothing, the clots
Of dung in corners of the rock, and used
Sheaths that make light love safe in the evenings: all the droppings of
    the summer
Idlers washed off in a winter ecstasy:
I think this cumbered continent envies its cliff then....But all seasons
The earth, in her childlike prophetic sleep,
Keeps dreaming of the bath of a storm that prepares up the long coast
Of the future to scour more than her sea-lines:
The cities gone down, the people fewer and the hawks more numerous,
The rivers mouth to source pure; when the two-footed
Mammal, being someways one of the nobler animals, regains
The dignity of room, the value of rareness.

Hands

Inside a cave in a narrow canyon near Tassajara
The vault of rock is painted with hands,
A multitude of hands in the twilight, a cloud of men's palms, no more,
No other picture. There's no one to say
Whether the brown shy quiet people who are dead intended
Religion or magic, or made their tracings
In the idleness of art; but over the division of years these careful
Signs-manual are now like a sealed message
Saying: "Look: we also were human; we had hands, not paws. All hail
You people with the cleverer hands, our supplanters
In the beautiful country; enjoy her a season, her beauty, and come down
And be supplanted; for you also are human."

Rock and Hawk

Here is a symbol in which
Many high tragic thoughts
Watch their own eyes.

This gray rock, standing tall
On the headland, where the seawind
Lets no tree grow,

Earthquake-proved, and signatured
By ages of storms: on its peak
A falcon has perched.

I think, here is your emblem
To hang in the future sky;
Not the cross, not the hive,

But this; bright power, dark peace;
Fierce consciousness joined with final
Disinterestedness;

Life with calm death; the falcon's
Realist eyes and act
Married to the massive

Mysticism of stone,
Which failure cannot cast down
Nor success make proud.

Fire on the Hills

The deer were bounding like blown leaves
Under the smoke in front of the roaring wave of the brush-fire;
I thought of the smaller lives that were caught.
Beauty is not always lovely; the fire was beautiful, the terror
Of the deer was beautiful; and when I returned
Down the black slopes after the fire had gone by, an eagle
Was perched on the jag of a burnt pine,

Insolent and gorged, cloaked in the folded storms of his shoulders.
He had come from far off for the good hunting
With fire for his beater to drive the game; the sky was merciless
Blue, and the hills merciless black,
The sombre-feathered great bird sleepily merciless between them.
I thought, painfully, but the whole mind,
The destruction that brings an eagle from heaven is better than mercy.

Carmel Point

The extraordinary patience of things!
This beautiful place defaced with a crop of suburban houses—
How beautiful when we first beheld it,
Unbroken field of poppy and lupin walled with clean cliffs;
No intrusion but two or three horses pasturing,
Or a few milch cows rubbing their flanks on the outcrop rockheads—
Now the spoiler has come: does it care?
Not faintly. It has all time. It knows the people are a tide
That swells and in time will ebb, and all
Their works dissolve. Meanwhile the image of the pristine beauty
Lives in the very grain of the granite,
Safe as the endless ocean that climbs our cliff.—As for us:
We must uncenter our minds from ourselves;
We must unhumanize our views a little, and become confident
As the rock and ocean that we were made from.

Hildegarde Flanner
(1899–1987)

June Hildegarde Flanner was a poet, playwright, and essayist best known for her lyrical poems celebrating California's natural beauty. Born in Indiana, she visited Pasadena in 1915, where she first met Olive Percival, a renowned book collector and gardener who would become her close friend and mentor. Briefly attending Sweet Briar College, Flanner moved to California in 1919 to attend the University of California, Berkeley, where she studied with poet Witter Bynner. After winning the Emily Chamberlain Cook Prize at Berkeley, Flanner saw her first book of poems, *Young Girl and Other Poems*, published in 1920. *This Morning* followed in 1921.

In 1923 the family home was destroyed in the great Berkeley fire, and Flanner and her mother moved to southern California. Three years later, Flanner married Frederick Monhoff, an artist and architect, and moved with him to Altadena, a pastoral suburb of Pasadena. She had one son, Jan (who later changed his name to John). Flanner became the central poet in Pasadena's thriving artistic community, writing as a dismayed witness to urban sprawl and environmental threats. By the age of forty, she was established in the long tradition of California nature poetry and an early feminist voice. By 1942 she had published eight volumes of poems, including *Time's Profile* (1929), *Valley Quail* (1929), and *If There is Time* (1942). Most of this work is in praise of California's landscapes and gardens, but there are also love poems and many proto-feminist poems. She also wrote several one-act plays, including *Mansions* (1920) and *The White Bridge* (1938).

In 1962, disgusted by the urbanization of southern California, Flanner and her family moved to the Napa Valley, where she published three more books of poetry before her death in 1987, including her first book in almost thirty years, *In Native Light* (1970), and *X* (1983). As with her earlier work, these poems use traditional forms and reflect her love for and connection with the natural world. In her later years, Flanner also published four books of poetic essays. *A Vanishing Land* (1980) was a call to preserve California's delicate landscapes, as was *Brief Cherishing: A Napa Valley Harvest* (1985). Her last publication, *Different Images: Portraits of Remembered People* (1987), contained profiles of women who had inspired her.

Noon on Alameda Street

Sun, when it shines on traffic, has a look
Of loaded radiance that might explode,
Yet keeps its kindle like a meaning known
Only to motors in the city road,

Only to fury lifted of all horns
Mourning to themselves a thing to come,
For we have heard delirium in a claxon,
Seen revelation lit on chromium.

On Alameda Street the earth is turning
Secret among old sluices and their kind:
The voice of men among machines at noon
Comes like a sigh from history to the mind,

For in this noon there is no light like light,
(Oh, tell us, dark on asphalt, of the sun)
But brightness spawning upon dirty glass,
But fever smoking at meridian,

But men and women riding in their graves
With hands upon a wheel they cannot keep
Clear in the rapt confusion of the crowd,
Crowd and the fate of motion and of sleep.

Prayer

With Him who sets the lily on the stem,
With Him who looses summer in the loam,
With Him who wakes the winds and hushes them,
With Him who calls the dead and brings them home,
With Him the nameless, unimportunate,
The utterly within us, beautiful,
With Him I leave tomorrow and too late
Regret I left not yesterday as well.
Unto what loveliness may we commend

The desolation of the flesh that weeps,
To what untellable and bitter end
Shall wake the soul that lifts from sleep...and sleeps?
Oh rouse me up, good God, and keep me so,
Washing my heart in water of the snow!

Janet Lewis
(1899–1998)

Poet, novelist, and librettist Janet Lewis was born in Chicago, the daughter of an English professor. She grew up in the nearby suburb of Oak Park, where she and her contemporary, Ernest Hemingway, both published their first works in the same high school literary magazine. Her family spent summers on an island in Michigan near an Ojibway family with whom they were very close, a connection that initiated Lewis's lifelong interest in American Indian folklore and mythology. She attended the University of Chicago, where she joined the Poetry Club and formed lasting friendships with writers such as Glenway Wescott and Elizabeth Madox Roberts. She would also eventually meet and marry a former member of the club, the poet-critic Yvor Winters, who was then staying at a tuberculosis sanitarium in New Mexico.

After graduation in 1920, Lewis lived briefly in Paris but returned to Chicago. In 1922 she contracted tuberculosis, which compelled her to enter the same Santa Fe sanitarium, Sunmount, that Winters had recently vacated. The two poets, who had met a year earlier in Chicago, began corresponding. During the five years that Lewis spent recuperating in Sunmount, the letters between the two young poets grew more passionate. In 1926 they married in a ceremony conducted at the sanitarium. The following year they moved to California, where Winters spent the rest of his life teaching at Stanford. Lewis had already published her first book of poems, *The Indians in the Woods* (1922), which reflected her twin debts to imagism and American Indian culture. Her second book, *The Wheel in Midsummer*, appeared in 1927.

She also began writing fiction. Her first novel, *The Invasion* (1932), was followed by four more novels, most notably *The Wife of Martin Guerre* (1941), which writer Evan Connell Jr. called "one of the greatest short novels in American literature." Lewis also wrote six opera libretti in verse, most notably *The Wife of Martin Guerre* (1956) for composer William Bergsma and *The Last of the Mohicans* (1976) and *Mulberry Street* (1987) for Alva Henderson. Lewis and Winters had two children. She lived in Los Altos, California, from 1931 until her death in 1998.

Never a prolific poet, Lewis continued to write verse throughout her long life. Deeply influenced by the imagist aesthetic of her youth, she never abandoned its insistence on compression, precision, and direct presentation. Her language remained economical and understated, and the central sensory image, usually visual, stayed in the forefront of her imagination. By mid-career she had begun to write in traditional forms, but she never relinquished free verse. Unlike her husband's fiercely articulated theories, Lewis's approach to writing poetry was practical and undogmatic. *Poems Old and New: 1918–1978* appeared in 1981.

Girl Help

Mild and slow and young,
She moves about the room,
And stirs the summer dust
With her wide broom.

In the warm, lofted air,
Soft lips together pressed,
Soft wispy hair,
She stops to rest,

And stops to breathe,
Amid the summer hum,
The great white lilac bloom
Scented with days to come.

Carmel Highlands

Below the gardens and the darkening pines
The living water sinks among the stones,
Sinking yet foaming, till the snowy tones
Merge with the fog drawn landward in the dim lines.
The cloud dissolves among the flowering vines,
And now the definite mountain-side disowns
The fluid world, the immeasurable zones.
Then white oblivion swallows all designs.

But still the rich confusion of the sea,
Unceasing voice, sombre and solacing,
Rises through veils of silence past the trees;
In restless repetition bound, yet free,
Wave after wave in deluge fresh releasing
An ancient speech, hushed in tremendous ease.

Yvor Winters
(1900–1968)

Arthur Yvor Winters was born in Chicago, the son of a successful stock and grain broker. When he was still a child, his family moved to Eagle Rock, a small town near Pasadena that his paternal grandfather and uncle had helped found. Now part of metropolitan Los Angeles, the area was then still rural. "I used to climb over the hills when I was about ten," he later told the writer Hisaye Yamamoto, "and wander around in La Cañada, which was uncontaminated live-oak forest, not a house in miles, and almost knee-deep in leaf mold." The California landscape would become a central presence in his poetry. By the time he was ready for college, however, his family had returned to Chicago. He entered the University of Chicago, where he joined the Poetry Club. (Janet Lewis, whom Winters would eventually marry, joined the club the year after he left.)

In late 1918, Winters contracted tuberculosis and had to leave college. He soon settled in the Sunmount Sanitarium in Santa Fe, New Mexico. The only available treatment was immobility, and the young poet slowly recuperated for three years—afflicted by "a fatigue so heavy that it was an acute pain, pervasive and poisonous." During this time Winters wrote his first book of poems, *The Immobile Wind* (1921), and most of his second, *The Magpie's Shadow* (1922). Both volumes show his absorption of the imagist aesthetic and the influence of Japanese haiku and American Indian poetry. Written mostly in free verse or syllabics, his early poems are mostly very short—sometimes only a single line of six syllables—and usually focus on one or two images that serve as an entryway into a state of heightened awareness. The young Winters was deeply committed to modernist experiment, and his early work also revealed the influence of Ezra Pound, Wallace Stevens, H. D., and William Carlos Williams.

By the time he left the sanitarium, Winters had quarreled with his parents and needed to support himself. He first became a schoolteacher in the mining town of Madrid, New Mexico. Isolated from intellectual life, he corresponded with Marianne Moore, then a librarian in New York City, who loaned him books, "very kindly," he later remarked, "but I am sure illegally." Living in the West and reclusive by nature, Winters would conduct several important literary friendships by mail. He and

Hart Crane met only once, but their letters had a decisive influence on both poets' lives.

After reconciling with his parents, Winters entered the University of Colorado, where he studied French, Latin, and Spanish and completed an M.A. in 1926. (Significantly, Winters's formal literary education consisted mostly of Romance language and classical poetry—supplemented by his passionate private reading of contemporary verse; he did not study premodern English-language poetry until he arrived at Stanford.) On a trip back to Chicago, Winters had met Janet Lewis. She, too, had contracted tuberculosis and went to the same sanitarium Winters had recently left. In 1926 he and Lewis were married at Sunmount, where she was still a patient.

Winters taught French and Spanish at the University of Idaho and then, in 1927, he entered Stanford as a graduate student in English. He remained there for the rest of his life, eventually becoming a full professor. Once resettled in California, Winters rarely left the West and never traveled abroad. For better and worse, he cultivated a distance between himself and the Eastern centers of literary opinion. He was the only major New Critic to live in the West. Rather than attending literary conferences, he raised Airedales and tended a small orchard.

In 1928 Winters experienced a radical aesthetic shift. He abandoned free verse and returned to traditional meters. The shift was initially pragmatic and not ideological; having decided that he could not equal the poets he most admired—Baudelaire, Rimbaud, Valéry, Hardy, Bridges, and Stevens—by the imagist methods he was using, he decided to try other techniques. Gradually, however, he began to develop a new theory of poetry based on his experiments with meter and form. "My shift from the methods of these early poems," he later wrote, "was not a shift from formlessness to form; it was a shift from certain kinds of form to others." Imagistic free verse, he felt, had proved too restrictive.

Winters had written reviews since leaving New Mexico, but in the late 1920s he began focusing enormous energy on criticism. He published prominent early essays on Hart Crane, Louise Bogan, Wallace Stevens, Marianne Moore, and the Fugitives. He also wrote dissenting essays on Robert Frost, Robinson Jeffers, and Archibald MacLeish that helped define and consolidate the New Critical rejection of populist modernism. In 1929 Winters and Lewis created *Gyroscope*, an influential small literary magazine dedicated to correcting the excesses of modernism. The journal lasted only four issues, but it

confirmed Winters's growing importance as a major poet-critic.
In his essays and reviews Winters articulated his dissatisfaction with
the subjectivity, irrationality, and vague mysticism of American poetry.
In three cantankerously contrarian and brilliantly iconoclastic
critical volumes, *Primitivism and Decadence* (1937), *Maule's Curse:
Seven Studies in the History of American Obscurantism* (1938), and
The Anatomy of Nonsense (1943), Winters chronicled and dissected
the philosophical contradictions inherent in romantic and modernist
poetry. Eventually collected as *In Defense of Reason* (1947), these
studies defined Winters's new sense of poetry as a means of
"comprehension on a moral plane" of human experience cast in
language that fully conveyed the feeling of the given experiences.

Winters's later poetry employed a lucid and exact neoclassical style
in tight formal meters. His imagery maintained the bright exactitude
of his early experimental work, but now it operated in an ordered
rational context. He created a style, which he called "post-Symbolist,"
in which complex associational poetry was written with "no sacrifice to
rational intelligence."

While Winters's brand of modernism was conservative and classical,
his personal politics were firmly leftist and progressive. He was a lifelong
member of the ACLU and NAACP and once contemplated joining
the Communist Party. His example reinforces the notion that among
modernists there was little connection between aesthetic and political
radicalism.

In 1946 Winters helped his Stanford colleague Wallace Stegner
create one of the nation's first graduate programs in creative writing.
Over the next two decades the demanding and opinionated professor
became one of the most influential poetry-writing teachers in the history
of American letters. Some of his students accepted his aesthetic; others
rejected it, but few left unchallenged or unchanged. A short list of
Winters's students includes Donald Justice, Edgar Bowers, Philip
Levine, Thom Gunn, Donald Hall, Robert Hass, N. Scott Momaday,
Robert Pinsky, and Ann Stanford. Winters's contrarian views kept him
from receiving most literary honors, but in 1960, just as he published his
Collected Poems, he won the Bollingen Prize for lifetime contribution
to American poetry. He died of cancer in 1968.

One Ran Before

I could tell
Of silence where
One ran before
Himself and fell
Into silence
Yet more fair.

And this were more
A thing unseen
Than falling screen
Could make of air.

The Slow Pacific Swell

Far out of sight forever stands the sea,
Bounding the land with pale tranquillity.
When a small child, I watched it from a hill
At thirty miles or more. The vision still
Lies in the eye, soft blue and far away:
The rain has washed the dust from April day;
Paint-brush and lupine lie against the ground;
The wind above the hill-top has the sound
Of distant water in unbroken sky;
Dark and precise the little steamers ply—
Firm in direction they seem not to stir.
That is illusion. The artificer
Of quiet, distance holds me in a vise
And holds the ocean steady to my eyes.

Once when I rounded Flattery, the sea
Hove its loose weight like sand to tangle me
Upon the washing deck, to crush the hull;
Subsiding, dragged flesh at the bone. The skull
Felt the retreating wash of dreaming hair.
Half drenched in dissolution, I lay bare.
I scarcely pulled myself erect; I came
Back slowly, slowly knew myself the same.

That was the ocean. From the ship we saw
Gray whales for miles: the long sweep of the jaw,
The blunt head plunging clean above the wave.
And one rose in a tent of sea and gave
A darkening shudder; water fell away;
The whale stood shining, and then sank in spray.

A landsman, I. The sea is but a sound.
I would be near it on a sandy mound,
And hear the steady rushing of the deep
While I lay stinging in the sand with sleep.
I have lived inland long. The land is numb.
It stands beneath the feet, and one may come
Walking securely, till the sea extends
Its limber margin, and precision ends.
By night a chaos of commingling power,
The whole Pacific hovers hour by hour.
The slow Pacific swell stirs on the sand,
Sleeping to sink away, withdrawing land,
Heaving and wrinkled in the moon, and blind;
Or gathers seaward, ebbing out of mind.

A Summer Commentary

When I was young, with sharper sense,
The farthest insect cry I heard
Could stay me; through the trees, intense,
I watched the hunter and the bird.

Where is the meaning that I found?
Or was it but a state of mind,
Some old penumbra of the ground,
In which to be but not to find?

Now summer grasses, brown with heat,
Have crowded sweetness through the air;
The very roadside dust is sweet;
Even the unshadowed earth is fair.

The soft voice of the nesting dove,
And the dove in soft erratic flight
Like a rapid hand within a glove,
Caress the silence and the light.

Amid the rubble, the fallen fruit,
Fermenting in its rich decay,
Smears brandy on the trampling boot
And sends it sweeter on its way.

At the San Francisco Airport

To my daughter, 1954

This is the terminal: the light
Gives perfect vision, false and hard;
The metal glitters, deep and bright.
Great planes are waiting in the yard—
They are already in the night.

And you are here beside me, small,
Contained and fragile, and intent
On things that I but half recall—
Yet going whither you are bent.
I am the past, and that is all.

But you and I in part are one:
The frightened brain, the nervous will,
The knowledge of what must be done,
The passion to acquire the skill
To face that which you dare not shun.

The rain of matter upon sense
Destroys me momently. The score:
There comes what will come. The expense
Is what one thought, and something more—
One's being and intelligence.

This is the terminal, the break.
Beyond this point, on lines of air,
You take the way that you must take;
And I remain in light and stare—
In light, and nothing else, awake.

Kenneth Rexroth

(1905–1982)

Poet, critic, translator, anarchist, and cultural impresario, Kenneth Rexroth, who would occupy the intellectual center of the San Francisco Renaissance, was born in South Bend, Indiana. The only child of affluent bohemian parents, Rexroth had a nourishing but unconventional childhood in a progressive Christian Socialist household. When he was four, his family relocated to Elkhart—the first of many moves his increasingly erratic parents would make as their fortunes rose and fell. Eventually Rexroth's parents separated, reuniting briefly before his mother's untimely death in 1916. In her final illness she refused to let her ten-year-old son attend school but read to him from her sickbed, urging him to be a writer. Three years later his alcoholic father died suddenly. The orphaned adolescent went to Chicago to live with an aunt, but he quickly rebelled in the conventional new setting. Dropping out of high school at sixteen, Rexroth frequented bohemian Chicago, supporting himself through odd jobs and journalism. Soon he began hitchhiking across the country, later working his way to Europe and Latin America aboard ships.

In 1927 Rexroth married Andrée Schafer, a painter, and the newlyweds soon moved to San Francisco, the city with which the poet would ever afterward be associated. "It is the only city in the United States," he observed, "which was not settled overland by the westward-spreading puritan tradition." Deciding to "stay and grow up in the town," Rexroth wrote, painted, and worked in radical politics—usually just scraping by on limited funds. He briefly joined the Communist Party but left because his own principles were pacifist and anarchist. His marriage also broke up; he would eventually marry four times. In 1932 his poems appeared in Louis Zukofsky's An "Objectivists" Anthology. His first book, In What Hour (1940), was published to largely hostile reviews by Eastern critics who either decried his political defection from the organized Left or considered his West Coast subject matter trivial. Despite his growing reputation and readership, Rexroth would never be read sympathetically by Eastern critics, and he never won a major establishment award.

A conscientious objector and pacifist, Rexroth engaged in antiwar activity during the early days of World War II, especially by helping

Japanese Americans resist internment, which made him the subject of an FBI investigation. He was eventually granted an exemption from the draft and escaped incarceration, though the strain of the situation contributed to the breakup of his second marriage. In 1944 he published a long poem, *The Phoenix and the Tortoise*, with New Directions, which began a lifelong partnership between him and poet James Laughlin, one of the greatest American publisher of modernist letters. Now at the height of his powers, Rexroth published a steady stream of poetry, prose, translations, and drama. His most notable collections of poetry include *The Signature of All Things* (1950), *The Dragon and the Unicorn* (1952), *In Defense of the Earth* (1956), *Natural Numbers* (1963), and *The Heart's Garden, the Garden's Heart* (1967). Rexroth also began translating Asian poetry in an influential series of books, most notably *One Hundred Poems from the Japanese* (1955) and *One Hundred Poems from the Chinese* (1956).

By 1950 Rexroth had established himself—through hard work and sheer ambition—at the center of San Francisco literary life. He not only published in national journals but also conducted a weekly book-review show on Berkeley's newly established KPFA, the nation's first listener-sponsored radio station. A public spokesman for modernist literature, political dissent, and alternate lifestyles, Rexroth became the elder statesman of the new Beat movement emerging in San Francisco. The Beats generated huge amounts of media coverage that turned several younger writers Rexroth had championed—most notably Allen Ginsberg, Lawrence Ferlinghetti, and Jack Kerouac—into international celebrities, but such fame never came to Rexroth himself; he was too mature, well read, and intellectual to fit the media's definition of the Beat identity. (Instead, *Time* magazine dubbed him "the Daddy of the Beat Generation," not a particularly cool title.) The media craze did allow Rexroth to develop with the other Beats a new form of poetry reading—not the academic lecture style still prevalent today but a performance spoken to the accompaniment of live jazz.

Rexroth's later years were secure and comfortable. In 1968 he took a teaching position at the University of California, Santa Barbara, which he held until his retirement in 1974. Also in 1974, Rexroth finally married his longtime companion, Carol Tinker, his fourth and final spouse. He wrote a popular literary column, "Classics Revisited," for *Saturday Review* and a twice-weekly column in the *San Francisco Examiner* in which he was free to discuss any topic, from avant-garde art to world politics. Rexroth died at seventy-six in Santa Barbara where, after a Catholic and Buddhist ceremony, he was buried facing the Pacific Ocean.

Although Rexroth's poetic style may have seemed unorthodox early in his career, it prefigured the mainstream American poetry of the 1960s and 1970s. Clarity, simplicity, accessibility, and intensity are the main characteristics of his style. Written in direct, plainspoken free verse, Rexroth's poetry makes its points through image and observation. His lines are usually end-stopped with line breaks coming at an obvious pause of syntax or sense—a technique that heightens their conversational quality without letting them ever appear unduly chatty or verbose. Rexroth is a master of pictorial depiction, especially when describing the Western landscape, with an easy command of precise naturalist detail. There is also usually a strong sense of personal voice in his work—the "I" in the poem almost always purports to be the poet himself, which is to say that it attempts to recreate a convincing persona of the poet in words.

Rexroth worked to establish a West Coast identity for American poetry, one that would reflect the unique geographical, historical, cultural, and ethnic qualities of the region. "I am not Ivy League," he once asserted, as if anyone could have ever confused his self-educated libertarian anarchism with Ivy League elitism or New Critical detachment. He was both a populist and an intellectual—a potent combination of cultural values in the right circumstances. Rexroth also understood that regional literary identity need not, indeed must not, be provincial. His international sense of literary enterprise led him to translate from Chinese, Japanese, French, Spanish, and Greek, all as relevant sources for a California literary identity. Rexroth's place in the American literary canon, like that of many Californian poets such as Robinson Jeffers, William Everson, Josephine Miles, Robert Duncan, and Jack Spicer, remains open to debate. Consistently ignored by the Eastern literary establishment, these poets continue to exercise an active influence on West Coast writers, and they continue to be read. Rexroth left a small but enduring body of original poems, elegant translations, and still potent essays out of the huge body of work he created. It remains impossible to discuss the changes in mid-twentieth-century American poetry responsibly without mentioning him.

Requiem for the Spanish Dead

The great geometrical winter constellations
Lift up over the Sierra Nevada,
I walk under the stars, my feet on the known round earth.
My eyes following the lights of an airplane,
Red and green, growling deep into the Hyades.
The note of the engine rises, shrill, faint,
Finally inaudible, and the lights go out
In the southeast haze beneath the feet of Orion.

As the sound departs I am chilled and grow sick
With the thought that has come over me. I see Spain
Under the black windy sky, the snow stirring faintly,
Glittering and moving over the pallid upland,
And men waiting, clutched with cold and huddled together,
As an unknown plane goes over them. It flies southeast
Into the haze above the lines of the enemy,
Sparks appear near the horizon under it.
After they have gone out the earth quivers
And the sound comes faintly. The men relax for a moment
And grow tense again as their own thoughts return to them.

I see the unwritten books, the unrecorded experiments,
The unpainted pictures, the interrupted lives,
Lowered into the graves with the red flags over them.
I see the quick gray brains broken and clotted with blood,
Lowered each in its own darkness, useless in the earth.
Alone on a hilltop in San Francisco suddenly
I am caught in a nightmare, the dead flesh
Mounting over half the world presses against me.

Then quietly at first and then rich and full-bodied,
I hear the voice of a young woman singing.
The emigrants on the corner are holding
A wake for their oldest child, a driverless truck
Broke away on the steep hill and killed him,
Voice after voice adds itself to the singing.
Orion moves westward across the meridian,
Rigel, Bellatrix, Betelgeuse, marching in order,
The great nebula glimmering in his loins.

Delia Rexroth

California rolls into
Sleepy summer, and the air
Is full of the bitter sweet
Smoke of the grass fires burning
On the San Francisco hills.
Flesh burns so, and the pyramids
Likewise, and the burning stars.
Tired tonight, in a city
Of parvenus, in the inhuman
West, in the most blood drenched year,
I took down a book of poems
That you used to like, that you
Used to sing to music I
Never found anywhere again—
Michael Field's book, *Long Ago*.
Indeed it's long ago now—
Your bronze hair and svelte body.
I guess you were a fierce lover,
A wild wife, an animal
Mother. And now life has cost
Me more years, though much less pain,
Than you had to pay for it.
And I have bought back, for and from
Myself, these poems and paintings,
Carved from the protesting bone,
The precious consequences
Of your torn and distraught life.

from *Andrée Rexroth*

Mt. Tamalpais

The years have gone. It is spring
Again. Mars and Saturn will
Soon come on, low in the West,
In the dusk. Now the evening
Sunlight makes hazy girders
Over Steep Ravine above

The waterfalls. The winter
Birds from Oregon, robins
And varied thrushes, feast on
Ripe toyon and madroñe
Berries. The robins sing as
The dense light falls.
                    Your ashes
Were scattered in this place. Here
I wrote you a farewell poem,
And long ago another,
A poem of peace and love,
Of the lassitude of a long
Spring evening in youth. Now
It is almost ten years since
You came here to stay. Once more,
The pussy willows that come
After the New Year in this
Outlandish land are blooming.
There are deer and raccoon tracks
In the same places. A few
New sand bars and cobble beds
Have been left where erosion
Has gnawed deep into the hills.
The rounds of life are narrow.
War and peace have passed like ghosts.
The human race sinks towards
Oblivion. A bittern
Calls from the same rushes where
You heard one on our first year
In the West; and where I heard
One again in the year
Of your death.

Vitamins and Roughage

Strong ankled, sun burned, almost naked,
The daughters of California
Educate reluctant humanists;

Drive into their skulls with tennis balls
The unhappy realization
That nature is still stronger than man.
The special Hellenic privilege
Of the special intellect seeps out
At last in this irrigated soil.
Sweat of athletes and juice of lovers
Are stronger than Socrates' hemlock;
And the games of scrupulous Euclid
Vanish in the gymnopaedia.

Aspen Meadows

Look. Listen. They are lighting
The moon. Be still. I don't want
To hear again that wistful
Kyriale of husbands and lovers.
Stop questioning me
About my women. You are
Not a schoolgirl nor I a
Lecturing paleobotanist.
It's enough that the green glow
Runs through the down on your arms
Like a grass fire and your eyes
Are fogs of the same endless light.
Let the folds and divisions
Of your anatomy envelop
All horizons. O my sweet
Topology and delusion,
You may be arrogant and feral
But no clock can measure
How long ago you fell asleep
In my arms in the midst of
Sliding doors, parting curtains,
Electric fishes and candy lotuses
And the warm wet moonlight.

George Oppen
(1908–1984)

Considered the quintessential "poet's poet" by many poets and scholars, George Oppen was born in New Rochelle, New York. His mother's suicide when he was four and his father's remarriage five years later combined to cause him childhood trauma, and Oppen also accused his stepmother of physical violence and sexual abuse. He attended a private preparatory school in California and in 1926 matriculated at Oregon State University at Corvallis. In his first months, he met Mary Colby, who would later become his wife. When they stayed out all night on their first date, the university dismissed them both. Supported by trust funds, they were inseparable for the rest of their lives. They worked their way across the United States for two years, hitchhiking and working short-term jobs, and were married in Dallas, Texas, in 1927. The following year they traveled to New York City, where they met Louis Zukofsky and Charles Reznikoff, poets who would become lifelong literary allies and significant partners in the founding of the objectivist movement.

The Oppens moved to France in 1929 and were invigorated by the artistic climate. They established To Publishers, which issued Ezra Pound's *How to Read* (1931), William Carlos Williams's *A Novelette and Other Prose 1921–1931* (1932), and Louis Zukofsky's *An "Objectivists" Anthology* (1932), an important text in American modernist poetry. Oppen was also at work on his own early poetry, and some appeared in the 1931 *Poetry* magazine, an objectivist issue edited by Louis Zukofsky. Including poetry by Oppen, Charles Reznikoff, and Carl Rakosi as well as his own, the editor defined objectivism as proceeding by "economy of presentation," emphasizing the poem as an object made of words. Oppen as well urged a poetry that recorded the material reality of the world outside of its own structure. Originating in Ezra Pound's early imagist work and William Carlos Williams's insistence on a verse that displayed "no ideas but in things" in vernacular language, objectivist poetics also had a hidden political dimension, leftist in aesthetic and informed by a Marxist insistence on laying bare the historical and material foundations of knowledge. These were concerns shared by many American intellectuals during the 1930s.

Back in the United States in 1933, in the depths of the Depression, Oppen founded Objectivist Press, a short-lived successor to To Publishers, and he again published influential books of his own (*Discrete Series*, 1934) and by Williams and Reznikoff. Oppen had long insisted that objectivism focused on the poem as object—separated from the poet's views or intentions—and in *Discrete Series*, he presented "empirical statements" about the dire social conditions of the Depression, an alternative to the overt political commentary of the more polemical Marxist poetry of the 1930s.

Oppen and his wife joined the Communist Party in 1935, and rather than choosing the path of a committed artist-intellectual, he left the life of a poet for that of a radicalized factory worker. As a result of his political activities and the anti-Communist crusades of the 1950s, the Oppens fled to Mexico for eight years and he abandoned poetry for twenty-five years.

Granted passports to return to the United States in 1958, the family came back for their daughter to attend Sarah Lawrence College, and Oppen began writing poetry again at the age of fifty. They lived mainly in San Francisco until he entered a nursing home in Sunnyvale with Alzheimer's disease. He died in 1984.

Oppen published seven books after he resumed his life as a poet: *The Materials* (1962), *This in Which* (1965), *Of Being Numerous* (1968), *Alpine: Poems* (1969), *Seascape: Needle's Eye* (1972), *The Collected Poems of George Oppen* (1975), and *Primitive* (1978). His remarkable achievements as a poet were acknowledged with a Pulitzer Prize in 1969, for *Of Being Numerous*, and with a 1980 award from the American Academy and Institute of Arts and Letters.

Oppen's central question was always if language could really engage the profound moral questions of the modern age, and he proceeded in a verse so spare and elliptical that his detractors saw it as private, arcane, a retreat into language. But from Ezra Pound to Louis Simpson, poets extolled his life and pared-down style as aesthetically unique and morally distinctive, the work of what Charles Tomlinson called "the most human of poets."

The Bicycles and the Apex

How we loved them
Once, these mechanisms;
We all did. Light
And miraculous,

They have gone stale, part
Of the platitude, the gadgets,
Part of the platitude
Of our discontent.

Van Gogh went hungry and what shoe salesman
Does not envy him now? Let us agree
Once and for all that neither the slums
Nor the tract houses

Represent the apex
Of the culture.
They are the barracks. Food

Produced, garbage disposed of,
Lotions sold, flat tires
Changed and tellers must handle money

Under supervision but it is a credit to no one
So that slums are made dangerous by the gangs
And suburbs by the John Birch Societies

But we loved them once,
The mechanisms. Light
And miraculous…

The Building of the Skyscraper

The steel worker on the girder
Learned not to look down, and does his work
And there are words we have learned
Not to look at,
Not to look for substance
Below them. But we are on the verge
Of vertigo.

There are words that mean nothing
But there is something to mean.
Not a declaration which is truth

But a thing
Which is. It is the business of the poet
'To suffer the things of the world
And to speak them and himself out.'

O, the tree, growing from the sidewalk—
It has a little life, sprouting
Little green buds
Into the culture of the streets.
We look back
Three hundred years and see bare land.
And suffer vertigo.

Psalm

Veritas sequitur...

In the small beauty of the forest
The wild deer bedding down—
That they are there!

                 Their eyes
Effortless, the soft lips
Nuzzle and the alien small teeth
Tear at the grass

                 The roots of it
Dangle from their mouths
Scattering earth in the strange woods.
They who are there.

                 Their paths
Nibbled thru the fields, the leaves that shade them
Hang in the distances
Of sun

                 The small nouns
Crying faith
In this in which the wild deer
Startle, and stare out.

Rosalie Moore

(1910–2000)

Winner of the Yale Series of Younger Poets Award, Rosalie Gertrude Moore (Brown) published just four books of poetry in her life. Born in Oakland in 1910, Moore was the daughter of Marvin, a railroad man, and Teresa, a teacher. She graduated magna cum laude from the University of California, Berkeley, in 1932 and returned to get her M.A. in 1934. She wrote for small weekly papers (her work included a book-review column for the San Francisco *Leader*) before landing a job as a copywriter and announcer for KLX, an Oakland radio station, from 1935 to 1937. She left radio for a position with the U.S. Census Bureau and began writing seriously during off hours, winning an award for poetry at the New York World's Fair in 1939.

She explains in *The Grasshopper's Man and Other Poems* (1949): "My writing career started seriously about the time I left the radio job, when I came in contact with Lawrence Hart, critic and writer, who at that time was teaching poetry in the San Francisco Bay region." Moore, Hart, and several other poets formed a group called the Activists, who held that successful poems must be "active" in every line. They accused the fashionable Beat poets of failing to do "the actual work which a poet should do," as Moore wrote in *Poetry* magazine.

Moore married William L. Brown, a newspaperman and writer, in 1942, and they had three children. In 1947 she and her family moved to Mendocino County, where they lived on a rustic eighty-acre "ranch" and she wrote much of the time; she and her husband began to write children's stories together as Bill Brown and Rosalie Brown, and she continued to write poetry as well. In 1948, W. H. Auden chose Moore's first book of poems, *The Grasshopper's Man*, for the prestigious Yale Series award and wrote a glowing foreword. She was awarded Guggenheim Fellowships in 1950 and 1951, but she didn't publish another book of poems for almost thirty years.

Moore and her family moved to Marin County to be closer to established schools, and she and her husband focused on children's books until his death in 1964. "I loved writing the children's books in the 1950s, when my children were growing up," she recalled. The team was very successful, authoring seven works for juveniles between 1954 and 1963, and many of their stories were carried over into school readers.

In 1965, Moore took a teaching position at the College of Marin, where she worked until 1976. She returned to poetry after another long hiatus, and in 1977 published *Year of the Children: Poems for a Narrative*, based on the Children's Crusade of 1212. In 1979, at age sixty-nine, she published her collected works, *Of Singles and Doubles: Collected Poems, 1952–1978*. Her last book of poems was *Gutenberg in Strasbourg* (1997), a cycle of poems about the invention of the printing press. She was an active member of the Marin poetry community until her death in 2000 at age ninety.

Still without Life

The mind's circle increases death,
Not weakly, but with
A close and capital waiting.

Death is your ignorance of constants
    and horribles, and surely
Your knowledge of this, and walking
    behind a friend,
Are the same thing.

Never touch, never see, never counter
    in all your life
The solid that owns everything;
Only the objects, not us, have
The purpose to live like people,
The patience to love like boards.

Shipwreck

Watching, watching from shore:
Wind, and the shore lifting,
The hands raising on wind
And all the elements rising.

Calmly the wreck rides,
Turns like leviathan or log,

And the moon-revealing white turns upward
(Upward of palms, the dead);
And all of the sea's attack, small tangents and traps,
Is wasted on it, the wind wasted,
Helpless to wreck or raise.

Often in sleep turning or falling
A dream's long dimension
I rock to a random ship:
The one like a broken loon,
Clapping its light and calling;
The one bug-black, signing its sign in oil;
The telegraph-tall, invented —
Moved by a whine of wires;
The *Revenge* riding its crossbar,
Raising its sword hilt:

And I know their power is ended, and all of the dreams
Too vacant and inhabited:
The ships with lights on their brows, the mementos, the messages,
The cardinals, couriers to Garcias; and after it all, they say,
The ships make more noise than the sea.

And I look again
At the equal ocean
With its great dead ship.

Ripeness Is Rapid

Ripeness is rapid as plum-drop, as invader.
Plume-fall of evening captures the Turk's
          East, and I wonder—
The bright-ribbed Alexander...

Many in the berried light, riper,
The women.
But he came with a stiffness of swan,
With a tongue thick with galleys.

As one with toads or jewels at mouth speaking,
(And the waves pounding at Cypress)
He came, left hanging in air
The shaking cliffs and carrions.

Moonlight, wilderness cover;
The small wind dries on the bush,
The sail folds in Marmora.

Oh when will he return to this wooden moonlight,
        when uncover
All we were ever to see—that unfilled tomb
The women murmur for.

Josephine Miles
(1911–1985)

Josephine Miles was born in Chicago but grew up in southern California, where her family moved when she was five in the hopes that a warmer climate would ease her rheumatoid arthritis. Severely afflicted by the painful and crippling disease throughout her life, Miles was confined to a wheelchair and sometimes needed to be carried from place to place. A person of enormous optimism and resolve, she argued that her disease gave her the time and determination to write, and she achieved distinction as both a poet and scholar. After mastering classical languages in high school, she graduated Phi Beta Kappa from the University of California, Los Angeles, in 1932. She then earned her Ph.D. in 1938 from the University of California, Berkeley.

In 1940 Miles received two letters on the same day—the first from the celebrated Pasadena Playhouse, offering her a playwright fellowship, the second from UC Berkeley, offering her a teaching job. Without hesitation, she chose the academic career. Her decision proved successful, and she taught at Berkeley until her retirement in 1978. In 1947 she became the first woman to be tenured in the English department. Her skill as a teacher may be judged by the list of her famous literary students, which includes A. R. Ammons, William Stafford, Jack Spicer, and Diane Wakoski. Except for two years in Michigan, Miles lived all of her adult life in California. She died in 1985 at seventy-three.

Miles's first book of poetry, *Lines at Intersection* (1939), revealed her mature style—concise, understated, and exact—already fully formed. Eight volumes of poetry followed before her *Collected Poems: 1930–1983* (1983) appeared. She was a maverick in both her poetry and scholarship, developing her voice and interests into a distinctive, compelling body of work that often chafes against the norms of her era. Oddly enough, in her scholarship, notably in her most influential study, *Eras and Modes in English Poetry* (1957, revised and enlarged 1964), she sought to define such norms. Through statistical analysis of patterns in poetic diction and syntax, she mapped stylistic changes and confluences from the Elizabethan age to the twentieth century.

Recognition came slowly for Miles. Although she won fellowships from the Guggenheim Foundation and the National Endowment for the Arts, she had to wait until the end of her life for a significant award—the Lenore Marshall/*Nation* Poetry Prize for her *Collected Poems* in 1983. Her books were generally well reviewed, but she was rarely mentioned in critical surveys of contemporary poetry. Although deeply informed by tradition, her work was too original and idiosyncratic to be linked to any particular school of poets. As poet Julia Randall has observed, Miles's work can most naturally be seen in the tradition of Emily Dickinson, Marianne Moore, Stevie Smith, and Elizabeth Bishop, "a company of eccentric, independent, and unabashedly single ladies" who stood apart from the literary fashions of their times. In Miles's poetry there is a mixture of boldness and modesty, humor and sorrow, but she never surrenders to the pain and isolation that her life exacted. Although it is personal in its tone and subject matter, her work is rarely overtly autobiographical. One could not easily construe the singular circumstances of her remarkable life from her poems, although her situation is often subtly reflected in them. Her quiet and compact poetry can initially seem unassuming, but repeated readings reveal its imaginative and emotional power.

Riddle

You are a riddle I would not unravel,
You are the riddle my life comprehends.
And who abstracts the marvel
Abstracts the story to its sorriest ends.

But not your riddle. It is patent,
Never more than it says, and since that is
Impossible, it is the marvel
Nobody, as I am nobody, believes.

Conception

Death did not come to my mother
Like an old friend.
She was a mother, and she must
Conceive him.

Up and down the bed she fought crying
Help me, but death
Was a slow child
Heavy. He

Waited. When he was born
We took and tired him, now he is ready
To do his good in the world.

He has my mother's features.
He can go among strangers
To save lives.

Album

This is a hard life you are living
While you are young,
My father said,
As I scratched my casted knees with a paper knife.
By laws of compensation
Your old age should be grand.

Not grand, but of a terrible
Compensation, to perceive
Past the energy of survival
In its sadness
The hard life of the young.

PART III

MID-CENTURY REBELS AND TRADITIONALISTS

William Everson (Brother Antoninus)
(1912–1994)

William Oliver Everson, who would briefly achieve immense celebrity
as Brother Antoninus at the height of the San Francisco Renaissance
while also becoming one of the greatest letterpress printers in American
history, was born in Sacramento. He was the second of three children
born to a mismatched couple. The poet's father, a Norwegian
immigrant, had come to America alone as a boy and worked as a
bandmaster and printer. His wife, who was twenty years younger, grew
more emotionally distant from her husband with the birth of each child.
"In the world of the myth," the poet later commented, "my mother
was a goddess and my father was an ogre." A few months after his
birth, the poet's parents moved to Selma, the small farming town in the
San Joaquin Valley, where Everson grew up. A poor student, Everson
graduated from Selma Union High School in 1931 and entered Fresno
State College but quickly dropped out. Soon he enlisted in the Civilian
Conservation Corps, a Roosevelt administration job program, working
on roads in Sequoia National Park.

Returning to Fresno State College in the fall of 1934, Everson made
the crucial literary discovery of his life—the poetry of Robinson Jeffers.
"Suddenly the whole inner world began to tremble," he later wrote,
describing his first reading of Jeffers's work. Thus began Everson's
lifelong devotion to the older writer's work, which eventually resulted in
two extraordinary and impassioned critical studies, *Robinson Jeffers:
Fragments of an Older Fury* (1968) and *The Excesses of God: Robinson
Jeffers as a Religious Figure* (1988). This first encounter also confirmed
the young man's literary vocation. "I couldn't believe it," he recalled.
"I began to write other poems and by the end of the semester I knew
what I was going to do." He dropped out of college to be a poet while
supporting himself laying irrigation pipes. He published his first two
volumes of poems, *These Are the Ravens* (1935) and *San Joaquin* (1939),
with small California presses. In 1938 he married his high school
girlfriend and soon bought a small farm.

In 1940 American men were required to register for possible military
conscription—Europe was already at war—but Everson filed as a
conscientious objector. After the United States declared war on the Axis
powers, the thirty-year-old Everson was called up and sent to Civilian

Public Service Camp 56 in Waldport, Oregon, where he worked with other COs, clearing trails and crushing rocks. The camp, which contained many other intellectuals and artists, including Kenneth Rexroth and Henry Miller, covertly published an underground newsletter, "The Untide" (to counter the official camp publication, "The Tide"), and eventually issued an anarchist journal, *The Illiterati.* Everson not only contributed to these illicit publications but also helped print them. This was his introduction to hand printing, a craft he would soon master.

During Everson's three years at the camp, his father died (his mother had died in 1940), and his wife left him for another man. At the time of his demobilization in 1946, he moved to Sebastopol (in Sonoma County, California), which was then a small farm town, to set up a press in an arts commune. He soon moved to Berkeley, both to learn more about printing and to court an Italian American artist who was in the process of rediscovering her Catholic faith. She gave Everson a copy of *The Confessions of Saint Augustine,* introducing him to the other author who would prove to be decisive in his life.

At a midnight mass on Christmas Eve, 1948, Everson underwent a mystical experience, and the following July he was baptized at St. Augustine's Church in Oakland. He soon began working on San Francisco's skid row for Dorothy Day's Catholic Worker House, which provided food and lodging for the homeless. In his private devotions, Everson continued to have mystical experiences. "I was seized with a feeling so intense as to exceed anything I had previously experienced," he recorded in a notebook about one such event. "It was a feeling of extreme anguish and joy, of transcendent spirituality and of great, thrilling physical character....From the tabernacle had issued to me something like an intense invisible ray, a dark ray, like a ray of light seen in the mind only." In 1951 Everson joined the Dominican order as a lay brother (a postulate with no intention of becoming a priest and no obligation to take the vows of poverty, obedience, and chastity). Given the name Brother Antoninus, the poet entered St. Albert's, a monastery in Oakland. He set up his press in the basement and started designing and printing a Latin psalter which would eventually be recognized as one of the masterpieces of American handpress printing.

Everson's conversion unleashed a torrent of poetic creation. Many critics rate the three major collections published under the name of Brother Antoninus as his finest poetic works—*The Crooked Lines of God*

(1959), *The Hazards of Holiness* (1962), and *The Rose of Solitude* (1967), which were later collected in *The Veritable Years: 1949–1966* (1978). In this rhapsodic, visionary poetry, Everson transcends his earlier influences to create an expansive lyrical mode. The poems often sprawl, reflecting the ebb and tide of the poet's religious exhilaration, ecstasy, and despair. William Stafford, the plainspoken and understated poet who in most ways seems Everson's opposite, admiringly described this poetry as offering "a shock and a delight to break free into the heart's unmanaged impulses."

As Brother Antoninus, Everson became one of the key figures of the San Francisco Renaissance — the "Beat Friar" featured in *Time* magazine dressed in Dominican robes — intoning his poems to huge audiences around the country. In 1969 he left the Dominican order to marry Susanna Rickson. With typical panache, he announced his new life by stripping off his religious robes at the end of a poetry reading. He soon took a position as poet in residence at Kresge College at the University of California, Santa Cruz, and started a fine press on campus. Also at Kresge College, he taught a course on the poetic vocation. He continued to publish poetry prolifically, most notably *Man-Fate* (1974), *River Root* (1976), and *The Masks of Drought* (1980). His most important later work, however, was perhaps his critical prose. Now deeply influenced by the archetypal ideas of Carl Jung, as well as his earlier literary and religious sources, Everson examined the nature of poetic creation. His critical methods may seem unconventional when compared to contemporary academic criticism, but they are firmly based in Catholic contemplative literature. "Suffice it to say," he explained in the foreword to *Birth of a Poet: The Santa Cruz Meditations* (1982), "that when I left the monastery for academe the method that I brought with me was meditative rather than discursive. For I had learned how concepts seemingly exhausted by endless repetition could suddenly, under the probe of intuition, blossom into life."

from *The Falling of the Grain*
VIII. Advent

Fertile and rank and rich the coastal rains
Walked on the stiffened weeds and made them bend;
And stunned November chokes the cottonwood creeks
For Autumn's end.

And the hour of advent draws on the small-eyed seeds
That spilled in the pentecostal drought from the fallen cup;
Swept in the riddled summer-shrunken earth;
Now the eyes look up.

Faintly they glint, they glimmer, they try to see;
They pick at the crust; they touch at the wasted rind.
Winter will pinch them back but now they know,
And will not stay blind.

And all creation will gather its glory up
Out of the clouded winter-frigid womb;
And the sudden Eye will swell with the gift of sight,
And split the tomb.

The Making of the Cross

Rough fir, hauled from the hills. And the tree it had been,
Lithe-limbed, wherein the wren had nested,
Whereon the red hawk and the grey
Rested from flight, and the raw-head vulture
Shouldered to his feed—that tree went over
Bladed down with a double-bitted axe; was snaked with winches;
The wedge split it; hewn with the adze
It lay to season toward its use.

So too with the nails: milleniums under the earth,
Pure ore; chunked out with picks; the nail-shape
Struck in the pelt-lunged forge; tonged to a cask,
And the wait against that work.

Even the thorn-bush flourished from afar,
As do the flourishing generations of its kind,
Filling the shallow soil no one wants.
Wind-sown, it cuts the cattle and the wild horse;
It tears the cloth of man, and hurts his hand.

Just as in life the good things of the earth
Are patiently assembled: some from here, some from there;

Wine from the hill and wheat from the valley;
Rain that comes blue-bellied out of the sopping sea;
Snow that keeps its drift on the gooseberry ridge,
Will melt with May, go down, take the egg of the salmon,
Serve the traffic of otters and fishes,
Be ditched to orchards…

So too are gathered up the possibles of evil.

And when the Cross was joined, quartered,
As is the earth; spoked, as is the Universal Wheel—
Those radials that led all unregenerate act
Inward to innocence—it met the thorn-wove Crown;
It found the Scourges and the Dice;
The Nail was given and the reed-lifted Sponge;
The Curse caught forward out of the heart corrupt;
The excoriate Foul, stoned with the thunder and the hail—
All these made up that miscellaneous wrath
And were assumed.

The evil and the wastage and the woe,
As if the earth's old cyst, back down the slough
To Adam's sin-burnt calcinated bones,
Rushed out of time and clotted on the Cross.

Off there the cougar
Coughed in passion when the sun went out; the rattler
Filmed his glinty eye, and found his hole.

These Are the Ravens

These are the ravens of my soul,
Sloping above the lonely fields
And cawing, cawing.
I have released them now,
And sent them wavering down the sky,
Learning the slow witchery of the wind,
And crying on farthest fences of the world.

James Broughton
(1913–1999)

Born in Modesto, California, in 1913, James Broughton was the son of
wealthy parents, banker Irwin Broughton and his wife, Olga (Jungbluth)
Broughton. Broughton claimed that when he was three years old, a
"glittering stranger" in the night told him he was a poet. Several years
later he entered military school, where he began writing imitations of
the poems in the *Oxford Book of English Verse*. He graduated from
Stanford University in 1936 with a B.A., and after two years at the New
School for Social Research in New York (1943–1945), he returned to
California, working first with Art in Cinema, an experimental film
group at the San Francisco Museum of Art, and then in the late 1950s
and early 1960s he was part of the San Francisco Renaissance poetry
movement. He was resident playwright at the Playhouse Repertory
Theater in San Francisco from 1958 to 1964. Broughton married
Suzanna Hart, an artist, in 1962, and they had two children, Serena and
Orion. Hart and Broughton divorced in 1978, and he later had both
male and female lovers.

A gifted writer, filmmaker, and teacher, Broughton was a lecturer
at San Francisco State University from 1964 to 1976 and a film teacher
at the San Francisco Art Institute from 1968 to 1982. Broughton was, in
his own words, "first and foremost a poet," but he received attention for
his work in experimental film as well. He was a member of the board of
directors for Farallone Films, which produced many of his independent
films, from 1948 until his death. He received film awards in Edinburgh
(1953) and Cannes (1954), for poetic fantasy. In 1975 he received *Film
Culture*'s Twelfth Independent Film Award for the body of his work,
and subsequent lifetime achievement awards followed. His writing also
received acclaim. He was awarded Guggenheim Fellowships in 1971 and
1973 and a National Endowment for the Arts grant in 1976. He received
a James D. Phelan Award (1948) and a Eugene O'Neill Theatre
Foundation playwright fellowship (1969) for his plays, and a National
Lifetime Achievement in Poetry Award from the National Poetry
Association in 1992.

Broughton published many books of poetry, including *Musical
Chairs* (1950), which echoes the deceptively simple poems of Blake.
In later works, such as *Erogeny* (1976) and *Ecstasies* (1983), Broughton
fused eroticism and spirituality. He described himself as "Anglican by

birth, Taoist by nature, Dionysian in sprit, and Apollonian in practice."
Steeped in the visionary influences of Blake and others and the
transcendental beliefs of Ralph Waldo Emerson, Broughton wrote
poetry that looked squarely at the difficulties of life but always affirmed
and celebrated love's power. In a radio interview conducted not long
before his death, Broughton discussed Big Joy, a term which was both
his own nickname and his name for the secret of the universe. "Love,"
he said, "rules the universe," and Big Joy "runs the whole machine."

Aglow in Nowhere

At a meadow in Golden Gate Park
I stepped through an invisible gate
into the mellow light of nowhere
stepped beyond time and greenery

What had become of the seventy years
since first I tumbled on this grass?
And now many prices had I paid for
the tough somersaults that followed?

No longer brash nor intimidated
no longer riddled with wishes
I loll on this lawn of nowhere
and hope for a beatific vision

I know I have conquered nothing
I have simply outgrown everything
My history is a balloon I've let go of
without realizing I held on to it

Now I lack only a chamber for
what's left of my toys and scribbles
There I could desiccate quietly
like an Egyptian mummy   waiting
    for the last boat

Ann Stanford

(1916–1987)

"It is important to know where a poet lives," wrote poet, librettist, translator, literary critic, and editor Ann Stanford, "for the region, the culture surrounds the poetry, gives it a context from which the imagination can move."

Born in La Habra, California, in 1916, Stanford lived in southern California—"the chaparral-covered hills that are subject to drenching rains in winter and sudden fires in summer"—until her death in 1987. The daughter of a dealer in oil-drilling tools and a homemaker, Stanford completed her undergraduate work at Stanford University in 1938 and became a James D. Phelan fellow that year.

While an undergraduate, Stanford made her debut as a writer in Yvor Winters's *Twelve Poets of the Pacific* (1937). In 1942, she married Roland Arthur White, an architect, with whom she had four children. Returning to school after the children had matured, she completed M.A.s in journalism (1958) and English (1961) at the University of California, Los Angeles, where she also received her Ph.D. in 1962, in English and American literature. She then began teaching in the English department at California State University, Northridge, where she remained until 1987.

Stanford published numerous volumes of poetry, including *Magellan: A Poem to Be Read by Several Voices* (1958), *In Mediterranean Air* (1977), and *The Countess of Forli: A Poem for Voices* (1985), all of which won medals from the Commonwealth Club of California. Her poetry also received the Borestone Mountain Award for Poetry, the Shelley Memorial Award, a National Institute and American Academy award in literature, the Alice Fay di Castagnola Award, and two National Endowment for the Arts grants. She also published an anthology of women poets (1973), a translation of the *Bhagavad Gita* (1970), and two books on Puritan poet Anne Bradstreet (1974, 1983).

Compared to Bradstreet for the directness, restraint, and clarity of her verse, Stanford wrote poems that cover a variety of topics but always display a formality and quiet intensity. Her finest work, *In Mediterranean Air*, divides into six parts, beginning with the comfort and security of "the house, the lake, the shore" and the dangers lurking outside. Maxine Scates noted that a central theme of Stanford's is "the vulnerability of the home space, the imminent presence of the intruder on the horizon threatening the inviolability of what we hold most dear."

Much of Stanford's work derives from classical poetry, which endows it with formality and precision, balanced by an eye for the dramatic and dynamic. Of California she said, "It is easy to imagine the myths and tales of the Mediterranean region recreated [here], for the climate, the kinds of plants, the total landscape are much the same." Thus, even in historical re-creations such as "Pandora" and "The Women of Perseus," which are founded on Greek and Roman myths, Stanford remained a poet based in her sense of place.

Double Mirror

As this child rests upon my arm
So you encircled me from harm,
And you in turn were held by her
And she by her own comforter.

Enclosed, the double mirror runs
Backward and forward, fire to sun.
And as I watch you die, I hear
A child's farewell in my last ear.

The Committee

Black and serious, they are dropping down one by one to the top of
    the walnut tree.
It is spring and the bare branches are right for a conversation.
The sap has not risen yet, but those branches will always be bare
Up there, crooked with ebbed life lost now, like a legal argument.
They shift a bit as they settle into place.
Once in a while one says something, but the answer is always the same,
The question is too — it is all *caw* and *caw*.
Do they think they are hidden by the green leaves partway up
    the branches?
Do they like it up there cocking their heads in the fresh morning?
One by one they fly off as if to other appointments.
Whatever they did, it must be done all over again.

Done With

My house is torn down—
Plaster sifting, the pillars broken,
Beams jagged, the wall crushed by the bulldozer.
The whole roof has fallen
On the hall and the kitchen
The bedrooms, the parlor.

They are trampling the garden—
My mother's lilac, my father's grapevine,
The freesias, the jonquils, the grasses.
Hot asphalt goes down
Over the torn stems, and hardens.

What will they do in springtime
Those bulbs and stems groping upward
That drown in earth under the paving,
Thick with sap, pale in the dark
As they try the unrolling of green.

May they double themselves
Pushing together up to the sunlight,
May they break through the seal stretched above them
Open and flower and cry we are living.

Adrien Stoutenberg
(1916–1982)

There are more people on the Authors Among Us website "Librarians
Who Are Authors of Children's Literature" than one might imagine,
but none as distinctive as Adrien Stoutenburg—prolific juvenile writer,
folklorist, birder, musician, and deeply passionate poet. "If I were to
characterize the tone of voice," James Dickey wrote in the preface
to Stoutenburg's collected poetry, *Land of Superior Mirages* (1986),
"I would call it that of sensitive outrage, quivering, powerful, and
delicate. Delicate: *therefore* powerful."

Born in Darfur, Minnesota, in 1916, Stoutenburg was the daughter of
a barber and a beautician. She attended the Minneapolis School of Arts
from 1936 to 1938 and began a long career as a freelance writer in 1940.
Although she contributed short stories to *Cross Section* in 1940, in the
1950s she was mainly writing children's books and working at related
jobs. She worked for the Hennepin County Library in Richfield,
Minnesota (1949–1950), and then as a reporter for the *Richfield News*
(1950–1952). After moving to California, she became editor of Parnassus
Press in Berkeley from 1956 to 1958.

Stoutenburg wrote at least forty books during her career, sometimes
collaborating with other authors. Most were for the juvenile market
(often tall tales and other folklore), and she published many under a
variety of pseudonyms: Barbie Arden, Nelson Minier, and Lace Kendall
(her father's name). Still, poetry was a constant in her life. Her poetry
appeared in *Best Poems of 1957* (Pacific Books) and again in 1960 and
1962, and in other anthologies as well. She won nine Borestone
Mountain Awards, an Edwin Markham Award (1961), a Lamont Poetry
Award (1964) for *Heroes, Advise Us*, and a silver medal from the
California Literature Medal Awards (1970) for *A Short History of the Fur
Trade*. In 1979 she published *Greenwich Mean Time*, her last book. She
died of esophageal cancer on April 14, 1982, in Santa Barbara, California.

Stoutenburg's distinctive poetry combines elements of modernism
with traditional expository prose virtues to create verse that is both lucid
and surprising. James Dickey wrote of her work, "Nothing about it is
standard, everything unexpected and telling." Relying on a strong sense
of narrative, Stoutenburg wrote long poems with a clear sense of story,
rich in detail. She used her vivid imagination to champion the natural

world and its inhabitants and to decry those who despoil it for profit and vanity. Her *Short History of the Fur Trade* uses bright images to bring readers into the world of ocelots and snow leopards, at the same time condemning "those who peddle such intense brocades" as fur, and those who wear it. Deeply moral and full of conviction, her poetry is as intense as it is sad for worlds vanishing from our lives. It becomes, Dickey says, "part of the reader's conscience."

Cicada

I lay with my heart under me,
under the white sun,
face down to fields
and a life that gleamed
under my palm like an emerald hinge.
I sheltered him where we lay alive
under the body of the sun.
Trees there dropped their shadows
like black fruit,
and the thin-necked sparrows came
crying through the light.

At my life line I felt
his bent, bright knee
work like a latch.
He was safe with me
in the room my round bones made—
or might have been—
but he sang like a driven nail
and his skinless eyes looked out,
wanting himself as he was.

Wisdom was imprecise,
my hand's loose judgement dark.
Some jewel work straining in his thigh
broke like a kingdom.
I let him go,
a jackstraw limping to the dynamo

of hunger under the hungering sun
and the world's quick gizzard.
High noon hummed,
all parts in place —
or nearly so.

Before We Drown

I have seen myself and others
rolling in this ocean,
and the arrows of fish in the surf,
and a shark walking upon the water,
and Noah sailing with trumpets,
and a giraffe limping ashore
like a mottled tree.

We are here to salute the sea,
to taste salt, to burn our eyes
with sunlight and the black smoke of driftwood
started from one match against the headlines.

We are here to measure waves
and the length of the marlin's gill
and to gather up into castles
the wandering, witless sand
before the tide turns
and we see our dead selves
mirrored, open-mouthed,
in its glass shoulders.

Violet Kazue de Cristoforo
(b. 1917)

Born as Kazue Yamane in Hawaii in 1917, Violet Kazue de Cristoforo moved to the U.S. mainland the same year. At age eight, she was sent to Hiroshima, Japan, to be educated. She returned to the United States at age thirteen and later attended high school in Fresno. Shortly after graduating, she married Shigeru Matsuda. During World War II, the family was interned with other Japanese Americans in a relocation camp in Jerome, Arkansas. The couple was separated after her husband refused to complete a questionnaire at the Jerome camp and was moved to a high-security Justice Department camp in Santa Fe, New Mexico. Deemed "disloyal," Violet de Cristoforo and her three children were then moved to Tule Lake, California, for security purposes. Hurt and angered by such treatment, the entire family later expatriated to Japan after the war, in 1946. The poet later returned to the United States and remarried, taking on the last name she is now known by.

Violet de Cristoforo is best known as a memoirist, oral historian, and haiku poet of the Japanese American relocation camps, which were established by Executive Order 9066 in 1943. Her *Poetic Reflections of the Tule Lake Internment Camp, 1944,* a short gathering of sharply etched vignettes and haiku from her own experience, was published in 1988, more than forty years after the painful events it recounts. Of the hundreds of haiku she wrote at Tule Lake, only fifteen survived.

De Cristoforo is also a scholar of early-twentieth-century haiku in Japan and of the haiku kais (poetry clubs) that flourished in California's Central Valley in the decades before World War II. She is the compiler and translator of *May Sky, There is Always Tomorrow: An Anthology of Japanese American Concentration Camp Kaiko Haiku* (1996).

Haiku

DOOSHI SOROU SOSHITE MATSU NO ME FUTORI SHOKA NO SORA

Like-minded people gather
new shoots sprout from pine tree
early summer sky

OROKASHISA TADA NI NATSU NO HI O KURASHI MUKOU CASTLE ROCK

Foolishly—simply existing
summer days
Castle Rock is there

Tenth Wedding Anniversary (July 3, 1944)

TSUKI OBORO TOTSUGISHI YORU NO SORA DATTA

Misty moon
as it was
on my wedding night

Stockade prisoners on hunger strike

NANI MO MITE INAI KOKORO NO HI GA TSUZUKI KOGEN NATSU TAKENAWA

My heart perceives nothing
day to day
summer at its peak in highland

KONCHU KAZU ARU YUBE AKO IYO-IYO SEICHO SHITARI

Myriad insects
in the evening
my children are growing

Wilma Elizabeth McDaniel
(b. 1918)

"By the time I was ten I was afflicted with poetry," Wilma McDaniel explains in *Down an Old Road,* Chris Simon's film documentary of her life and work. "I was in its grips," she continues, "and I remain there today." The self-proclaimed spinster and Okie was born December 22, 1918, the fourth of eight children, near Stroud, Oklahoma. She was the daughter of a sharecropper father and a mother whom McDaniel refers to as an "artist without watercolors." The family moved to California's Central Valley in 1936, where McDaniel worked the fields for years not far from Tulare, where she presently lives.

After years of stuffing a shoebox with poems written on paper bags and scraps of paper, McDaniel finally took her shoebox portfolio to the editor of the *Tulare Advance Register.* Struck by the originality of McDaniel's verse, he began to publish something nearly each week. She never wrote the lovesick verse she felt her readers expected of a spinster such as herself, but instead insisted on strong images, the use of vernacular, slices of life set in cotton fields or K-mart. Almost legally blind, she still writes daily. Of her poetry she says, "there's nothing in there that's fake or false."

McDaniel always lived with her mother, from whom she inherited her poetry "affliction," and whom she nursed her through long periods of illness. When her mother died, McDaniel said it was as if "the great presence of God had gone out of the world." Much of her poetry is rich in biblical allusion. Raised in a Protestant fundamentalist home, she entered the Catholic church at twenty-one, after three years of study. "If I'd been free to do so…I would have chosen to be a Carmelite nun," she explains. "I have spoken about this to God at times, and he gave me something much harder." Her mother's long sicknesses taught her to endure a life of frequent poverty and pain, and she asserts that "nothing works full-time but God."

In the 1970s, McDaniel abandoned a life of privacy and enclosure to publish the collections *The Red Coffee Can* and *A Prince Albert Wind.* She has since written a memoir, more collections of poetry, short stories, and a regular newspaper column. Her most recent collections are *A Primer for Buford* (1994), *The Last Dust Storm* (1995), and *Borrowed Coats* (2001). In a style *The American Book Review* called "scraped clean," in memorable poems like "First Spring in California,"

McDaniel captures the nobility of those trapped in the Great Depression and encapsulates the lives of the children and grandchildren who have never known the hunger that was a constant in the lives of the "old folks." Her poetry, "indeed, Wilma herself," Gerald Haslam writes of the Dust Bowl migrants, "represents well the great contribution made — however unwillingly — to California."

First Spring in California, 1936

The Okies wrapped their
cold dreams in army blankets
and patchwork quilts
and slept away the foggy
winter nights of 1935

From doorways of tents
and hasty shacks
now and then a boxcar
they watched for spring
as they would watch for
the Second Coming of Christ

And saw the Valley change
from skim milk blue
still needing sweaters
to palest green that filled
their eyes with hope

As they waited for odd jobs
the Valley burst forth
with one imperial color
poppies flung their gold
over acres of sand
like all the bankers in California
gone raving mad

Women wept in wonder
and hunted fruit jars to can

the precious flowers
in case next year
did not produce a bumper crop

Burned in the Test

I have wasted so much
sunrise
scraping burned oatmeal
from a charred pot

I have often profaned
bright noon
into three pm
waiting by the telephone
for a call that never came

Why can't I be satisfied
to soak a pot overnight
and be content with new shoestrings
when the old ones snap

I have spent a cat's lifetime
tying short pieces together

I have glued broken handles
on many cups
waited days to find out
they never hold
and been burned in the test

Lawrence Ferlinghetti
(b. 1919)

The poet who rose to international acclaim as Lawrence Ferlinghetti was born in Yonkers, New York, as Lawrence Monsanto Ferling, the youngest son of Charles and Clemence Ferling. He never knew his father, who purportedly died before he was born, and his mother was soon hospitalized for a nervous disorder. The young Lawrence Ferling spent several years living with relatives in France, then in an orphanage in New York, and finally with a wealthy family in Bronxville. He studied journalism at the University of North Carolina and was an officer in the Naval Reserve during World War II. After the war he took his M.A. at Columbia and his Ph.D. at the University of Paris. In 1952 he cofounded City Lights Bookstore in the North Beach section of San Francisco. He has lived in San Francisco ever since. In 1998 he was named the city's first official poet laureate.

As co-owner of the City Lights Bookstore and editor in chief of City Lights Publishing, Ferlinghetti has been an outspoken and influential figure in contemporary poetry as well as one of the prime movers of the Beat movement. He published Allen Ginsberg's *Howl* in 1956 and was soon charged with "printing and selling lewd and indecent material." He prevailed in court, and this victory against censorship lifted publisher and poet to national attention, energizing the Beats. City Lights Bookstore has become one of California's major literary landmarks.

In a 1955 essay about getting poetry out of the classroom and into the streets, Ferlinghetti wrote, "The printed word has made poetry so silent." No longer the vocal "outsider," Ferlinghetti has become increasingly aware that he is part of mainstream American poetry: "Herbert Marcuse once noted the enormous capacity of society to ingest its own dissident elements….It happens to everyone successful within the system. I'm ingested myself." His poems display an oral performance aesthetic, the best of them offering a charming but pointed irreverence reminiscent of E. E. Cummings.

Ferlinghetti published his first book, *Pictures of the Gone World,* in 1955. A prolific poet, he made the greatest impression with his early books, especially *A Coney Island of the Mind* (1958), which became one of the best-selling poetry books of the century. His later books include

Starting from San Francisco (1961) and *The Secret Meaning of Things*
(1968). He also coauthored, with Nancy J. Peters, a comprehensive,
illustrated history of northern California literary life, *Literary San
Francisco* (1980). He has published more than thirty collections of
poems, an autobiographical novel, and several plays.

Untitled

In Goya's greatest scenes we seem to see
                                        the people of the world
            exactly at the moment when
                        they first attained the title of
                                        'suffering humanity'
            They writhe upon the page
                    in a veritable rage
                                        of adversity
                    Heaped up
                        groaning with babies and bayonets
                                        under cement skies
                in an abstract landscape of blasted trees
                    bent statues bats wings and beaks
                                slippery gibbets
                    cadavers and carnivorous cocks
            and all the final hollering monsters
                    of the
                            'imagination of disaster'
            they are so bloody real
                            it is as if they really still existed

And they do

        Only the landscape is changed

They still are ranged along the roads
        plagued by legionnaires
                        false windmills and demented roosters

They are the same people
                         only further from home
          on freeways fifty lanes wide
                         on a concrete continent
                                   spaced with bland billboards
                    illustrating imbecile illusions of happiness

The scene shows fewer tumbrils
                         but more maimed citizens
                                             in painted cars
          and they have strange license plates
and engines
               that devour America

Untitled
          Constantly risking absurdity
                                   and death
               whenever he performs
                         above the heads
                                   of his audience
          the poet like an acrobat
                    climbs on rime
                         to a high wire of his own making
and balancing on eyebeams
                         above a sea of faces
          paces his way
                    to the other side of day
          performing entrechats
                         and sleight-of-foot tricks
          and other high theatrics
                         and all without mistaking
               any thing
                    for what it may not be

For he's the super realist
                    who must perforce perceive
          taut truth
                    before the taking of each stance or step
          in his supposed advance
                              toward that still higher perch
     where Beauty stands and waits
                              with gravity
                                   to start her death-defying leap
               And he
               a little charleychaplin man
                              who may or may not catch
                    her fair eternal form
                              spreadeagled in the empty air
                    of existence

Robert Duncan
(1919–1988)

Edward Howard Duncan was born in Oakland in 1919, to day laborer Edward Duncan and mother Marguerite Carpenter, who died in childbirth. His father gave him up, and Duncan was adopted by Edwin and Minnehaha (Harris) Symmes, who raised him as Robert Edward Symmes.

Duncan was raised in a theosophical household, in a climate of séances and spirit meetings, free to use an extensive library of the occult, which he did regularly. A childhood accident struck him cross-eyed and afflicted with double vision, leaving him with a startling mien and a misfortune he transmuted metaphorically to a mode of seeing the doubleness of all life, spirit and waking.

Duncan graduated from Kern High School in Bakersfield, and when he let it be known he planned to be a poet, his freethinking professional parents were appalled. He spent two years at the University of California, Berkeley, then followed a lover to New York, where he was part of the bohemian group that encircled Anais Nin.

Drafted into the U.S. Army in 1941, Duncan was discharged for homosexuality, on psychiatric grounds. Having asserted one new identity, he returned to an older one, "re-christening" himself Robert Duncan in a fusion of birth and adoptive names. Duncan would spend the rest of his life baring occult truths and revealing the unity of things camouflaged by the dazzle of modern life. We often see the poet addressing the one beneath the many, and the many alive in the one, in his poetry: below the surface of the ruined peaceable kingdom of "The Temple of the Animals," for example, runs an anxiety over interior and exterior loss. And even in the flux of "Poetry, A Natural Thing," there is faith in the power of the poet's mind to make what rushes through the moment a whole thing.

After his discharge from the Army, Duncan returned to the Bay Area. He met Kenneth Rexroth, and the older author brought him into his literary circle. Duncan wrote poetry, published in journals, and helped edit a little magazine. When John Crowe Ransom accepted one of his poems for *The Kenyon Review* in 1944, it appeared that Duncan had entered the literary mainstream. But when Ransom read "The Homosexual in Society," Duncan's trailblazing essay in *Politics*, Ransom had second thoughts and declined to publish the poem.

Duncan's essay was one of the first frank analyses of the rights denied homosexuals—much as they were denied African Americans and Jews—and the social and psychic effects of such displacement. Moreover, having declared his own sexual identity, Duncan was now free to explore it near the center of his poetry for the next forty years.

Duncan soon joined poets such as Rexroth and Jack Spicer in a "poetic renaissance" in San Francisco, a decade before the Beat generation came into the spotlight. By 1947, after the publication of *Heavenly City, Earthly City,* he was already respected as an enormously learned poet, one so steeped in appropriating arcane traditions into a new mythology that he was challenging and daunting. In 1951, he fell in love with painter Jess Collins, and they made a home together for almost forty years, until Duncan's death in 1988.

While teaching at North Carolina's Black Mountain College in 1956, Duncan was profoundly influenced by Charles Olson, the "father" of "projective verse," and the result yielded *The Opening of the Field* (1960), in which Duncan saw poetry as an ongoing process, a "building form" that wove all the elements within reach of his consciousness together. *Roots and Branches* (1964) and *Bending the Bow* (1968) solidified his reputation as a revolutionary mythopoeic artist in the tradition of Yeats.

Duncan was embroiled with other intellectuals in the crusade against the war in Vietnam, but unlike most, he insisted that he, too, was implicated in the creation of a national culture of violence. He did not publish for almost fifteen years, and by the time *Ground Work: Before the War* (1984) and *Ground Work II: In the Dark* (1987) appeared, he had fallen out of favor. Yvor Winters was repelled by his lack of "moral fiber," and James Dickey pronounced him "unpityingly pretentious." Most of the prominent poets who came of age in the 1970s and 1980s ignored him, and many readers saw him as an archaic ornament.

More recently, Duncan's literary stock has risen considerably. For many poets and scholars, he is a fascinating California cultural figure who lived as an unfettered poet and brought homosexuality and the homosexual artist into dominant discourse. Others see a figure who made major contributions to at least three significant literary movements and forged a revolutionary poetics in the process, finally establishing himself as a major American modernist poet and intellectual.

The Temple of the Animals

The temple of the animals has fallen into disrepair.
The pad of feet has faded.
The panthers flee the shadows of the day.
The smell of musk has faded but lingers there...
lingers, lingers. Ah, bitterly in my room.
Tired, I recall the animals of last year—
the altars of the bear, tribunals of the ape,
solitudes of elephantine gloom, rare
zebra-striped retreats, prophecies of dog,
sanctuaries of the pygmy deer.

Were there rituals I had forgotten? animal calls
to which those animal voices replied,
calld and calld until the jungle stirrd?
Were there voices that I heard?
Love was the very animal made his lair,
slept out his winter in my heart.
Did he seek my heart or ever
sleep there?

I have seen the animals depart,
forgotten their voices, or barely remembered
—like the last speech when the company goes
or the beloved face that the heart knows,
forgets and knows—
I have heard the dying footsteps fall.
The sound has faded, but lingers here.
Ah, bitterly I recall
the animals of last year.

Poetry, A Natural Thing

Neither our vices nor our virtues
further the poem. "They came up
    and died
just like they do every year
    on the rocks."

The poem
feeds upon thought, feeling, impulse,
   to breed   itself,
a spiritual urgency at the dark ladders leaping.

This beauty is an inner persistence
   toward the source
striving against (within) down-rushet of the river,
   a call we heard and answer
in the lateness of the world
   primordial bellowings
from which the youngest world might spring,

salmon not in the well where the
   hazelnut falls
but at the falls battling, inarticulate,
   blindly making it.

This is one picture apt for the mind.

A second: a moose painted by Stubbs,
where last year's extravagant antlers
   lie on the ground.
The forlorn moosey-faced poem wears
   new antler-buds,
   the same,

"a little heavy, a little contrived",

his only beauty to be
   all moose.

This Place Rumord to Have Been Sodom

   might have been.
Certainly these ashes might have been pleasures.
Pilgrims on their way to the Holy Places remark

this place. Isn't it plain to all
that these mounds were palaces? This was once
a city among men, a gathering together of spirit.
It was measured by the Lord and found wanting.

It was measured by the Lord and found wanting,
destroyd by the angels that inhabit longing.
Surely this is Great Sodom where such cries
as if men were birds flying up from the swamp
ring in our ears, where such fears that were once
desires walk, almost spectacular,
stalking the desolate circles, red eyed.

This place rumord to have been a City surely was,
separated from us by the hand of the Lord.
The devout have laid out gardens in the desert,
drawn water from springs where the light was blighted.
How tenderly they must attend these friendships
or all is lost. All *is* lost.
Only the faithful hold this place green.

Only the faithful hold this place green
where the crown of fiery thorns descends.
Men that once lusted grow listless. A spirit
wrappd in a cloud, ashes more than ashes,
fire more than fire, ascends.
Only these new friends gather joyous here,
where the world like Great Sodom lies under fear.

The world like Great Sodom lies under Love
and knows not the hand of the Lord that moves.
This the friends teach where such cries
as if men were birds fly up from the crowds
gatherd and howling in the heat of the sun.
In the Lord Whom the friends have named at last Love
the images and loves of the friends never die.
This place rumord to have been Sodom is blessd
in the Lord's eyes.

Roots and Branches

Sail, Monarchs, rising and falling
orange merchants in spring's flowery markets!
messengers of March in warm currents of news floating,
    flitting into areas of aroma,
tracing out of air unseen roots and branches of sense
    I share in thought,
filaments woven and broken where the world might light
    casual certainties of me. There are

echoes of what I am in what you perform
this morning. How you perfect my spirit!
    almost restore
an imaginary tree of the living in all its doctrines
    by fluttering about,
intent and easy as you are, the profusion of you!
awakening transports of an inner view of things.

Charles Bukowski
(1920–1994)

No California writer in recent times has attracted a greater cult following than Charles Bukowski. In an era obsessed with good looks, youth, and smoothness, "the Buk" made his reputation as the bard of lowlife Los Angeles, trading on his ugliness and celebrating the world of barflies, whores, bookies, petty thieves, and racetrack touts.

Born in West Germany in 1920 of a German mother and an American G.I. father, he immigrated with them to L.A. at age two and suffered with them through the Depression as an adolescent. Details of a poor and dysfunctional family always filtered through in countless variations in Bukowski's prose and poetry—especially the novel *Ham on Rye* (1982)—and the father characters were extremely physically abusive. Young Bukowski took refuge in secret reading and claimed it saved him. At thirteen he discovered alcohol, which almost killed him many times. Disfigured as an adolescent by terrible acne and boils and beaten by his father, he became a loner, and only "the poor and the lost and the idiots" were willing to befriend him. He found their honesty, candor, verve for living at the lower registers, and familiarity with violence exhilarating. He saw life as empty and bleak—or at least he said he did—and he admired those who went out brawling. In almost seventy books of poetry, fiction, and essays, he became their spokesman and champion, and the rawness of his celebrations of "real life" and attacks on phoniness in every guise made him internationally famous.

Bukowski attended Los Angeles City College from 1939 to 1941, but at twenty-one he began a succession of manual-labor jobs—dishwasher, truck driver, parking lot attendant, warehouseman, mail carrier—that inspired his characters and themes. In reality, he had only one literary protagonist: himself, usually thinly disguised as Henry Chinaski. He moved to New York to write in earnest in the early 1940s, but the response was so negative that he went on a ten-year drunk across three continents that almost took his life. He eventually got a job with the U.S. Postal Service, where he worked from the mid-50s to late 60s, and the experience was recorded in all its bleakness and hilarity in *Post Office* (1971), one of the novels that made him famous.

Bukowski wrote every day, but his work was not professionally published and distributed to an audience until midlife. Starting in 1959, he published a profusion of small-press books of poems, and in the late 1960s he gained his first following as a columnist for underground papers, including the *Los Angeles Free Press*. If there was a sacred cow, Bukowski tortured it in his column, and he began to receive snide swipes in New York, especially from academic critics. The worse the establishment attention, the more his legend flourished. In 1969 he quit his postal job to scratch out a living from his literary endeavors, but it wasn't until the publication of the novels *Post Office* and *Factotum* (1975) did he live comfortably, a station that seemed to enrage him all the more.

Charles Bukowski never mined his adopted state for metaphors, and his lowlife settings could have been taken from any American city, but he felt that Los Angeles—because of its grandness of promises impossible to fulfill—had more of the brokenhearted, crazed, and nothing-left-to-losers per capita than any other American city. He made poetry from the detritus of broken lives, and if many found what he drew ugly, violent, and depressing, it was controlled and orchestrated by a distinctive voice—writer John William Corrington called it "the spoken voice nailed to paper." His work was pared down without a trace of fake emotion, surprisingly sharp, imagistic and evocative on the page, always driven by a scalding vision and a near-Eastern control of language and poetic line. If he thought life was pointless, he was tender and elegiac with those who lived and left with style, as in "eulogy to a hell of a dame." By the time he died of diabetes in 1994, a low-rent legend in Los Angeles, he had thirty books in print and his work had been translated into twenty languages.

the tragedy of the leaves

I awakened to dryness, and the ferns were dead,
the potted plants yellow as corn;
my woman was gone
and the empty bottles like bled corpses
surrounded me with their uselessness;
the sun was still good, though,
and my landlady's note cracked in fine
and undemanding yellowness; what was needed now

was a good comedian, ancient style, a jester
with jokes upon absurd pain; pain is absurd
because it exists, nothing more;
I shaved carefully with an old razor
the man who had once been young and
said to have genius; but
that's the tragedy of the leaves,
the dead ferns, the dead plants;
and I walked into a dark hall
where the landlady stood
execrating and final,
sending me to hell,
waving her fat, sweaty arms
and screaming
screaming for rent
because the world had failed us
both.

my old man

16 years old
during the depression
I'd come home drunk
and all my clothing—
shorts, shirts, stockings—
suitcase, and pages of
short stories
would be thrown out on the
front lawn and about the
street.

my mother would be
waiting behind a tree:
"Henry, Henry, don't
go in...he'll
kill you, he's read
your stories..."

"I can whip his
ass…"

"Henry, please take
this…and
find yourself a room."

but it worried him
that I might not
finish high school
so I'd be back
again.

one evening he walked in
with the pages of
one of my short stories
(which I had never submitted
to him)
and he said, "this is
a great short story."
I said, "o.k.,"
and he handed it to me
and I read it.
it was a story about
a rich man
who had a fight with
his wife and had
gone out into the night
for a cup of coffee
and had observed
the waitress and the spoons
and forks and the
salt and pepper shakers
and the neon sign
in the window
and then had gone back
to his stable
to see and touch his
favorite horse

who then
kicked him in the head
and killed him.

somehow
the story held
meaning for him
though
when I had written it
I had no idea
of what I was
writing about.

so I told him,
"o.k., old man, you can
have it."
and he took it
and walked out
and closed the door.
I guess that's
as close
as we ever got.

eulogy to a hell of a dame —

some dogs who sleep at night
must dream of bones
and I remember your bones
in flesh
and best
in that dark green dress
and those high-heeled bright
black shoes,
you always cursed when you
drank,
your hair coming down you
wanted to explode out of

what was holding you:
rotten memories of a
rotten
past, and
you finally got
out
by dying,
leaving me with the
rotten
present;
you've been dead
28 years
yet I remember you
better than any of
the rest;
you were the only one
who understood
the futility of the
arrangement of
life;
all the others were only
displeased with
trivial segments,
carped
nonsensically about
nonsense;
Jane, you were
killed by
knowing too much.
here's a drink
to your bones
that
this dog
still
dreams about.

Leonard Nathan
(b. 1924)

Poet, translator, essayist, and professor of rhetoric Leonard Nathan was born in Los Angeles, the son of Israel and Florence (Rosenberg) Nathan. He briefly attended the Georgia Institute of Technology before joining the Army in 1943 to serve in the European Theatre of Operations. After the war, he returned to Los Angeles to take classes at the University of California, Los Angeles, but soon moved north to Berkeley, where he has lived since. He completed his education at the University of California, Berkeley, earning a B.A. (1950), an M.A. (1952), and a Ph.D. (1961). He joined the faculty at Berkeley in 1960 and has been a professor emeritus since 1992. He lives a few miles north of campus in Kensington.

Nathan published his first book, *Western Reaches,* in 1958, and following his second book, *The Glad and Sorry Seasons* (1963), he published prolifically, completing more than a dozen volumes by the time he published *Carrying On: New and Selected Poems* (1985). Nathan did not publish a collection for fourteen years after *Carrying On,* but with *The Potato Eaters* (1999), he not only broke the silence but found his widest audience and critical acclaim. Several of the poems in *The Potato Eaters* have appeared in *The New Yorker,* and the book won the coveted Silver Medal for Poetry from the Commonwealth Club of California. On winning the award, Nathan commented, "The older I get, the more I find myself revisiting childhood in my poetry and discovering myself at home again in a world like that of folk or faery tales, where the strange can become familiar, the familiar strange. Thus, in the poem 'The Potato Eaters,' a boring supper becomes a ritual meal containing a meaning beyond itself."

While his verse seems conversational, it is aesthetically formal — regularly rhymed and often in an understated iambic pentameter. The voice is calm and reflective, that of a mature and wise mind, and it takes on special energy in considering the wild and natural world. An avid birder, he wrote the popular *Diary of a Left-Handed Birdwatcher* (1996), a blend of poetry and prose that has captured the imaginations of nontraditional readers of poetry (naturalists and birdwatchers) as well as readers who know and value his work.

In addition to writing poetry, Leonard Nathan is a successful translator, with nine volumes to his credit, including three with Czeslaw Milosz. He is also the author of *The Tragic Drama of William Butler Yeats: Figures in the Dance* (1965) and, with Arthur Quinn, *The Poet's Work: An Introduction to Czeslaw Milosz* (1991).

Letter

Dear Antigone,
after going over all the arguments
pro and con, I'm as divided as ever,
but when the last word dies away,
I know you're right.

Everybody does,
that's why Creon has to bury you
every time the state can't make children
obey the letters of the law
that don't spell love.

And that's why I stand here watching it all,
glad no one has asked me to help,
my littlest daughter's hand in mine,
her eyes looking up with a sad trust,
already forgiving.

Coup

That chair
isn't yours anymore.

Noon
when bells shed iron
on the dusty sleep of the poor
we took your chair.

The Republic
is now a wall
for you to die against
and (after a whitewash)
a background
for our smiles.

No hard feelings.

Hole

The mouse crawled through it,
the snake after him
and you're next.

Did you think
because Socrates went through
and Saint Francis
it was going to be bigger?

They also squeezed every hope
into its least possibility,
shedding layer after layer
to slide, tongue flicking,
into the rank darkness.

O yes,
the self is that small.

Edgar Bowers
(1924–2000)

A master of poetic form, Edgar Bowers was born in 1924 in Rome, Georgia. His father, William, was an agronomist and nurseryman; his mother, Grace, was a teacher. Early years at his father's nursery near Stone Mountain imprinted the Georgia landscape on the young Bowers, and it later provided the foundation for many later poems. He started classes at the University of North Carolina, Chapel Hill, but left after a year to serve in the Army during World War II. From 1943 to 1946 he was a member of the Counter Intelligence Corps, serving as an interpreter and counterintelligence officer in the Bavarian Alps, Hitler's home region. His duties took him from one fine house to another, where he listened as citizens recounted their war memories. One of his most memorable war poems, "The Stoic: For Laura Von Courten," issued from a countess's recollections of the bombing of Munich. Similarly, a visit to a castle housing Mozart's claviers led to the early sonnet "For W. A. Mozart."

After his discharge, Bowers returned to Chapel Hill, where he completed his B.A. in 1947. He moved shortly thereafter to Stanford University to study poetry. His mentor was Yvor Winters, and under his guidance, Bowers abandoned experiment and free verse for a formal style and rhymed, metric verse. His work continued the lineage of Winters's Stanford School of poets, and Bowers and a circle including J. V. Cunningham, Turner Cassity, Helen Pinkerton Trimpi, and Timothy Steele keep Winters's formalist legacy alive today.

A meticulous editor of his own work, he published just six books during his career. As his friend and former Santa Barbara colleague H. Porter Abbott recalled in the *Los Angeles Times*, "His output was not great in number, but everything he published was polished within an inch of its life. It was the most important thing to him, writing a poem." Bowers's first book, *The Form of Loss*, was published in 1956. He was awarded two Guggenheim Fellowships (1959 and 1969) and was included in *Five American Poets* (edited by Ted Hughes and Thom Gunn) before releasing his second full-length collection, *The Astronomers* (1965). A dozen years passed before he published *Living Together: New and Selected Poems* (1977), and more than a decade after that, *For Louis Pasteur* won the prestigious Bollingen Prize in 1989. His *Collected Poems* appeared in 1997.

Bowers completed his Ph.D. at Stanford and held several teaching positions before moving to the University of California, Santa Barbara, in 1958, where he stayed until retirement in 1991. He spent his Santa Barbara years in a small beach house in the exclusive community of Montecito, where he watched the dolphins and the surf from his deck over the sand. He had a long love affair with life on the California coast, and several of his finest poems ("The Beach" and "An Afternoon at the Beach") owe a debt to the seascape. When he retired, he moved to San Francisco, where he died of non-Hodgkin's lymphoma in 2000.

A recent conference and exhibit at the University of California, Los Angeles, summarized his legacy: curator Kevin Durkin wrote, "He was intensely private and devoted to the craft of poetry during a period that generally favored formless self-expression. He believed that reason should balance emotion, that elegance should temper spontaneity, and that the traditions of the past should guide one beyond the fashions of the present. Ironically, as a result of his stubborn adherence to what many of his contemporaries deemed outmoded virtues, Bowers's poetry continues to gain admirers today and will be read for centuries to come."

An Afternoon at the Beach

I'll go among the dead to see my friend.
The place I leave is beautiful: the sea
Repeats the winds' far swell in its long sound,
And, there beside it, houses solemnly
Shine with the modest courage of the land,
While swimmers try the verge of what they see.

I cannot go, although I should pretend
Some final self whose phantom eye could see
Him who because he is not cannot change.
And yet the thought of going makes the sea,
The land, the swimmers, and myself seem strange,
Almost as strange as they will someday be.

In the Last Circle

You spoke all evening hatred and contempt,
The ethical distorted to a fury
Of self-deception, malice, and conceit,
Yourself the judge, the lawyer, and the jury.
I listened, but, instead of proof, I heard,
As if the truth were merely what you knew,
Wrath cry aloud its wish and its despair
That all would be and must be false to you.

You are the irresponsible and damned,
Alone in final cold athwart your prey.
Your passion eats his brain. Compulsively,
The crime which is your reason eats away
Compassion, as they both have eaten you,
Till what you are is merely what you do.

The Stoic: For Laura Von Courten

All winter long you listened for the boom
Of distant cannon wheeled into their place.
Sometimes outside beneath a bombers' moon
You stood alone to watch the searchlights trace

Their careful webs against the boding sky,
While miles away on Munich's vacant square
The bombs lunged down with an unruly cry
Whose blast you saw yet could but faintly hear.

And might have turned your eyes upon the gleam
Of a thousand years of snow, where near the clouds
The Alps ride massive to their full extreme,
And season after season glacier crowds

The dark, persistent smudge of conifers.
Or seen beyond the hedge and through the trees
The shadowy forms of cattle on the furze,
Their dim coats white with mist against the freeze.

Or thought instead of other times than these,
Of other countries and of other sights:
Eternal Venice sinking by degrees
Into the very water that she lights;

Reflected in canals, the lucid dome
Of Maria della Salute at your feet,
Her triple spires disfigured by the foam.
Remembered in Berlin the parks, the neat

Footpaths and lawns, the clean spring foliage,
Where just short weeks before, a bomb, unaimed,
Released a frightened lion from its cage,
Which in the mottled dark that trees enflamed

Killed one who hurried homeward from the raid.
And by yourself there standing in the chill
You must, with so much known, have been afraid
And chosen such a mind of constant will,

Which, though all time corrode with constant hurt,
Remains, until it occupies no space,
That which it is; and passionless, inert,
Becomes at last no meaning and no place.

Jack Spicer
(1925–1965)

Jack Spicer was born in Los Angeles in 1925, the elder of two sons of
Midwestern parents. His father, a former radical labor unionist, managed
hotels and apartment buildings, and the family lived comfortably even
during the Great Depression. A bookish and unattractive child with poor
eyesight who was teased by other boys, Spicer sought refuge in local
libraries, where he read escapist detective novels and thrillers. Declared
physically unfit to serve in the military during World War II, Spicer
attended the University of Redlands for two years before transferring in
1945 to the University of California, Berkeley, where he majored in
philosophy and literature. In the thriving nonconformist Berkeley
community, the young Spicer gradually reinvented himself as a poet,
a bohemian, a radical, and—very slowly and timidly—a gay man. His
first English teacher at Berkeley was the poet Josephine Miles, who
generously encouraged his literary ambitions. Spicer also became
interested in radical politics and joined San Francisco's Libertarian
Circle, a group of "philosophical anarchists" led by Kenneth Rexroth.

The decisive encounter for Spicer, however, came in 1946 when he
met Robert Duncan, whose flamboyant and self-assured public persona
as poet and homosexual so dazzled the younger writer that he declared
afterward that 1946 was the true year of his birth. The two young poets
soon announced—only half-seriously at first—"The Berkeley Renaissance,"
which essentially consisted of a group of their literary friends gathered
around bookstore owner George Leite, who published the international
arts magazine *Circle*.

Amid this bohemian ferment, Spicer continued his academic studies.
After earning an M.A. in linguistics at Berkeley in 1950, he entered a
doctoral program in Anglo-Saxon and Old Norse, but never finished
a dissertation. For the rest of his short life Spicer eked out a living as a
research linguist working on scholarly projects. He taught at the University
of Minnesota for two years but returned to California in 1952. A few years
later he moved briefly to New York and then Boston, but in late 1956 he
returned to San Francisco. He would never leave the West again.

Working part-time as a researcher in Berkeley, he also taught a
"Poetry as Magic" workshop at the San Francisco Public Library.
During the next few years, Spicer finally came into his own as a poet.

The key to his artistic development was his concept of the "serial poem." Unhappy with his earlier work, Spicer decided that it had failed because he had tried to write poems that stood alone. "There is no single poem," he eventually realized. "Poems should echo and reecho against each other….They should create resonances." Spicer then began to conceive of his work in terms of individual books or booklets of interrelated poems. A serial poem, he explained in a lecture, uses the book as its unit of composition. Unlike traditional poetic sequences, however, these books were not necessarily conceived as progressive sequences of individual poems; rather, they existed as a competitive community of synchronous alternatives.

The first of Spicer's serial books was *After Lorca* (1957), an ingenious and moving compilation of genuine translations, fake translations, and prose letters to the dead Spanish poet Federico García Lorca, who also supposedly provided an introduction from beyond the grave. *After Lorca* was published by the newly created White Rabbit Press, which printed the stapled chapbook on a mimeograph press on a Saturday night at the San Francisco Greyhound Bus offices—a representative genesis for books in the bohemian North Beach of that era. Other books quickly followed, many of which were published only after Spicer's death in 1965. *A Book of Music*, for example, was finished in 1958 but not published until 1969. *Billy the Kid* (1959) appeared with drawings by Jess, the Bay Area artist who was Robert Duncan's lover. *The Heads of the Town Up to the Aether* (1962), Spcier's longest book, was followed by *The Holy Grail* (1964) and *Language* (1965)—as well as half a dozen other books published posthumously. Unreviewed and hardly noticed at the time of their creation, these playful and profoundly inventive collections today provide the most exuberant and accessible entry into the experimental West Coast poetry of the era. Spicer never fell into the common fallacy that experimental art need not be interesting. His poems eagerly charm, cajole, argue, and amuse the reader, and they gleefully adopt every available technique to accomplish their task. Depending on what works one cites, the dexterously diverse Spicer can with equal justice be classified as a Beat or surrealist, a late modernist or early postmodernist, a protolanguage poet or premature New Formalist.

Until the posthumous publication of *The Collected Books of Jack Spicer* (1975), edited by his friend Robin Blaser, the poet's reputation was confined to San Francisco and Berkeley. This situation was mostly Spicer's doing. He printed his books in tiny editions and did not allow them to be sold outside San Francisco—often giving them away free at readings. He also broke bitterly with Duncan after his mentor joined with the Black Mountain School, which Spicer found abstract and humorless. He was happiest in his small "magic circle" of friends talking drunkenly late into the night at North Beach bars. As the national media touted the San Francisco Renaissance and catapulted many friends and former friends into international fame as Beat poets in the late 1950s, Spicer knew he had become a marginal figure. After being injured in an automobile crash sometime in the winter of 1962–1963, the poet increased his already heavy drinking, which eventually led to his being fired from his research job. In July 1965, at the age of forty, Spicer collapsed and fell into a coma. Waking only intermittently, he died three weeks later in the alcoholic ward of the public hospital.

Improvisations on a Sentence by Poe

"Indefiniteness is an element of the true music."
The grand concord of what
Does not stoop to definition. The seagull
Alone on the pier cawing its head off
Over no fish, no other seagull,
No ocean. As absolutely devoid of meaning
As a French horn.
It is not even an orchestra. Concord
Alone on a pier. The grand concord of what
Does not stoop to definition. No fish
No other seagull, no ocean—the true
Music.

Orfeo

Sharp as an arrow Orpheus
Points his music downward.
Hell is there
At the bottom of the seacliff.
Heal
Nothing by this music.

Eurydice
Is a frigate bird or a rock or some seaweed.
Hail nothing
The infernal
Is a slippering wetness out at the horizon.
Hell is this:
The lack of anything but the eternal to look at
The expansiveness of salt
The lack of any bed but one's
Music to sleep in.

Conspiracy

A violin which is following me

In how many distant cities are they listening
To its slack-jawed music? This
Slack-jawed music?
Each of ten thousand people playing it.

It follows me like someone that hates me.

Oh, my heart would sooner die
Than leave its slack-jawed music. They
In those other cities
Whose hearts would sooner die.

It follows me like someone that hates me.

Or is it really a tree growing just behind my throat
That if I turned quickly enough I could see
Rooted, immutable, neighboring
Music.

A Book of Music

Coming at an end the lovers
Are exhausted like two swimmers. Where
Did it end? There is no telling. No love is
Like an ocean with the dizzy procession of the waves' boundaries
From which two can emerge exhausted, nor long goodbye
Like death.
Coming at an end. Rather, I would say, like a length
Of coiled rope
Which does not disguise in the first twists of its lengths
Its endings.
But, you will say, we loved
And some parts of us loved
And the rest of us will remain
Two persons. Yes,
Poetry ends like a rope.

Bob Kaufman
(1925–1986)

A legendary figure known as "The Original Be-Bop Man" and "The Black American Rimbaud," Bob (Garnell) Kaufman was born in New Orleans in 1925. He shrouded his origins in romantic mystery, but he was apparently the tenth of thirteen children, and his father was half African American, half German Orthodox Jew, and his mother was a black Catholic with family from old New Orleans roots. In addition to participating in both Jewish and Catholic religious services, the young Kaufman was influenced by his grandmother's voodoo beliefs. He ran away to sea when he was thirteen and spent twenty years as a Merchant Marine, surviving shipwrecks and circling the globe nine times during his service. These "facts" are controversial and open to many interpretations, as are the life, talent, and poetry of Bob Kaufman.

Docking in New York City in the early 1950s and inspired by a shipmate who had become his unofficial tutor, Kaufman enrolled in the New School for Social Research. He fell for the hard bop and improvisational jazz that was sweeping the avant-garde American scene, and he met and befriended Charlie Parker, Thelonious Monk, and Charles Mingus. His work was thereafter powered by the rhythms and phrasing of improvisational jazz, and Kaufman (with Jack Kerouac a close second) was singular among Beats in truly injecting jazz into his own poetry.

Kaufman met William S. Burroughs and Allen Ginsberg in New York, and they traveled together to San Francisco's North Beach to join the flowering of the Beat generation and to meet Lawrence Ferlinghetti, Jack Kerouac, and Gregory Corso. Inspired by the rhythms and improvisations of jazz, Kaufman began reciting spontaneous poems, working as a bard familiar on the streets. "Crootey Songo" is only one of his numerous poems written as much to be played on a saxophone as shouted on a corner.

Standing for the spontaneity of the spoken word, Kaufman did not seek to publish his work, but friends nevertheless transcribed and submitted versions of his performances for print. Lawrence Ferlinghetti of City Lights Bookstore published three broadsides of his work in 1959: "Abomunist Manifesto," "Second April," and "Does the Secret Mind Whisper?", the first of which remains famous as a generational manifesto. By the time he returned to the East again, Kaufman was both famous and infamous in San Francisco. He was invited to read at Harvard in 1960 and nominated for the prestigious Guinness Poetry Award, but literary recognition masked a cycle of personal disintegration marked by poverty, addiction, imprisonment, and hospitalization.

When John F. Kennedy was assassinated in 1963, Kaufman took a Buddhist vow of silence and withdrew from society for a decade. His broadsides were gathered into *Solitudes Crowded with Loneliness* (1965), which went largely unnoticed in the United States but was translated into Arabic, Danish, French, German, Italian, Polish, Russian, and Spanish, and was a major influence in spreading Beat culture through Europe. Friend Mary Beach also collected some of Kaufman's poems and published *Golden Sardine* in 1967. In 1975, on the day the Vietnam War was declared over, Kaufman broke his silence and stunned people in a coffee shop by reciting "All Those Ships that Never Sailed." For three years, he was intensely active and productive, writing many of the poems that would be collected in *The Ancient Rain: Poems, 1956–1978* (1981).

In 1978 Kaufman once again withdrew, isolated from all but a handful of friends. He was an infrequent, troubled, and troubling sight in San Francisco, and his downward spiral was broken only by his death from emphysema in 1986. In more recent times, the puzzle of Bob Kaufman has been rediscovered by poets and scholars alike, and his poetry and the details of his life are the subject of serious re-evaluation.

Round About Midnight

Jazz radio on a midnight kick.
Round about Midnight.

Sitting on the bed,
With a jazz type chick
Round about Midnight,

Piano laughter, in my ears,
Round about Midnight.

Stirring laughter, dying tears,
Round about Midnight.

Soft blue voices, muted grins,
Exciting voices, Father's sins,
Round about Midnight.

Come on baby, take off your clothes,
Round about Midnight.

No More Jazz at Alcatraz

No more jazz
At Alcatraz
No more piano
for Lucky Luciano
No more trombone
for Al Capone
No more jazz
at Alcatraz
No more cello
for Frank Costello
No more screeching of the
Seagulls
As they line up for
Chow
No more jazz
At Alcatraz

Myra Cohn Livingston
(1926–1996)

One of the major children's poets in the United States, Myra Cohn Livingston was born in Omaha, Nebraska, in 1926. Her family moved to Los Angeles during the Depression, and Livingston fancied herself more a budding musician than a nascent poet. In high school, she took a summer class taught by the French composer Darius Milhaud. A stern taskmaster, Milhaud insisted the rules of music be understood and respected before they could be broken in the name of creativity. "If I have remembered nothing else in my life, it was that principle and I have lived by it," Livingston wrote in her autobiography for the Something about the Author series. "Learn first that there are rules, and then learn patiently when to leave them behind."

Livingston worked as a professional French horn player until she graduated from Sarah Lawrence College in 1948, when she returned to California. She began writing book reviews, first for the *Los Angeles Daily News* (1948–1949), then for the *Los Angeles Mirror* (1949–1950). She also worked as personal secretary for singer Dinah Shore and later for renowned violinist Jascha Heifetz. Livingston married and moved to Dallas, where she lived for twelve years, raising three children. She was also a creative writing teacher for the Dallas Public Library and the public school system from 1958 to 1963.

In 1958 Livingston published her first book, *Whispers and Other Poems*, written earlier when she was in college. *Wide Awake and Other Poems* followed soon after in 1959. In 1963, appalled by John F. Kennedy's assassination in Dallas, her family returned to California, where she wrote prolifically, publishing forty books of children's poetry before her death from cancer in 1996. In addition to writing hundreds of original poems, Livingston edited more than three dozen children's and theme anthologies and also published several books on writing, including *When You Are Alone / It Keeps You Capone: An Approach to Creative Writing with Children* (1973), *The Child As Poet: Myth or Reality?* (1984), and *Climb into the Bell Tower: Essays on Poetry* (1990).

Livingston was also an active and beloved teacher. She resumed teaching when she returned to California in 1963, and she was poet in residence for the Beverley Hills Unified School District from 1966 to 1984. Like her artistic mentor Milhaud many years earlier, she was an outspoken critic, especially of the thousands "who call themselves poets" but have no understanding of their craft and end up teaching their students little more than wordplay. She was also a popular lecturer in the University of California, Los Angeles's Extension program from 1973 until 1996. One former student, poet Jenny Factor, remembers Livingston's lesson to her and fellow young students: "To trust our crazy eyes, to believe in our unique way of seeing the world, and not to be afraid to speak out even when the vision we see is new and different."

Coming from Kansas

Whenever they come from Kansas
they stay for nearly a week
and they live with Grandma in Council Bluffs
because her house has room enough,
and we go over the day they arrive.
Everyone shouts when they pull in the drive.
We kiss and hug and I get to play
with my cousin Joan most every day
    and the grown-ups cry when they leave.

Whenever they say they're coming,
we make a lot of plans.
Joan and I like to put on a play
and we start to write it the very first day.
There're costumes and sets and curtains to do;
we write a part for the neighbor boy, too,
Denny, who comes in the very first scene
to introduce Joan, who's always the queen
    and I have to be the king.

And when it's hot in the afternoons
we get a big glass of Kool-Aid
and play cribbage or jacks on the vestibule floor
and Denny, the boy who lives next door,
comes over and dares us to go up the hill
where the cemetery, dark and still,
lies spooky with ghosts. We go before night,

but Denny and Joan always get in a fight
  and I have to take Joan's side.

Whenever they come in summer,
Joan tells me about her friends.
She says that Kansas is better, too,
there's always more fun and things to do.
But when we visited there last year
I saw her friends, and they all were queer,
And I told her so, and her face got tight
And then we had a terrible fight
  and we pulled each other's hair.

When we go to Grandma's in autumn,
Joan isn't there any more,
and Denny comes over. There's so much to do
like racing down North Second Avenue
or daring each other to slide down the eaves
or sloshing the puddles and jumping in leaves
and if we decide to write out a scene
Denny will always let me be queen
  and I don't have to bother with Joan!

An Angry Valentine

If you won't be my Valentine
I'll *scream*, I'll *yell*, I'll *bite!*
I'll cry aloud, I'll start to whine
If you won't be my Valentine.
I'll frown and fret, I'll mope and whine,
And it will serve you right—
If you won't be my Valentine
I'll *scream*, I'll *yell*, I'll *bite!*

Birds Know

Birds know how to lift their wings,
                to fold their feet
                to fly

                across the air
                to other lands
                fighting the windy sky.

Birds know how to leave the cold.

One day, so will I.

Lew Welch
(1926–1971)

One of the lesser-known members of the Beat generation, Lew Welch was born in Phoenix, Arizona, in 1926. His father, Lewis Barrett Welch Sr., was a prominent surgeon, wed to Dorothy Brownfield Welch. After their marriage dissolved, Dorothy set off with their children for California when Lew was only three. The family moved often within the state, and Lew Welch attended schools in many different towns, finally graduating high school in Palo Alto. But even before these transitory days, he felt himself psychologically fragile. As he later told poet David Meltzer, "I went to the loony bin when I was fourteen months old….It is the world's record, even among my beat generation friends. I copped out, I went crazy, split, I said 'forget it.'" He experienced numerous psychic breaks from then on and was subject to profound bouts of depression, one of which led to his mysterious disappearance in 1971.

Welch entered Reed College in 1948 and soon met Gary Snyder and Philip Whalen. By 1949 the three young men were sharing a house and exploring a world of poetry and alternative lifestyles. Welch was co-editor of the Reed literary magazine, wrote poetry and incisive criticism that he revealed only to friends, and was clearly a talented young man. And troubled as well. For the next three years, Welch moved often, hatching elaborate plans for a fresh start to his life with each new geographic locale. On one of his trips back to Portland, he met William Carlos Williams, who was lecturing at Reed College.

Depression and mental agitation seemed to stalk Welch. During a sunny spell, he took a job with Montgomery Wards in Chicago, started psychoanalysis, and married Mary Garber. But San Francisco, the burgeoning Beat movement (led by his former roommates), and his hopes of being a poet seemed to call his name, and he moved back to the Bay Area.

His poetry thrived. Donald Allen's influential anthology *The New American Poetry* (1960) included a poem by Welch, and the same year saw the publication of Welch's first book, *Wobbly Rock*.

The last decade of Lew Welch's short life was marked by a significant poetic output and considerable personal turmoil. He was a handsome and magnetic figure, sufficiently impressive to Jack Kerouac, who modeled his *Big Sur* character Dave Wain after the hard-drinking poet.

Amidst a succession of short love affairs and frequent breakdowns, Welch wrote verse admired by many, enough to produce more then a dozen chapbooks, including the proto-environmental poetry of *The Song Mt. Tamalpais Sings* (1969). Welch led a cautionary life and left a healthy handful of fine poems. They include "Ring of Bone" and "Not Yet 40, My Beard Is Already White," clear, imagistic poems in a firm voice, about the healing powers of the Western outdoors well before the rise of late-twentieth-century California nature poetry.

His life apparently ended in May 1971, while he was recuperating at his friend Gary Snyder's Sierra Nevada foothill farmstead near Nevada City. Welch walked off from his remote campsite with a rifle, never to be found. A last note read: "I never could make anything work out right and now I'm betraying my friends. I can't make anything out of it— never could. I had great visions but never could bring them together with reality. I used it all up. It's all gone."

The Basic Con

Those who can't find anything to live for,
always invent something to die for.

Then they want the rest of us to
die for it, too.

Not Yet 40, My Beard Is Already White

Not yet 40, my beard is already white.
Not yet awake, my eyes are puffy and red,
　　　　　　like a child who has cried too much.

What is more disagreeable
than last night's wine?

I'll shave.
I'll stick my head in the cold spring and
look around at the pebbles.
Maybe I can eat a can of peaches.

Then I can finish the rest of the wine,
write poems till I'm drunk again,
and when the afternoon breeze comes up

I'll sleep until I see the moon
and the dark trees
and the nibbling deer

and hear
the quarreling coons

Henri Coulette
(1927–1988)

Poet, editor, and educator Henri Coulette was born in Los Angeles
in 1927. Coulette melded seamless metrics with a lifelong devotion to
California icons like the LBG-30 (a pioneer Glendale computer),
the noir Los Angeles memorialized by Raymond Chandler, and the
gravesites of Hollywood movie stars. He received his B.A. from Los
Angeles State College (now California State University, Los Angeles) in
1952, two years after his marriage to Jacqueline Meredith, and he spent
his entire life in California, save for two years in military service
(1945–1946) and his years at the University of Iowa completing his
M.F.A. (1954) and Ph.D. (1959). Upon receiving his doctorate, he
returned to his undergraduate alma mater, where he was a professor of
English until his death of an apparent heart attack in 1988.

Although Coulette's themes are contemporary, his poetics are classic
through and through. A master of meter and formal elegance, he was
widely praised for his control of the technical art of poetry and his
ability to translate the modern world into classical stanzas. He was,
Robert Mezey and Donald Justice wrote, "a master of syllabics," and his
poetry is unique in their eyes for its "ability to get wildly different types
of words to lie down together."

During his lifetime, Coulette published only two books. His second,
The Family Goldschmitt (1971)—which had most of its edition
accidentally shredded by the publishing house, never to be reprinted—
was praised for its depths of emotion, its compression of pain, agony,
and tension into "supportable thought." *The War of the Secret Agents
and Other Poems* (1965), Coulette's only widely available volume of
poetry, articulates a fascinating vision of California. He won two coveted
awards for the collection: the Lamont Poetry Award of the Academy of
American Poets and the James D. Phelan Foundation Award. While
the title poem is about a literal secret agent, much of the book invokes
Hollywood's metaphoric ideas of secret agents, spies and spy novels,
and ultimately, webs of intrigue and duplicity. Such subjects were, for
Coulette, part of what makes California a land of dreams in which the
real and the surrogate are endlessly mingled and confused. Noting that
he was intrigued by the general idea of double agents—those who led
several lives—Justice and Mezey observed that in an age of confessional

poets, Coulette understood that the self is composed of multiple
identities, that "he saw himself in some respects as an agent, under
orders, in disguise, with code name and cover story ready; it was,
perhaps, his metaphor for the life of a poet."

Night Thoughts
in memory of David Kubal

Your kind of night, David, your kind of night.
The dog would eye you as you closed your book;
Such a long chapter, such a time it took.
The great leaps! The high cries! The leash like a line drive!
The two of you would rove the perfumed street,
Pillar to post, and terribly alive.

Your kind of night, nothing more, nothing less;
A single lighted window, the shade drawn,
Your shadow enormous on the silver lawn,
The busy mockingbird, his rapturous fit,
The cricket keeping time, the loneliness
Of the man in the moon—and the man under it.

The word *elsewhere* was always on your lips,
A password to some secret, inner place
Where Wisdome smiled in Beautie's looking-glass
And Pleasure was at home to dearest Honour.
(The dog-eared pages mourn your fingertips,
And vehicle whispers, *Yet once more*, to tenor.)

Now you are elsewhere, *elsewhere* comes to this,
The thoughtless body, like a windblown rose,
Is gathered up and ushered toward repose.
To have to know this is our true condition,
The Horn of Nothing, the classical abyss,
The only cry a cry of recognition.

The priest wore purple; now the night does, too.
A dog barks, and another, and another.
There are a hundred words for the word *brother*.
We use them when we love, when we are sick,
And in our dreams when we are somehow you.
What are we if not wholly catholic?

Postscript

There are some questions one should know by heart.
A world without them must be shadowless.
Who was it said, Come let us kiss and part?

The one who asked, Why is this apple tart?
And dreamed the serpent was the letter S?
There are some questions one should know by heart.

It was the thorn that plotted to outsmart
The cunning of the rose with such success.
Who was it said, Come let us kiss and part?

There are interiors none may map or chart:
In your voice, crying, was a wilderness.
There are some questions one should know by heart.

Your ape and echo from the bitter start,
This mirror mourns your image's caress.
Who was it said, Come let us kiss and part?

We had too little craft and too much art.
We thought two noes would make a perfect yes.
There are some questions one should know by heart.
Who was it said, Come let us kiss and part?

Philip Lamantia
(b. 1927)

Praised by French surrealist André Breton as "a voice that rises once
in a hundred years," Philip Lamantia was born in San Francisco in
1927, the son of Sicilian immigrants. He began writing poetry in
elementary school, and in junior high, having immersed himself in
the work of Edgar Allan Poe and H. P. Lovecraft, he was briefly expelled
for "intellectual delinquency." At fourteen, inspired by the surrealist
paintings of Salvador Dali and Joan Miró at the San Francisco Museum
of Art, Lamantia began studying surrealist literature, which shaped his
own poetry. Revolutionary surrealism, with its dreamlike and oddly
juxtaposed imagery, immediately appealed to Lamantia, who claimed
that the influence, "even before [his] knowledge of surrealist theory,
was part of [his] own individual temperament." In 1943, when he was
just fifteen years old, he saw a group of his poems published in *View:
A Magazine of the Arts.*

Lamantia dropped out of high school at sixteen and went to New
York, where many European surrealists had fled Nazism and fascism
during World War II. But he became disillusioned with the circle (he
would take it up again years later), finding it stagnant and dated, and
returned to California to complete his high school diploma. Lamantia
enrolled at the University of California, Berkeley, and was quickly
absorbed in the radical social and intellectual ferment that swirled
around the region. He developed two new passions, mysticism and
eroticism, and they were reflected in his first book, *Erotic Poems* (1946).

He left Berkeley after two years to wander the world in search of
mystical experience, often summoned through drug-induced states of
altered consciousness. He lived with Indian tribes in Nevada and Mexico,
traveled through France and Morocco, and spent time in avant-garde jazz
clubs when he returned to cities in the United States. He joined forces
with the Beats, whose work blended jazz and everyday speech into
political statement, and he was immortalized by Jack Kerouac as Francis
da Pavia in *Dharma Bums* and David D'Angeli in *Desolation Angels.* He
was an important player at the historic Six Gallery evening of October 7,
1955, at which the Beat movement first found public fame. While
Lamantia found the Beats kindred, his thought and poetry maintained
stylistic and thematic differences that widened further as he developed.

After a decade of wandering, Lamantia moved to Spain, where he studied philosophy and mathematics. In 1966 he published his second book, *Touch of the Marvelous*, which included work from *Erotic Poems*. Critics seized the opportunity to consider his full career to that point. Tom Clark describes the early poetry as finding "illumination in the infernal image of violence and pain," while the best of his later poems "cohere psychically and verbally in a rare, surprising clarity." In 1967, City Lights released another collection, *Selected Poems: 1943–1966*. His next book, *Blood of the Air* (1970), represented a return to his surrealist roots. His most recent book is *Bed of Sphinxes: New and Selected Poems 1943–1993*, published in 1997.

Lamantia lives in San Francisco, where he guards his privacy. Long a spiritual quester, he returned to the Catholic Church in 1998. His spiritual convictions remain deeply rooted in mysticism.

HIGH

O beato solitudo! where have I flown to?
stars overturn the wall of my music
as flight of birds, they go by, the spirits
opened below the lark of plenty
ovens of neant overflow the docks at Veracruz
This much is time
summer coils the soft suck of night
lone unseen eagles crash thru mud
I am worn like an old sack by the celestial bum
I'm droppng my eyes where all the trees turn on fire!
I'm mad to go to you, Solitude—who will carry me there?
I'm wedged on this collision of planets/Tough!
I'm ONGED!
I'm the trumpet of King David
the sinister elevator tore itself limb by limb

> You can not close
> you can not open
> you break yr head
> you make bloody bread!

Helen Pinkerton
(b. 1927)

Helen Pinkerton was born in 1927 in Butte, Montana. Her father was a copper miner who died in a work-related accident when she was eleven, leaving her mother to rear four children by herself. His death drove the young Pinkerton—a devout Catholic—into a decade-long crisis of faith, and that theme continues to be central to her poetry. Pinkerton edited her Mount Vernon, Washington, high school newspaper and yearbook and later attended Stanford University to study journalism. When fellow students at the *Stanford Daily* went on and on about a demanding poet-critic named Yvor Winters, she took a class with him. The experience changed the course of her life, and she earned her undergraduate degree (1948) and master's degree (1950) studying with him as her mentor. She received a Ph.D. from Harvard (1966) as a Herman Melville scholar, and her first academic book was *Melville's* Confidence Man *and American Politics in the 1850s.*

Pinkerton taught at several universities, returning to teach at Stanford for more than a decade prior to retirement. The demands of teaching, family (she married and reared children with poet Wesley Trimpi, from whom she is now divorced), as well as a stern streak of self-criticism has limited the publication of her poetry to a handful of scholarly journals, and *Taken in Faith*, her first collection of poetry, did not appear until 2002. "I've never seen any reason to publish a lot," she has said. "I throw away a lot of half-finished poems and drafts. It does not make for quantity. But I'm afraid that's my temperament."

Her subjects are often spiritual and philosophic, and she has long favored a rigorously controlled verse defined by attention to classic forms and regular metrics and rhymes. This formality in a time of distinct self-expression has limited her appeal mainly to enthusiasts of the New Formalist school. Pinkerton is also a vocal critic of recent poetry, decrying the current "breakdown in the notion of what a poem can be. Not everybody is capable of being a poet—just like everybody isn't capable of being a fine ballet dancer or a fine pianist."

Estimations of her poetic talent by a core of stubborn enthusiasts were not laggard, and Yvor Winters wrote in 1967 that "she is a master of poetic style. No poet in English writes with more authority." Poet Timothy Steele, who wrote the afterword to *Taken in Faith*, said flatly,

"She has written some of the best poems of her generation." Pinkerton currently lives and writes in Menlo Park.

For an End

Had I not loved,
I had not believed,
And not believing,
Had been deceived.

Had I not loved,
I had not known
Either your being
Or my own.

Had I not loved,
I had not known
That you could love
Both mind and bone.

Had you not loved,
When your decree
Seemed total loss,
You had lost me.

Nature Note: The California Poison Oak

Dry summers flaw the leaf to a rose flame,
Where, as a vine, it seems to flicker higher
Than live-oaks it consumes, or where it leaps
As a free-standing shrub or tree—ablaze
In wild-oat hayfields. Yet, with winter come,
The stems shrink back and almost disappear
In sinuous tangles, while a few white drupes
That look like snowberries hang to trick the eyes.

Nothing will warn but old experience
The ignorant damp hand that comes to dig
In winter rain the dormant trillium:
Seeking to bring a wild spring beauty home
It finds, as parasitic as a drug,
Pain stinging flesh that brushed the stems but once.

Philip Levine
(b. 1928)

Called "a large ironic Whitman of the industrial heartland" and "one of our quintessentially urban poets," Philip Levine has fashioned a major reputation as a poet of the working class. He was born in Detroit, Michigan, in 1928, the son of middle-class Russian Jewish immigrants, his father a businessman, his mother a bookseller. Levine and his twin brother were five when their father died suddenly and the family was slowly financially drained. Levine's childhood was colored by money worries during the Great Depression, a sympathy for radical politics and American workers, and a fascination with the Spanish Civil War.

Levine was educated at Wayne State College (now University), receiving his A.B. in 1950, and he immediately got a job in an automotive factory, working for several years at such firms as Chevrolet Gear and Axle and Detroit Transmission. His experiences there have played vividly in his poetry since. Levine earned a mail-order master's degree in 1954, writing his thesis on Keats's "Indolence" ode.

Levine's true career as a poet began in 1953, when he went to the University of Iowa to study with Robert Lowell and John Berryman. He was especially influenced by the latter, then far less well known than Lowell, and Levine remembers Berryman as "the most brilliant, intense, articulate man I've ever met." Donald Justice, Henri Coulette, and Jane Cooper were among his more prominent classmates. Levine married Frances Artley and, after several years off, returned to Iowa to complete his M.F.A. in 1957. Following a year with Yvor Winters at Stanford, he moved to Fresno to take an academic position at California State University, Fresno, where he taught from 1958 until 1992. Under Levine's guidance, CSU Fresno became a major graduate center for the study of poetry writing and the home of the Fresno Poets.

Levine's poetry had long appeared in magazines and limited editions when, at forty, he published his first full-length collection, *Not This Pig* (1968), with Wesleyan University Press. He created poems in a streetwise vernacular, an early version of the mythologized working-class persona for which he would later be appreciated. Levine brought out *They Feed They Lion* in 1972, the title poem of which scrambled grammar and syntax to evoke surreal disorientation. His next book, *1933* (1974), took its title from the year of his father's death, and many continue to find the mining of his childhood in an industrial wasteland as the source of best work to date. Levine's imaginative obsession with the Spanish Civil War led him to compose the poems of *The Names of the Lost* (1976). Collections that followed were *7 Years from Somewhere* (1979), *Ashes: Poems New and Old* (1979), *One for the Rose* (1981), and *Selected Poems* (1984).

As his later poetry evolved, Levine's voice became more direct, his lines less energetic or ironic, which caused some critics to express reservations even as his readership and reputation continued to grow. For many readers and scholars, Levine is now *the* artful and compelling voice of urban American, dispossessed blue-collar life. *New Selected Poems* and *What Work Is* (both 1991, the latter winning his second National Book Award) brought Levine true national prominence, and *The Simple Truth* (1994), which won the Pulitzer Prize, solidified his standing as a major contemporary American poet.

They Feed They Lion

Out of burlap sacks, out of bearing butter,
Out of black bean and wet slate bread,
Out of the acids of rage, the candor of tar,
Out of creosote, gasoline, drive shafts, wooden dollies,
They Lion grow.

Out of the grey hills
Of industrial barns, out of rain, out of bus ride,
West Virginia to Kiss My Ass, out of buried aunties,
Mothers hardening like pounded stumps, out of stumps,
Out of the bones' need to sharpen and the muscles' to stretch,
They Lion grow.

Earth is eating trees, fence posts,
Gutted cars, earth is calling her little ones,
"Come home, Come home!" From pig balls,
From the ferocity of pig driven to holiness,
From the furred ear and the full jowl come
The repose of the hung belly, from the purpose
They Lion grow.

From the sweet glues of the trotters
Come the sweet kinks of the fist, from the full flower
Of the hams the thorax of caves,
From "Bow Down" come "Rise Up,"
Come they Lion from the reeds of shovels,
The grained arm that pulls the hands,
They Lion grow.

From my five arms and all my hands,
From all my white sins forgiven, they feed,
From my car passing under the stars,
They Lion, from my children inherit,
From the oak turned to a wall, they Lion,
From they sack and they belly opened
And all that was hidden burning on the oil-stained earth
They feed they Lion and he comes.

Animals Are Passing from Our Lives

It's wonderful how I jog
on four honed-down ivory toes
my massive buttocks slipping
like oiled parts with each light step.

I'm to market. I can smell
the sour, grooved block, I can smell
the blade that opens the hole
and the pudgy white fingers

that shake out the intestines
like a hankie. In my dreams
the snouts drool on the marble,
suffering children, suffering flies,

suffering the consumers
who won't meet their steady eyes
for fear they could see. The boy
who drives me along believes

that any moment I'll fall
on my side and drum my toes
like a typewriter or squeal
and shit like a new housewife

discovering television,
or that I'll turn like a beast
cleverly to hook his teeth
with my teeth. No. Not this pig.

Genius

Two old dancing shoes my grandfather
gave the Christian Ladies,
an unpaid water bill, the rear license
of a dog that messed on your lawn,
a tooth I saved for the good fairy
and which is stained with base metals
and plastic filler. With these images
and your black luck and my bad breath
a bright beginner could make a poem
in fourteen rhyming lines about the purity
of first love or the rose's many thorns
or the dew that won't wait long enough
to stand my little gray wren a drink.

Waking in March

Last night, again, I dreamed
my children were back at home,
small boys huddled in their separate beds,
and I went from one to the other
listening to their breathing—regular,
almost soundless—until a white light
hardened against the bedroom wall,
the light of Los Angeles burning south
of here, going at last as we

knew it would. I didn't waken.
Instead the four of us went out
into the front yard and the false dawn
that rose over the Tehachipis and stood
in our bare feet on the wet lawn
as the world shook like a burning house.
Each human voice reached us
without sound, a warm breath on the cheek,
a dry kiss.
                    Why am I so quiet?
This is the end of the world, I am dreaming
the end of the world, and I go from bed
to bed bowing to the small damp heads
of my sons in a bedroom that turns
slowly from darkness to fire. Everyone
else is gone, their last words
reach us in the language of light.
The great eucalyptus trees along the road
swim in the new wind pouring
like water over the mountains. Each day
this is what we waken to, a water
like wind bearing the voices of the world,
the generations of the unborn chanting
in the language of fire. This will be
tomorrow. Why am I so quiet?

Bert Meyers
(1928–1979)

Bert Meyers was born in Los Angeles into a strongly Jewish household in 1928. Meyers himself was a workingman with socialist sympathies, and he toiled as a ditchdigger, janitor, and warehouseman before becoming a picture framer and gilder. In 1957 he married a college teacher, Odette Miller, who was born in Paris to Polish immigrants and survived the Holocaust in hiding, arriving in Los Angeles in 1949. Meyers and his wife had two children, one of whom, Daniel, is a film director.

Meyers did not have an advanced education and taught himself to write through reading and talking with other poets at coffee houses. He stole time to compose poetry at night and published his first book, *Early Rain,* in 1960. He enjoyed his work as a framer and fine carpenter, but emphysema forced him to give it up and move from Los Angeles at age thirty-six. He then threw himself into poetry, applying to Claremont Graduate School, where, despite having no undergraduate credits, he was accepted on the recommendations of poets Marianne Moore, Robert Bly, and Denise Levertov. Meyers flourished immediately, receiving grants from the Ingram Merrill Foundation in 1964 and 1965 and the National Endowment for the Arts in 1967, the same year he received his M.A.

From 1967 until his death from lung cancer in 1979, Meyers taught at Pitzer College, outside of Los Angeles. Many students recall his influence, including poet Garrett Hongo, who, in "Postcards for Bert Meyers," remembers him fondly as a wild spirit with a passionate gift for making and understanding poetry. Before his death, he published four more collections of poetry: *The Dark Birds* (1968), *Sunlight on the Wall: Selected Poems* (1977), *Windowsills* (1979), and *The Wild Olive Tree* (1979), later expanded to *The Wild Olive Tree and Blue Café* (1982). He also translated, with his wife, *Lord of the Village* by François Dodat (1973).

"The most exquisite poetry by any of the L.A.-born poets was written by Bert Meyers," Philip Levine wrote in 2003. "A colossal talent and a protégé of Tom McGrath,…he brought a remarkably precise physicality to poems of an unusual spiritual dimension, poems unlike anything else spawned by the fifties."

The Garlic

Rabbi of condiments,
whose breath is a verb,
wearing a thin beard
and a white robe;
you who are pale and small
and shaped like a fist,
a synagogue,
bless our bitterness,
transcend the kitchen
to sweeten death—
our wax in the flame
and our seed in the bread.

Now, my parents pray,
my grandfather sits,
my uncles fill
my mouth with ashes.

Arc de Triomphe

Nothing but grey seen through the arch—
as if triumph were an abyss
into which a nation marches.

Thom Gunn

(b. 1929)

Born Thomson Gunn in Gravesend, England, in 1929, Thom Gunn
was the son of journalists Kent Gunn and Ann Charlotte Thomson
Gunn, who shelved her career with the birth of Thom and his brother,
Ander. Gunn speaks rarely of his childhood, but describes it as a happy
one until his parents divorced when he was ten; his mother committed
suicide five years later. He was a voracious reader of poetry in
adolescence, well before he arrived at Cambridge after two years of
National Service. He completed his degree at Trinity College in 1953.
Fighting Terms (1954) was his first full collection of poetry, and it was so
finished and demonstrative that one critic called it "one of the few
volumes of postwar verse that all serious readers of poetry need to
possess and to study." Of the generation of British poets who emerged
in the 1950s (Philip Larkin, Ted Hughes, and Charles Tomlinson among
them), Gunn is regarded as Anglo-American, in the tradition of Eliot,
Pound, and Auden. The straddling of national cultures has made for an
uneasy peace: traditional British critics have often regarded his
California connections with embarrassment. Mainly out of uncertainty,
scholars of American and Californian poetry have often overlooked him
as one of the West Coast's major literary figures.

Gunn first came to the United States in 1954 to study with Yvor
Winters at Stanford, and he initially found Winters's intellectual rigor
and formal aesthetics exhilarating, staying on for the Ph.D. program,
which he left in 1958. Since 1960, Gunn has made his permanent home
in San Francisco, a city he took to quickly for its openness and the
freedom it afforded him to shape his life and craft. His early work was
metrical and rhymed, but after his move, he began to explore syllabic
scansion and free verse. *My Sad Captains* (1961), half metric and rhymed
and half in free verse, reflects this artistic evolution, but he never
abandoned metrics for prosier forms, and paradoxically, has treated his
most turbulent subjects—notably LSD and AIDs—in formal verse. He
works in both modes and, as Timothy Steele points out, Gunn is one of
the few substantial poets of the last half-century to write in meter *and*
free verse, combining the best of two opposing aesthetic camps.

Gunn has written about every stage of cultural development in
California. In the 1950s he immortalized the Hell's Angels, black leather,

and muscle culture in *The Sense of Movement* (1957). He took more than a hundred "trips" on LSD in the late 1960s, and these experiences figured powerfully in *Moly* (1971), named for the herb Odysseus ate to foil Circe's power to turn men into swine. In *Jack Straw's Castle* (1976), he treated his homosexuality in print, and he has since been regarded by many as the most eloquent poetic voice of gay life. His verse of the 1980s explored street life, randy cruising, and bathhouses, but as the AIDs scourge swept San Francisco late in the decade, his poetry took on an elegiac tone, reflecting the suffering and death of his friends and acquaintances; in one month alone he lost four close friends. Out of this personal and public crisis grew *The Man with Night Sweats* (1992), a volume that will stand as the central poetic testament of those plague years.

Gunn's genius has been to embody the human and artistic contradictions of his age. Reading his extravagantly diverse *Collected Poems* (1994), one finds treatments of LSD, video games, and street hustlers next to lyrics on Catholic saints, Keats, and Caravaggio—all of them not only perfectly achieved but recognizably drawn from the same imagination. Gunn is the prince of paradox, the quintessential San Franciscan who still holds a British passport, a Romantic entranced by classical control, an experimentalist who never renounced rhyme and meter, and an antiauthoritarian populist with mandarin standards.

Ranging from his mother's suicide and cannibal Jeffrey Dahmer to sex with strangers in public places and the story of David and Bathsheba, the subjects of *Boss Cupid* (2000) further confirm Gunn's status as a poet of singular originality and range. He has made his way without an academic sinecure (he left a permanent post with the University of California, Berkeley, in 1966 on gaining tenure) or self-publicizing school, and he stands alone as a writer who witnessed the most painful events of our age with gravity and compassion. He has made a poetry of life on the edges, a body of artful work distinguished by powerful observation, freshness of voice, philosophic depth, and wit.

On the Move

The blue jay scuffling in the bushes follows
Some hidden purpose, and the gust of birds
That spurts across the field, the wheeling swallows,
Has nested in the trees and undergrowth.

Seeking their instinct, or their poise, or both,
One moves with an uncertain violence
Under the dust thrown by a baffled sense
Or the dull thunder of approximate words.

On motorcycles, up the road, they come:
Small, black, as flies hanging in heat, the Boys,
Until the distance throws them forth, their hum
Bulges to thunder held by calf and thigh.
In goggles, donned impersonality,
In gleaming jackets trophied with the dust,
They strap in doubt—by hiding it, robust—
And almost hear a meaning in their noise.

Exact conclusion of their hardiness
Has no shape yet, but from known whereabouts
They ride, direction where the tyres press.
They scare a flight of birds across the field:
Much that is natural, to the will must yield.
Men manufacture both machine and soul,
And use what they imperfectly control
To dare a future from the taken routes.

It is a part solution, after all.
One is not necessarily discord
On earth; or damned because, half animal,
One lacks direct instinct, because one wakes
Afloat on movement that divides and breaks.
One joins the movement in a valueless world,
Choosing it, till, both hurler and the hurled,
One moves as well, always toward, toward.

A minute holds them, who have come to go:
The self-defined, astride the created will
They burst away; the towns they travel through
Are home for neither bird nor holiness,
For birds and saints complete their purposes.
At worst, one is in motion; and at best,
Reaching no absolute, in which to rest,
One is always nearer by not keeping still.

Flying Above California

Spread beneath me it lies—lean upland
sinewed and tawny in the sun, and

valley cool with mustard, or sweet with
loquat. I repeat under my breath

names of places I have not been to:
Crescent City, San Bernardino

—Mediterranean and Northern names.
Such richness can make you drunk. Sometimes

on fogless days by the Pacific,
there is a cold hard light without break

that reveals merely what is—no more
and no less. That limiting candour,

that accuracy of the beaches,
is part of the ultimate richness.

San Francisco Streets

I've had my eye on you
   For some time now.
You're getting by it seems,
   Not quite sure how.
But as you go along
   You're finding out
What different city streets
   Are all about.

Peach country was your home.
   When you went picking
You ended every day
   With peach fuzz sticking
All over face and arms,

Intimate, gross,
Itching like family,
    And far too close.

But when you came to town
    And when you first
Hung out on Market Street
    That was the worst:
Tough little group of boys
    Outside Flagg's Shoes.
You learned to keep your cash.
    You got tattoos.

Then by degrees you rose
    Like country cream—
Hustler to towel boy,
    Bath house and steam;
Tried being kept a while—
    But felt confined,
One brass bed driving you
    Out of your mind.

Later on Castro Street
    You got new work
Selling chic jewelry.
    And as sales clerk
You have at last attained
    To middle class.
(No one on Castro Street
    Peddles his ass.)

You gaze out from the store.
    Watching you watch
All the men strolling by
    I think I catch
Half-veiled uncertainty
    In your expression.
Good looks and great physiques

Pass in procession.
You've risen up this high—
    How, you're not sure.
Better remember what
    Makes you secure.
Fuzz is still on the peach,
    Peach on the stem.
Your looks looked after you.
    Look after them.

The Man with Night Sweats

I wake up cold, I who
Prospered through dreams of heat
Wake to their residue,
Sweat, and a clinging sheet.

My flesh was its own shield:
Where it was gashed, it healed.

I grew as I explored
The body I could trust
Even while I adored
The risk that made robust,

A world of wonders in
Each challenge to the skin.

I cannot but be sorry
The given shield was cracked
My mind reduced to hurry,
My flesh reduced and wrecked.

I have to change the bed,
But catch myself instead

Stopped upright where I am
Hugging my body to me

As if to shield it from
The pains that will go through me,

As if hands were enough
To hold an avalanche off.

Gary Snyder

(b. 1930)

Born in San Francisco, Gary Snyder grew up mostly in Oregon and
Washington State. Even as a child, the future poet loved the landscape
of the Pacific Northwest—the woods, mountains, and tidal flats. While
attending public schools in Seattle and Portland, he also became
interested in Native American lore. In high school he began climbing
mountains and learning about wilderness survival. He took his B.A.
in anthropology from Reed College in 1951, studied briefly at Indiana
University (where he read Kenneth Rexroth, another West Coast
naturalist poet who loved the outdoors), and from 1953 to 1956 studied
Asian languages at the University of California, Berkeley. His life
became an effort to balance physical labor and work in the woods
with more intellectual and spiritual pursuits. When not studying, he
worked as a lumberjack, trail maker, and forest fire lookout in the
Cascade Mountains.

While living in the Bay Area, Snyder became part of the Beat
movement through his friendships with Philip Whalen (his Reed
roommate), Allen Ginsberg, and Jack Kerouac (he served as the model
for Japhy Ryder in Kerouac's 1958 novel *The Dharma Bums*), and he
took part in the famous reading at the Six Gallery in October 1955,
when Ginsberg read "Howl" and Snyder read his poem "The Berry
Feast." Snyder's deep interest in Zen Buddhism influenced the reading
of his friends, and these poets also benefited from translations of
Oriental poetry by Ezra Pound, Arthur Waley, Rexroth, and others.
In 1956, with a scholarship from the First Zen Institute of America,
Snyder moved to Japan. He lived abroad most of the next twelve years,
writing and studying while the Beat movement in America progressed
into the political and social turmoil of the 1960s. He also visited India
and sailed to Istanbul on an oil tanker. After his return to the United
States, Snyder built a house in the Sierra Nevada mountains of
northern California, where he has lived ever since, except when
teaching at various institutions throughout the country. Snyder has been
married four times and has two sons, Kai and Gen, by his third wife.

While in Japan, Snyder published his first book of poems, *Riprap*
(1959), as well as *Myths and Texts* (1960) and *Riprap and Cold
Mountain Poems* (1965), which included his translations of Han Shan,
the T'ang dynasty poet. Upon his return to the United States, his main

publisher became New Directions, the influential modernist house founded by Pound's disciple James Laughlin, who also published Rexroth, Duncan, Levertov, Merton, and many other American poets. New Directions brought out many volumes of Snyder's work, including *The Back Country* (1968), *Regarding Wave* (1970), and *Turtle Island* (1974). Later collections from other publishers include *Axe Handles* (1983), *No Nature: New and Selected Poems* (1992), and his long poem *Mountains and Rivers Without End* (1996). For the most part, Snyder's books do not display the sort of notable stylistic or intellectual development that can be traced in the careers of other poets. Snyder's primary concerns—spiritual attunement, nature and the environment, and alternative definitions of community—were very much with him from the start. As for technique, his meditative stance came with a quietude and mistrust of language. The body of the poem was a kind of allusion to the primary experience that engendered it rather than an embodiment of such experience.

Unlike Kerouac, who drank himself to death, and Ginsberg, who reveled in publicity, Snyder has led a quieter life that critics have called remarkably healthy. His spiritual stance allowed him to appreciate establishment poets such as T. S. Eliot, whom his peers had denigrated. He has also been consistent in his devotion to environmental causes. As a result, he has become one of the enduring heroes of the literary counterculture and possibly the most widely respected individual in the Beat generation. His honors include grants from the Bollingen and Guggenheim Foundations, the Levinson Prize from *Poetry* magazine (1968), and even the Pulitzer Prize (1975) for *Turtle Island*. He is an emblematic figure of the American West, a role model for those who share his belief that materialism has endangered the planet. "As a poet," he once wrote, "I hold the most archaic values on earth. They go back to the late Paleolithic: the fertility of the soil, the magic of animals, the power-vision in solitude, the terrifying initiation and rebirth, the love and ecstasy of the dance, the common work of the tribe."

Riprap

Lay down these words
Before your mind like rocks.
        placed solid, by hands

In choice of place, set
Before the body of the mind
in space and time:
Solidity of bark, leaf, or wall
riprap of things:
Cobble of milky way,
straying planets,
These poems, people,
lost ponies with
Dragging saddles —
and rocky sure-foot trails.
The worlds like an endless
four-dimensional
Game of Go.
ants and pebbles
In the thin loam, each rock a word
a creek-washed stone
Granite: ingrained
with torment of fire and weight
Crystal and sediment linked hot
all change, in thoughts,
As well as things.

Marin-An

sun breaks over the eucalyptus
grove below the wet pasture,
water's about hot,
I sit in the open window
& roll a smoke.

distant dogs bark, a pair of
cawing crows; the twang
of a pygmy nuthatch high in a pine —
from behind the cypress windrow
the mare moves up, grazing.

a soft continuous roar
comes out of the far valley
of the six-lane highway—thousands
and thousands of cars
driving men to work.

Dick Barnes

(1932–2000)

Born in San Bernardino, Dick Barnes spent his childhood days in "the wilds" of eastern California. Much of it was passed in a modest woodstove-heated house in Running Springs, followed by several years in even smaller towns in the Mojave Desert. He went from a one-room schoolhouse to Pomona College, Harvard University, and Claremont Graduate School, where he took his Ph.D. in Renaissance literature. He taught for an extended period at Pomona College until his death in 2000. Barnes was survived by his wife of many years, Pat, and several children.

Barnes was a poet, occasional dramatist, musician, translator, editor, and college professor. His poetic output consisted of two books, *A Lake on the Earth* (1982) and *Few and Far Between* (1994), both of which were published by Ahsahta Press. He was anthologized only occasionally, most recently in Robert Mezey's *Poems of the American West* (2002). He was also an able translator, from the Italian and Spanish, and with longtime friend and fellow poet Mezey, he rendered the collected poems of the Argentine Jorge Luis Borges into English.

A demanding critic of his own work and a devoted and much-admired teacher, Barnes's output was small and his readers apparently relatively few, but they numbered prominent poets among them, including William Stafford, Miller Williams, and Donald Justice. If he was a very well-kept secret as a poet, Dick Barnes attracted the highest praises from those knowledgeable about the craft and writing of poetry. "By the late 1970s," Mezey recalls, "some of us thought him to be an exceptional poet, one of the wisest and most original poets writing in English."

Every Man His Own Cross

My father wept aloud in the night. My mother
tried to comfort him, but couldn't. O,

the world would have to be intricately cruel
to make him cry like that, cruel in its need

and he alone, unable in the face of it, and don't think
there was anything he could do he hadn't tried:

you'd never find a more unsparing man than he.
"And what about the boy?" he cried out, meaning me:

I was listening dismayed in my bed. I
was a coward, and lazy, and no help, he said.

He put me on his list of failures, or of the cruel things
the world had done to him, that night. And I agreed.

Looking back now, I think he saw me in his place, unspared,
unworthy, doomed to defeat like him no matter how eagerly

and angrily, or even how patiently, and for how long a time
I would try. Like him. And he was right.

There'd be more to say, and there will be, but I
would just as soon start from that. I do, still, agree.

Few and Far Between

If only we could forgive ourselves, and didn't
have to have somebody else forgive us—

Where I came from everybody could see anyone coming,
even storms: and out there the etiquette

was not to say right off what you came for when you did
or ask anybody why, if they came where you were

in all space, and time; it made for a kind
of trust, or—well, it was like trust.

I remember some of those storms, how the dust
would kick up before them in the wild wind, and behind it

the blueblack cloud piled high white on top
with lightning flaring inside, and maybe only a few miles wide,

coming over the desert sort of slow and grand:
you could have got out of the way if you wanted to

but nobody did; as I said, seldom enough is welcome.
Didn't I say that? One night when mother was away

my dad and I followed a storm clear down
to Needles in the state car. His job

was to take care of the highway, so it was work, sort of,
for us to ride along behind that cloud we could see by its own light

through the wild fragrance the desert has after a rain
in the lone car on the road that night, to keep track

of the damage it did. He showed me a place near Essex
where a flash flood had ripped out three hundred feet of roadbed

two years before, where it hadn't rained
in fifty years before that. The foreman said so,

Billy Nielson, and he'd been there fifty years
without seeing the ground wet.

My dad and I stopped on the grade below Goffs
and watched the storm go on out of his territory

across the river into Arizona
where the sky was getting gray,

and turned for home as the sun rose behind us
back across the clean desert in slant light

that lit the smoke trees in washes that were churned smooth
where the water went, and sharpened along the edges

through Essex and Cadiz Summit, great tamarisked Chambless,
Ludlow for breakfast with the humorous Chinaman, Lee,

Newberry Springs, Daggett and Elephant Butte, Nebo hidden by wire,
on home over the hill to Bartsow on the good road.

Michael McClure
(b. 1932)

Best known as a member of San Francisco's Beat movement, Michael McClure was born in Marysville, Kansas, in 1932. His early years were divided between the farmlands of Kansas and the lush landscape of Seattle, Washington, where he took long walks with his grandfather, a physician and naturalist. McClure wanted to become a biologist or naturalist, and his poetry and poetics derive powerfully from contemporary science. Nobel laureate Francis Crick has written an extremely favorable "scientist's view" of his work. After brief stops at the University of Wichita and the University of Arizona, McClure enrolled at San Francisco State University in 1954, where he studied with Robert Duncan.

Duncan had a powerful influence on McClure's sense and practice of poetic craft, and he introduced him to San Francisco's vibrant poetry community. In 1955, McClure met Allen Ginsberg, who invited him to read as one of five poets at the Six Gallery reading, where Ginsberg performed "Howl" for the first time and the Beat movement was born. From this, his first public reading, McClure has made the relationship between the natural environment and the union of man's mind and animal nature (what he calls "spiritmeat") the dominant themes in his work. He famously wrote that "when a man does not admit that he is an animal, he is less than an animal. Not more but less."

McClure published his first book, *Passage* (1956), a year after the Six Gallery reading. His poems are often centered on the page, a technique he uses to give them "the lengthwise symmetry found in higher animals," and he has continued radical innovations with space, typography, and the kernels of language on the page. McClure's poetry, essays, and plays share the central philosophy developed in his first book of essays, *Meat Science Essays* (1961): "all are finally creatures of Meat and Spirit." Like many Beats, McClure used psychomimetic drugs in the 1960s to explore altered states of consciousness, and he reported on his findings regularly in essays and poetry. By 1965, he had ten poetry publications to his credit, including *Hymns to St. Geryon and Other Poems* (1959) and *Ghost Tantras* (1964).

McClure has been a prolific poet and essayist, and he has also had a continuing interest in performance. His controversial play *The Beard* (1965) was performed to mingled howls of complaint and claims of genius. A reviewer for *Newsweek* called the dialogue "without question the 'filthiest' ever heard on a commercial stage in the English-speaking nations." McClure spent much of his time and energy for the next three years defending himself against obscenity charges. Serious scholars of the theater differ on this work, and many define it as significant in the development of contemporary drama. His subsequent plays include the award-winning *Josephine: The Mouse Singer* (1980). McClure has also worked with productions mixing music and poetry, and for the last decade, he has conducted a long-term collaboration with Ray Manzarek, keyboardist for the iconic rock band of the late 1960s The Doors. He also co-wrote the hit song "Mercedes Benz" with Janis Joplin.

With over sixteen full-length collections of poetry, six books of essays, two novels, and ten plays, McClure is one of the most prolific of the Beat-era poets. He has been awarded two grants from the National Endowment for the Arts (1964 and 1974), a Guggenheim Fellowship (1973), and other honors. Since 1962 he has taught at the California College of Arts and Crafts in Oakland. He lives in the East Bay hills with his wife, the sculptor Amy Evans McClure.

Canticle

The sharks tooth is perfect for biting. The intent
matters./ I am sick of beautiful things
/ and I would make a robe of gestures

without beauty except for the beauty inherent
in words and motion.

Listen/ Listen/ listen/ Listen/ Listen

to the words as waves/ pressures
all is destruction—without it there is
no strength.   The muscle builds
itself double   by destruction of cells.

The tendons whisper to the skeleton

Listen/ Listen/ listen/ Listen/ Listen
and only the nerves hear.

The field and seed are one thing destroying
the other. Intent, enwrapped with one another

Erethism is love. Love

Inventing a thing of leaves and flowers

'retractions devour' the thing burgeoning
is the thing intent/ Love/ Strength/ Light
and Dark/ spring to blossoms.

The Flowers of Politics, One

THIS IS THE HUGE DREAM OF US THAT WE ARE
HEROES THAT THERE IS COURAGE
in our blood! That we are live!
That we do not perpetuate the lie of vision
forced upon ourselves
by ourselves. That we have made the nets of vision real!
AND SNARED THEM

OH I AM BLIND AS A FLOWER AND SENSE LESS
we see nothing but banality.
Break in the forms and take real postures!

This is the real world clear and open.
The flower moves and motion is its sense,
and transference of ions,
all that it does is perception
and vision.
OH BREAK UP THE FORMS AND FEEL NEW THINGS
I declare that I am love who have never known
it and I make new love.
My hand is pink and white and blue and great
to me. My eyes are bright
and I know that love is air. An act
and nothing more. That we are seraphs,
cherubim and heroes, chieftains and gods.

This is the blind senseless thing of knowing
that unconscious we walk in it, and strive
among all things. This is
A CANDLE
and shape of light.
The hand and arm annunciate all things

and draw the eye upon the speaking face

declaring from the inner body.
We are wrought on a bending shaft of air and light
and make an animal around it

and spread a radiance from ourselves that melts
in light.

John Ridland
(b. 1933)

Poet, professor, and translator John Ridland was born in London in 1933 and spent his first three years in India and Scotland. His earliest memory is of looking up at the enormous side of an ocean liner from a dock, the ship having just carried him into San Pedro Harbor and the United States in 1936. He grew up in the Flintridge Hills near Pasadena, and in 1943 his parents moved to Spokane, Washington, to create a British vice-consulate. Ridland stayed behind with his aunt and uncle in Pasadena to continue attending Flintridge Prep School, spending summers with his parents in Spokane.

Ridland graduated with honors from Swarthmore College in 1953, where he was a competitive swimmer. He was drafted into the Army and spent two years stationed in Puerto Rico from 1954 to 1955. In 1957, he married Muriel Thomas, a New Zealander who had come to Berkeley as a Fulbright scholar. The Ridlands' first son had severe developmental defects and died when he was six, and they wrote about their experiences as parents of a disabled child in *And Say What He Is: The Life of a Special Child* (1975). They have two other children.

Ridland earned an M.A. from the University of California, Berkeley, in 1958 and returned to southern California to attend Claremont Graduate School, where he completed his Ph.D. in 1964. He began teaching at UC Santa Barbara in 1961 and continues there in the English department and the College of Creative Studies. He has been a visiting professor in Melbourne, Australia, and was director of the University of California education abroad program in Australia.

From 1966 to 1972, he edited the *Little Square Review*, an elegant, if petite (six inches square) quarterly ("weather permitting") printed by Noel Young. The first issues featured early work by such poets as Barry Spacks, Robert Peters, and Robert Pinsky. He also served as the faculty advisor for UCSB's literary journal, *Spectrum*, from 1969 to 1999.

He has been best known as a translator since his 1999 verse translation of Sándor Petőfi's Hungarian epic poem *János Vitéz*. While he hadn't previously read Hungarian, he was inspired to translate *John the Valiant* after seeing murals based on the poem decorating a restaurant he visited in Budapest. Ridland's translation has been honored in Hungary and by Hungarian Americans as a significant contribution to their cultural heritage, and it has been published in bilingual and multilingual editions. His books of poetry include *Ode on Violence* (1969), *In the Shadowless Light* (1978), *Elegy for My Aunt* (1981), *Palms* (1993), and *Life with Unkie* (1999)—a companion to *Elegy for My Aunt*. A chapbook inspired by his time in Puerto Rico, *(Un)extinguished Lamp/Lampara (An)apagada: Letters to Hugo Margenat, Puerto Rican Poet (1933–1957)*, was published in 2000.

The Lazy Man's Haiku

out in the night
a wheelbarrowful
of moonlight.

A New Person

There is a new person in the world today.
I have given him a name, but that is not his name,
He must make it, his own, and be what he says he is,
And say what he is. And if he is my son,
That is not what he must become.

Richard Brautigan
(1933–1984)

The turbulent life of Richard Brautigan, whose classic experimental novel, *Trout Fishing in America* (1967), embodied the sensibility of an American generation, began in Tacoma, Washington, in 1933. His mother moved the family to Eugene, Oregon, where he spent childhood in poverty. At twenty he was arrested for throwing a rock through a police station window, explaining that he wanted to go to jail so that he could eat. Instead he was sent to Oregon State Hospital, where he was diagnosed as paranoid schizophrenic and treated with electroshock therapy. He left Oregon soon after his release and moved to San Francisco sometime around 1955.

In San Francisco, Brautigan became involved in the Beat movement. His first known poem, "The Second Kingdom" was published in 1956, and his first poetry chapbook, *Four New Poets*, was published by Inferno Press in 1957. His first book was *Lay the Marble Tea* (1959), a collection of twenty-four poems. Brautigan published seven more books of poetry, alternating them with distinctive novels and collections of short fiction. As the Beats subsided in influence and elided into the hippie movement in the late sixties, Brautigan flourished and his literary reputation grew, first by broadsides, small press publications, and word of mouth. Then New York found him and published his most popular works, including *A Confederate General from Big Sur* (1964), *Trout Fishing in America* (1967), and *In Watermelon Sugar* (1968). Brautigan's fiction reached huge audiences, particularly *Trout Fishing in America*, which established him as a whimsical counterculture icon and unwitting spokesman for the "California dreamin'" of the generation of love. Poems such as "The Galilee Hitch-Hiker" and "All Watched Over by Machines of Loving Grace" drew nontraditional young readers to poetry, and collections such as *The Pill* versus *the Springhill Mine Disaster* (1968) also grew his audience. Lacking any formal education, and on the strength of his published work alone, Brautigan was awarded a National Endowment for the Arts grant and became poet in residence at the California Institute of Technology.

In the early 1970s he continued publishing poetry and prose but found fame overbearing, and he sought escape by moving to Pine Creek, Montana, for a reclusive life among the Rocky Mountain chic.

He refused to give interviews or do readings for the next eight years. By the late 1970s, Brautigan found himself ignored by critics and nearly forgotten by audiences who had hailed him as a major new voice a decade earlier. He had protracted bouts with drugs and alcohol, and as his bitterness grew and he developed an affinity for weapons, he alienated all but a few friends. In 1978, he was briefly back in the public eye when five of his works were banned from a California high school and the subsequent ACLU court case was decided in favor of Brautigan and his publisher.

By 1980, his popularity had waned further, his talent was eroded by drugs and alcohol, and Montana acquaintances were relieved when he moved back to California. But his erratic habits isolated him there even more, and on October 25, 1984, Richard Brautigan's body was found at home in Bolinas, California, a suicide by gunshot. He had apparently been dead for some time.

Whether writing poetry or prose, Brautigan was near-Asian in evocative restraint, working in a spare but witty style. At its best, his work captured the sensibilities of an entire counterculture generation: stylistically unadorned, whimsical in voice, endowed with a doe-eyed innocence, imbued with a deadpan sense of gentle satiric humor that caused one critic to liken him to Mark Twain high on marijuana.

All Watched Over by Machines of Loving Grace

I like to think (and
the sooner the better!)
of a cybernetic meadow
where mammals and computers
live together in mutually
programming harmony
like pure water
touching clear sky.

I like to think
    (right now, please!)
of a cybernetic forest
filled with pines and electronics
where deer stroll peacefully

past computers
as if they were flowers
with spinning blossoms.

I like to think
(it has to be!)
of a cybernetic ecology
where we are free of our labors
and joined back to nature,
returned to our mammal
brothers and sisters,
and all watched over
by machines of loving grace.

Robert Mezey
(b. 1935)

Born in Philadelphia, Pennsylvania, in 1935, Robert Mezey was a frequent visitor to California before settling in 1976 in Claremont, California, as professor and poet in residence at Pomona College. A poet who names as his influences writers as diverse as Catullus, Cabeza de Vaca, and Sam Cooke, Mezey once wrote, "It is possible I'm not a poet at all. But I am a man, a Piscean, and unhappy, and therefore I make up poems." The son of Ralph and Claire Mezey, he attended Kenyon college in Ohio before entering the Army in 1953. By his own account, he was discharged as a "subversive" in 1955, and he re-entered college at the University of Iowa, where he earned his B.A. in 1960. Mezey moved to Palo Alto in 1960, where he was a Stanford University Poetry Fellow. In 1963, he married Ollie Simpson, with whom he has three children. That same year, he started working as an instructor at Western Reserve University in Ohio. After one year there and two in Pennsylvania, Mezey returned to California as an assistant professor at Fresno State University in 1967. He spent the next three years as an associate professor at the University of Utah and returned to California a final time to accept the Pomona position. He currently divides his time between California and Washington, D.C.

Author of almost a dozen collections, most recent of which is *Collected Poems: 1952–1999* (2000), Mezey has edited the work of others, including the poems of Henri Coulette, E. A. Robinson, and Thomas Hardy. He was co-editor (with Stephen Berg) of the influential anthology *Naked Poetry* (1969). Mezey's third book, *The Lovemaker* (1961), displays his early admiration of formalist critic and poet Yvor Winters. While the book won the Lamont Poetry Award, Mezey would later turn away from its formalism, saying, "When I was quite young I came under unhealthy influences—Yvor Winters, for example, and America, and my mother, though not in that order." In his subsequent collections, *White Blossoms* (1965) and *A Book of Dying* (1970), Mezey sought to retain his love of the metaphysical poets with a freer naturalism, something he and his contemporary and collaborator Stephen Berg called "open form." Even without traditional meter and rhyme, Mezey's poetry retains tight control over rhythm through stresses and accents, a technique that suggests a light grip on his emotions. The Scholar E. L. Mayo praises his use of sharp images, his rhythmic control, and especially his ability to write lines "shaping the raw emotion…toward the extraordinary clarity they achieve."

Touch It

Out on the bare grey roads
I pass by vineyards withering toward winter,
cold magenta shapes and green fingers,
the leaves rippling in the early darkness.
Past the thinning orchard the fields
are on fire. A mountain of smoke
climbs the desolate wind, and at its roots
fire is eating dead grass with many small teeth.
When I get home, the evening sun
has narrowed to a filament. When it goes
and the dark falls like a hand on a tabletop,
I am told that what we love most is dying.
The coldness of it is even on this page
at the edge of your fingernail. Touch it.

from *Couplets*

She thinks if she puts out, her sainthood will be recognized.
He figures his wit and pathos entitle him to love.

She laughs and cries, showing her small teeth;
He lifts her dress and buries his face in her bush.

She loves somebody else, who doesn't give a shit.
He does too, but that's different.

It was all good clean fun that had no future
And now it doesn't even have a past.

Neither of them is even alive at this point—
There's just me, and you, I suppose, wherever you are.

What a mess, the meat burnt, the sink overflowing,
The kid won't stop crying, he wants his milk.

Kathleen Fraser

(b. 1937)

"From as early in my life as I can remember, I resisted others' categories and imperatives, perhaps because there were so many of them," Kathleen Fraser has observed about herself. "I didn't like being identified too readily or absolutely, nor did I wish to represent anything that could be described ahead of time." An avant-garde poet with a fascination for deconstructing language, she is surely one of the knottier presences in contemporary poetry. She was born in Oklahoma in 1937, the daughter of a Presbyterian minister. She attended high school in Covina, and then went on to Occidental College, where she began to write poetry while earning a B.A. in English literature (1958). Shortly after graduating, Fraser went to New York City to work as an editorial associate for *Mademoiselle*. She began studying at the 92nd Street YMCA's Poetry Center with Stanley Kunitz and at the New School for Social Research with Kenneth Koch and Robert Lowell. She won the Frank O'Hara Poetry Prize at the New School and was featured on the first "Young Poets" bill at the 92nd Street Y. Fraser met her first husband, the poet Jack Marshall, in Kunitz's poetry workshop. They married in 1960, and their son, David, was born in 1966.

Fraser was living in San Francisco when her first book, *Change of Address*, was published in 1968. The next year, she and her husband were offered teaching positions at the Iowa Writer's Workshop. They separated in 1970, and she taught briefly at Reed College before she returned to California as a professor of creative writing at San Francisco State University. She taught there for twenty years, serving as director of the Poetry Center from 1972 to 1975 and founding the American Poetry Archives. From 1983 to 1991, she published and edited *HOW(ever)*, a feminist journal of avant-garde and modernist writers. She has won the Frank O'Hara Poetry Prize (1964), two grants from the National Endowment for the Arts (1971 and 1978), and a Guggenheim Fellowship (1981).

Fraser has published fifteen volumes of poems, including *What I Want* (1974), *New Shoes* (1978), *Each Next: Narratives* (1980), and *Il Cuore: The Heart: Selected Poems 1970–1995* (1997). She has also published two children's books, several translations of Italian poetry, and a collection of essays, *Translating the Unspeakable: Poetry and the Innovative Necessity* (2000). Fraser divides her time between San Francisco and Rome, where she lives with her husband, the philosopher and playwright Arthur Bierman, whom she married in 1985.

Change of Address

When the ring gleamed white and your chair hugged the edge of it,
and I led an elephant into the tent
with my skin like gold lamé, and black mesh snaking
the length of my legs, and hair of pomaded waves curling red
to the waist; when I leaped to the back of the elephant,
scaling his five thousand wrinkles,
yes, feeling his huge bones lurch
and the canvas ripping up
night near my neck (and all the lights blazing);
when I slid down his hairy trunk
to lie flat in the sawdust under the five-cloved foot,
waiting, with the old silk handkerchief over my face —
did you think you were at a circus?

Or the year I wore purple velvet and a torn wedding veil
with a little blue fan spread over my pale thighs,
and hovered near the ceiling pouring tea (and good omens
were predicted when the oatmeal cookies were passed),
and you cried out: the recipe, the recipe!
And then when I hitched a ride on that Spanish rooster, waving
goodbye with one hand, the other holding tight to his blazing
comb, and seven candles burned on the wedding canopy —
did you think it was a painting you were looking at?

You can tear up your lecture notes now, erase every phone
number under my name, and go shopping in someone else's suitcase.
I've changed my address again. And don't waste your money
on bilingual road maps. After a six-day ocean voyage,
a train ride, and three Métro transfers, you'd only find nights
where the breath churns to snow after dark,

and a bench with a man making blankets of his arms, his wife
in her black wool nightgown, and a three-legged cat
in her lap. And then, would you recognize me?

[1963]

The History of My Feeling
for D.

The history of my feeling for you (or is it the way you change
and are blameless like clouds)
                                        reminds me of the sky in Portland

and the morning I unpacked
and found the white plates from Iowa City
broken,
                consistently surprising with cracks,
petals like new math theories smashed
                                with the purposeful fingers of chance.
I loved the plates. They were remnants from an auction
which still goes on in my head because of the auctioneer's body
and his sexy insinuations about the goods he was selling.

But to Ruth, who talked them into their thin wraps of newspaper,
what we were sharing was departure and two lives breaking
and learning
                to mend into new forms.

We had loved our husbands,
                                torn our bodies in classic ways to bear
                                children: Sammy, David, Wesley—
Now we loved new men and wept together
so that the plates weren't important and hadn't been packed
with the care I might have given had I been alone.
But Ruth was with me.

You were gone, like this storm that's been arriving and
                                    disappearing
all morning.

I awoke to hear heavy rain in the gutters.
The light was uncertain and my feelings had grown less sure.
Last night, pinned by a shaft of pain —
                    your presence and your absence —
I knew clearly that I hated you
for entering me profoundly, for taking me inside you,
for husbanding me, claiming all that I knew
                                    and did not know,
yet letting me go from you
into this unpredictable and loneliest of weathers.

[1971]

PART IV

CONTEMPORARY POETS

Steve Kowit
(b. 1938)

Poet, teacher, and activist Steve Kowit was born in New York City and grew up in Brooklyn, where his father was a teacher and an attorney. He decided in high school that he wanted to be a poet and did undergraduate work at Brooklyn College, studying with Robert Lowell at the New School for Social Research and Stanley Kunitz at the 92nd Street YMCA in Manhattan. The politically minded Kowit came to San Francisco in 1967 both to avoid Army Reserve meetings to which he was committed in New York and to join in what he calls a "small but sincere religious flowering" in the Haight Ashbury district. He enrolled at San Francisco State University, earned a master's degree, and went to work at the Rincon Annex Post Office, where he met his wife-to-be, Mary, an artist. When the Army threatened to send the recalcitrant reservist to Vietnam, Kowit and his wife left the country for six years, living in Central and South America, occasionally returning to the United States to teach.

After the Vietnam War ended, Kowit returned to California to teach at the University of California, San Diego, and San Diego State University. He published his first collection, *Climbing the Walls*, in 1977 and he has written, edited, and translated over a dozen books since then, including Pablo Neruda's *Incitement to Nixonicide and Praise for the Chilean Revolution* (1979). His other collections include *Lurid Confessions* (1983), *Passionate Journey: Poems and Drawings in the Erotic Mood* (1984), and most recently *The Dumbbell Nebula* (2000).

Kowit earned an M.F.A. from Warren Wilson College in 1990 and has been awarded a National Endowment for the Arts fellowship and a Pushcart Prize for his poetry. His poems are included in U.S. Poet laureate Billy Collins's "Poetry 180 Project." Self-decribed as "Jewish by birth, Buddhist by inclination," he lives and writes poetry with an awareness of suffering and a belief in compassion, treating both with gusto, wit, and sensuality.

A veteran of twenty years of leading poetry workshops, Kowit published a popular writing guide for student poets, *In the Palm of Your Hand: The Poet's Portable Workshop* (1995), and he also edited *The Maverick Poets: An Anthology of 40 Contemporary Poets* (1988). He currently teaches at Southwestern College and lives in the small town of Potrero, near the

Mexican border in east San Diego County. He continues to be an activist; after years of involvement in animal rights issues as the founder of the Animal Rights Coalition of California, he now focuses on working with other American Jews to end Israeli violence toward Palestinians.

Hell

I died & went to Hell & it was nothing like L.A.
The air all shimmering & blue. No windows
busted, gutted walk-ups, muggings, rapes.
No drooling hoodlums hulking in the doorways.
Hell isn't anything like Ethiopia or Bangladesh or Bogota:
beggars are unheard of. No one's starving. Nobody
lies moaning in the streets. Nor is it Dachau
with its ovens, Troy in flames, some slaughterhouse
where squealing animals, hung upside down, are bled & skinned.
No plague-infested Avignon or post-annihilation Hiroshima.
Quite the contrary: in Hell everybody's health is fine
forever, & the weather is superb—eternal spring.
The countryside all wildflowers & the cities
hum with commerce: cargo ships bring all the latest
in appliances, home entertainment, foreign culture, silks.
Folks fall in love, have children. There is sex
& romance for the asking. In a word, the place is perfect.
Only, unlike Heaven, where when it rains
the people are content to let it rain,
in Hell they live like we do—endlessly complaining.
Nothing as it is is ever right. The astroturf
a nuisance, neighbors' kids too noisy, traffic
nothing but a headache. If the patio were just
a little larger, or the sunroof on the Winnebago worked.
If only we had darker eyes or softer skin or longer legs,
lived elsewhere, plied a different trade, were slender,
sexy, wealthy, younger, famous, loved, athletic.
Friend, I swear to you as one who has returned
if only to bear witness: no satanic furies
beat their kited wings. No bats shriek overhead.
There are no flames. No vats of boiling oil

wait to greet us in that doleful kingdom.
Nothing of the sort. The gentleman who'll ferry you across
is all solicitude & courtesy. The river black but calm.
The crossing less eventful than one might have guessed.
Though no doubt you will think it's far too windy on the water.
That the glare is awful. That you're tired, hungry, ill
at ease, or that, if nothing else, the quiet is unnerving.
That you need a drink, a cigarette, a cup of coffee.

Ishmael Reed
(b. 1938)

Satirist, innovator, and iconoclast Ishmael Reed was born in Chattanooga, Tennessee, but grew up in the working-class neighborhoods of Buffalo, New York. After graduating from high school in 1956, he attended the University of Buffalo but left in his junior year. Reed then worked as a journalist—first for Buffalo's *Empire Star Weekly*, a black community newspaper, and then in New York City, where in 1965 he helped establish the *East Village Other*, one of America's earliest underground newspapers. In 1967 Reed published his first novel, *The Free-Lance Pallbearers*. That same year, he moved to the West Coast to teach at the University of California, Berkeley. Establishing himself as one of the leading African American novelists of his generation with books like *Mumbo Jumbo* (1972), *The Last Days of Louisiana Red* (1974), and *Flight to Canada* (1976), Reed developed an audacious and experimental approach, mixing elements from high and low culture with comic ingenuity, a combination one also finds in his poetry. Although best known as a novelist, Reed is quintessentially a man of letters, adept at the full range of literary enterprises—fiction, poetry, criticism, editing, and organizing. He is undoubtedly one of the most active and resourceful figures in contemporary literary life.

Reed played an early, continuing, and decisive role in articulating the literary ethos now known as multiculturalism. He founded *Yardbird Reader* (1972–1976), a highly influential and inclusive African American literary journal, which represented a lively forum for what Reed's co-editor, Al Young, called "a non-white establishment." In the United States's bicentennial year of 1976, Reed also cofounded the Before Columbus Foundation, a "multi-ethnic organization dedicated to promoting a pan-cultural view of America." These values were further articulated in 1995 when Reed served as general editor for HarperCollins's four-volume "Literary Mosaic Series" of anthologies. "Once these voices have been heard," Reed remarked in his preface to the groundbreaking multicultural series, "there is no turning back." His career has frequently been characterized by public controversy. Reed's sharp satire and outspoken views have outraged critics on the right, left, and middle, and he has usually handled these literary battles with a humor and grace not always found among his detractors.

Reed's first collection of poems, *Catechism of D Neoamerican Hoodoo Church* (1970), parodied everything from Marx and Engels's *Communist Manifesto* and Eurocentric literary standards, to Ralph Ellison and other mainstream black intellectuals. The volume's most celebrated poem, "I am a cowboy in the boat of Ra," presents a black gunslinger outlaw journeying to battle the ancient Egyptian deity Set, a symbol of the repressive and moribund in Western culture. His subsequent collections, *Conjure* (1972), *Chattanooga* (1973), *A Secretary to the Spirits* (1978), and *New and Collected Poems* (1988), demonstrate Reed's eclectic aesthetic and restless energy. He currently lives in Oakland, California.

I am a cowboy in the boat of Ra

The devil must be forced to reveal any such physical evil (potions, charms,
        fetishes, etc.) still outside the body and these must be burned.
    (RITUALE ROMANUM, PUBLISHED 1947, ENDORSED BY COAT-OF-ARMS AND
        INTRODUCTORY LETTER FROM FRANCIS CARDINAL SPELLMAN)

I am a cowboy in the boat of Ra,
sidewinders in the saloons of fools
bit my forehead   like   ○
the untrustworthiness of Egyptologists
who do not know their trips. Who was that
dog-faced man? they asked, the day I rode
from town.

School marms with halitosis cannot see
the Nefertiti fake chipped on the run by slick
germans, the hawk behind Sonny Rollins' head or
the ritual beard of his axe; a longhorn winding
its bells thru the Field of Reeds.

I am a cowboy in the boat of Ra. I bedded
down with Isis, Lady of the Boogaloo, dove
down deep in her horny, stuck up her Wells-Far-ago

in daring midday getaway. 'Start grabbing the
blue,' I said from top of my double crown.

I am a cowboy in the boat of Ra. Ezzard Charles
of the Chisholm Trail. Took up the bass but they
blew off my thumb. Alchemist in ringmanship but a
sucker for the right cross.

I am a cowboy in the boat of Ra. Vamoosed from
the tempe i bide my time. The price on the wanted
poster was a-going down, outlaw alias copped my stance
and moody greenhorns were making me dance; while my mouth's
shooting iron got its chambers jammed.

I am a cowboy in the boat of Ra. Boning-up in
the ol West i bide my time. You should see
me pick off these tin cans whippersnappers. I
write the motown long plays for the comeback of
Osiris. Make them up when stars stare at sleeping
steer out here near the campfire. Women arrive
on the backs of goats and throw themselves on
my Bowie.

I am a cowboy in the boat of Ra. Lord of the lash,
the Loup Garou Kid. Half breed son of Pisces and
Aquarius. I hold the souls of men in my pot. I do
the dirty boogie with scorpions. I make the bulls
keep still and was the first swinger to grape the taste.

I am a cowboy in his boat. Pope Joan of the
Ptah Ra. C/mere a minute willya doll?
Be a good girl and
bring me my Buffalo horn of black powder
bring me my headdress of black feathers
bring me my bones of Ju-Ju snake
go get my eyelids of red paint.
Hand me my shadow

I'm going into town after Set

I am a cowboy in the boat of Ra

look out Set   here i come Set
to get Set   to sunset Set
to unseat Set   to Set down Set

                        usurper of the Royal couch
                        imposter RAdio of Moses' bush
                        party pooper O hater of dance
                        vampire outlaw of the milky way

Oakland Blues

Well it's six o'clock in Oakland
and the sun is full of wine
I say, it's six o'clock in Oakland
and the sun is red with wine
We buried you this morning, baby
in the shadow of a vine

Well, they told you of the sickness
almost eighteen months ago
Yes, they told you of the sickness
almost eighteen months ago
You went down fighting, daddy. Yes
You fought Death toe to toe

O, the egrets fly over Lake Merritt
and the blackbirds roost in trees
O, the egrets fly over Lake Merritt
and the blackbirds roost in trees
Without you little papa
what O, what will become of me

O, it's hard to come home, baby
To a house that's still and stark

O, it's hard to come home, baby
To a house that's still and stark
All I hear is myself
thinking
and footsteps in the dark

Lawson Fusao Inada
(b. 1938)

Lawson Fusao Inada is third-generation Japanese American from an immigrant family of humble origins; his mother was born in the back of her family's fish store, and his father, in a noodle factory in Watsonville before going on to dental school. Inada was born in West Fresno, an impoverished community he calls a "continental crossroads," a mix of Chicano, black, and Asian cultures. In 1942 the entire Inada family was gathered at the Fresno County Fairgrounds along with other Japanese Americans to be sent to internment camps, which, in their case, were located in Arkansas and, later, Colorado. His camp experiences are detailed in the long poem "Camp," the first section of his collection *Legends from Camp* (1993).

After the War, Inada returned to high school in Fresno. "A non-Buddhist," he says, "I joined the black and Chicano set. The main thing then was music." He became heavily interested in jazz and, after a year at Fresno State College, he enrolled at the University of California, Berkeley, largely to be closer to the famous Blackhawk Club in San Francisco. Underage, Inada regularly sneaked in to the jazz club where he met Billie Holiday, Miles Davis, and John Coltrane. "They made me want to 'say' something," he recalls. By the time he returned to Fresno, he was studying bass guitar.

He returned to Fresno in 1957, where he worked with poet Philip Levine, the founder of the Fresno Poets group. Encouraged by Levine, Inada was soon writing poems rooted in his Japanese American experience, work infused with the bluesy rhythms he loved and the jazz legends he so admired. In his first book, *Before the War: Poems as They Happened* (1971), he opens with a Japanese American character playing "air bass," offers tributes to Charlie Parker and Billie Holiday, and terms himself a "campsman...blowing shakuhachi versaphone," grafting his bittersweet internment experiences onto American jazz roots. Jazz and blues are recurrent influences in his work, as both subject and in the aesthetics of diction (slang and argot), musical phrasing and repetition, and an emphasis on poetry as a declaimed and performed art. Poet Leslie Silko hails him as "a poet-musician in the tradition of Walt Whitman."

Co-editing the influential anthology *Aiiieeeee! An Anthology of Asian American Writers* (1991) established him on the forefront of the movement to recover lost Asian American literary talents and introduce vigorous new generations. He extended his interests in the Japanese American experience in editing *Only What We Could Carry: The Japanese American Internment Experience* (2000). His second book of poetry, *Legends from Camp* (1993), won an American Book Award, and his most recent collection is *Drawing the Line* (1997). As a poet, teacher, and public spokesperson, Inada has been a major presence in the movement to tell the lost stories of those interned and to examine the human consequences of such tragic uprooting, while acknowledging that the spirit and art can endure and even thrive in such trauma.

from *Legends from Camp*

IV. The Legend of Lost Boy

Lost Boy was not his name.

He had another name, a given name—
at another, given time and place—
but those were taken away.

The road was taken away.
The dog was taken away.
The food was taken away.
The house was taken away.

The boy was taken away—
but he was not lost.
Oh, no—he knew exactly where he was—

and if someone had asked
or needed directions,
he could have told them:

"This is the fairgrounds.
That's Ventura Avenue over there.
See those buildings? That's town!"

This place also had buildings—
but there were all black, the same.
There were no houses, no trees,
no hedges, no streets, no homes.

But, every afternoon, a big truck
came rolling down the rows.
It was full of water, cool,
and the boy would follow it, cool.
It smelled like rain, spraying,
and even made some rainbows!

So on this hot, hot day,
the boy followed and followed,
and when the truck stopped,
then sped off in the dust,
the boy didn't know where he was.

He knew, but he didn't know
which barrack was what.
And so he cried. A lot.
He looked like the truck.

Until Old Man Ikeda
found him, bawled him out.
Until Old Man Ikeda
laughed and called him
"Lost Boy."
Until Old Man Ikeda
walked him through
the rows, and rows,
the people, the people,
the crowd.

Until his mother
cried and laughed
and called him
"Lost Boy."

Until Lost Boy
thought he was found.

Al Young
(b. 1939)

Born in 1939 in Ocean Springs, Mississippi, on the Gulf Coast near
Biloxi, Al Young grew up in the South and in Detroit. From 1957 to
1960 he attended the University of Michigan, where he co-edited
Generation, the campus literary magazine. In 1961 he migrated to the
San Francisco Bay Area. Settling at first in Berkeley, he held a variety
of colorful jobs (folksinger, lab aide, disk jockey, medical photographer)
before graduating from the University of California, Berkeley, in
Spanish. From 1969 to 1976 he was the Edward B. Jones Lecturer in
Creative Writing at Stanford University near Palo Alto, where he lived
and worked for three decades. Young has taught poetry, fiction, and film
writing at University of California campuses at Berkeley, Santa Cruz,
and Davis, as well as at many other colleges and universities.

Young's honors include Guggenheim, Wallace Stegner, Fulbright,
and National Endowment for the Arts Fellowships, the PEN-Library of
Congress Award for Short Fiction, the PEN-USA Award for Nonfiction,
two American Book Awards, and two *New York Times* Notable Book of
the Year citations. Young's almost twenty books include novels, poetry,
essays, and anthologies, and his work has been translated into more than
ten langauges. He has also written film scripts for Sidney Poitier, Bill
Cosby, and Richard Pryor and has lectured extensively for the U.S. State
Department, most recently in Kuwait and Bahrain. With Jack Hicks,
James D. Houston, and Maxine Hong Kingston, he was co-editor of the
anthology *The Literature of California, Volume I* (2001), which won a
California Commonwealth Club medal. Young's major collections of
poetry are *Heaven* (1992) and *The Sound of Dreams Remembered* (2001),
which won his second American Book Award.

A former professional guitarist, Young has a memorable voice and
often sings during his readings. His nonfiction includes several musical
memoirs, and he cites music as a major influence on his poetry and
poetry itself as a major force in his prose: "Some knowledge of poetry
or skills acquired by composing poetry can put any writer in an
advantageous position. Poetry sweetens the tongue, deepens the heart,
and expands the mind. Just as a singer, a cellist, a trombonist, a
saxophonist, an arranger or composer can sit down at the keyboard, then
sound and observe all of the chordal and harmonic relationships crucial

to a piece of music, so a novelist, an essayist, a journalist, even a writer of annual reports, may draw richly from the conventions and techniques of poetry."

Conjugal Visits

By noon we'll be deep into it—
    up reading out loud in bed.
Or in between our making love
    I'll paint my toenails red.

Reece say he got to change his name
    from Maurice to Malik.
He think I need to change mine too.
    Conversion, so to speak.

"I ain't no Muslim yet," I say.
    "Besides, I like my name.
Kamisha still sounds good to me.
    I'll let you play that game."

"I'd rather play with you," he say,
    "than trip back to the Sixties."
"The Sixties, eh?" I'm on his case.
    "Then I won't do my striptease."

This brother look at me and laugh;
    he know I love him bad
and, worse, he know exactly how
    much loving I ain't had.

He grab me by my puffed up waist
    and pull me to him close.
He say, "I want you in my face.
    Or on my face, Miss Toes."

What can I say? I'd lie for Reece,
    but I'm not quitting school.

Four mouths to feed, not counting mine.
    Let Urban Studies rule!

I met him in the want ads,
    we fell in love by mail.
I say, when people bring this up,
    "Wasn't no one up for sale."

All these Black men crammed up in jail,
    all this I.Q. on ice,
while governments, bank presidents,
    the Mafia don't think twice.

They fly in dope and make real sure
    they hands stay nice and clean.
The chump-change Reece made on the street
    —what's that supposed to mean?

"For what it costs the State to keep
    you locked down, clothed and fed,
you could be learning Harvard stuff,
    and brilliant skills," I said.

Reece say, "Just kiss me one more time,
    then let's get down, make love.
Then let's devour that special meal
    I wish they'd serve more of."

They say the third time out's a charm;
    I kinda think they're right.
My first, he was the Ace of Swords,
    which didn't make him no knight.

He gave me Zeus and Brittany;
    my second left me twins.
This third one ain't about no luck;
    we're honeymooners. Friends.

I go see Maurice once a month
    while Moms looks after things.
We be so glad to touch again,
    I dance, he grins, he sings.

When I get back home to my kids,
    schoolwork, The Copy Shop,
ain't no way Reece can mess with me.
    They got his ass locked up.

In the Sierras
for Oakley & Barbara Hall

Way up here, where sky comes close
to calling all the shots, where
photographers, geographers and gopher-
loathing golfers and creature-comfort joggers,
where bikers, hikers, wrecking crews and
hoarse writers alike mount slow invasions;
here, where whole fields, whole hills heal
and mountains make big money mean,
peace speaks its native tongue.

Way up here, where sky comes close,
where stakes grow vast, where the last
and first run neck and neck, where loveliness
lays herself on every line at once;
up here, where far and close dissolve,
where the Sierras do not err and terror
cheapens. Sleeplessness like formlessness
must nest at midnight-lighted height.
Peace gets and takes its chances.

James McMichael

(b. 1939)

James McMichael was born in 1939 in Pasadena, where his father, James M. McMichael, was a realtor and his mother, Elva, was a teacher. He received a bachelor's degree from the University of California, Santa Barbara, in 1961, and married Barbara Cress the same year. He proceeded to graduate school at Stanford University, where he studied with Yvor Winters. Classmate John Matthias gathered McMichael's poems with his own and those of three other poets in *Five American Poets: Robert Hass, John Matthias, James McMichael, John Peck, Robert Pinsky* (1979). Two members of the group—Hass and Pinsky—later served as poet laureate of the United States. McMichael completed his Ph.D. in 1965 and took a teaching position at UC Irvine, where he has taught since. He has been married three times and has two sons.

McMichael's first work was a critical book, *The Style of the Short Poem* (1967), and he continued the practice of being a poet-critic with *Ulysses and Justice* (1991). He published his first collection of poems, *Against the Falling Evil*, in 1971. He was awarded a Guggenheim Fellowship in 1977 and published his second collection, *The Lover's Familiar*, the same year. The long poems *Four Good Things* (1980) and *Each in a Place Apart* (1994) brought him considerable attention in a demanding genre, and he received the Shelley Memorial Award "for genius and need" in recognition of his accomplishment. He has also received the Eunice Tietjens Memorial Prize and a Whiting Foundation Writers' Award.

McMichael's poetry is often schematically fractured and novelistically detailed, characterized by a careful balance of candor and detachment. His powerful poem *Each in a Place Apart* provides a harrowing examination of the author's marriage, fatherhood, and marital breakup. As one critic comments, "The poem's very exactness of detail, together with the self-effacing polish of its lines, can make McMichael appear a person almost terrifyingly withdrawn from the facts of his own life. This strangely well-aimed book about human estrangement is telling, painful, beautiful." McMichael's *The World at Large: New and Selected Poems 1971–1996* came out in 1996.

Lutra, the Fisher

The otter is known
for the way his face turns up
anywhere.

On silver coins
or from behind mahogany bureaus

he wears the aspect of a suckling,
innocent
and helplessly

shocked that he should be caught so,

napkin under chin,
his dinner folded
head to tail between his jaws
like a limp bow.

When he goes to work

the surprise is
that he is there at all.

His long neck of a body
streams like sunken
weed-strands,

rises and trails the quiet wake
of any log or stone.

Even in the shallows

he is the thought of his own
absence
and can be found at home

as water would be found there,

filling the den
or strewing over the kitchen floor

bones and vermillion gills.

Art Beck
(b. 1940)

The pseudonymous poet Art Beck was born Dennis Dybeck in Chicago, Illinois, in 1940. He attended John Carroll University in Cleveland and the University of San Francisco. Except for a brief return to Chicago, Beck has lived in California since 1960, when he first established his home in San Francisco, where he still lives and works. Married to Kathleen Phelan since 1963, Beck and his wife have three children.

Beck's literary career has been conducted while the poet worked in the business world. After starting out as a collections agent and a "repo man," he is now a credit administrator at a California subsidiary of a major international bank. His assumption of a pseudonym stems in part from his work situation; he writes under a pen name to avoid any conscious or unconscious compromise of his workplace priorities. But the topic of work is important to him, and he finds it difficult to understand how poets who subsist on grants and live in artists' colonies can relate to the real world. Pointing out how the post–World War II economy shifted the average urban American away from unionized labor or small business and into the corporate setting, Beck insists, "You can't hold up corporate life as unusual or necessarily precluding an involvement in the arts." Indeed, to ignore what people do in their work life, he maintains, is to separate poetry from the reality of their being.

Beck has published two collections of verse, *The Discovery of Music* (1977) and *North Country (New Works)* (1981), and a long narrative poem, *Enlightenment: Notes for a Scurrilous Life, The Rediscovered Poems of Giacomo Casanova* (1977). He has also published two books of translations: *Simply to See*, a translation of Luxorius (1982), and *Rilke* (1983). He translates poetry by taking a long time to internalize the original, bringing it to the point that the English finds its own way to write the poem, he says. Ideally he seeks out not simply the source text "but the emotional source of the original poem." Whether writing his own verse or translating that of others, Beck finds himself believing that poetry is "a language itself, indifferent to whatever language is used to invoke it," and so whatever he is writing, he is always translating, "reaching down beneath language to tap another tongue."

Castro Street

*For in the resurrection, they neither marry nor are given in marriage,
but are like the angels in heaven.*

It certainly won't be heaven, in fact
I'm beginning to suspect the next world
will be something on the order of
Castro Street. At first, I'll try looking

for you everywhere. I'll stalk the frantic
bars and chic delicatessens. I'll search
for you behind the mirrors that hang
on the walls of every likely curio store.

I'll try not to be frightened by the shop
windows full of leather sex masks I know
couldn't cover your smile, but I'll
make a point of using only the deserted

women's toilets in the bars, not just
because it's safer but hoping
for the odd chance you might
be hiding there. Only what hope do we

have? The next world will be
the real thing. The wild Halloween
impersonators barely sense the shadows
moving in the crowd, or how absolutely

orderly and flawless the final process
is. Tonight, Death's a Nazi Peter Lorre.
He won't put up with any mixing
of the sexes. It makes him sick,

and, beyond that, bores him to despair.
He has a nice clean world where everybody
pays their rent on time and little kids
only get to show their guilty faces on the street

after they've learned their lesson. We'll never
find each other there. The women have to live together
in tough condominium complexes on the other
side of town. They won't let you out, and I'll be lost

where we're not wanted, in the forest of broken
buildings, basement passageways, sheds with hidden doors,
and ladders inside walls they've set between us.
That same obsessed prick who snatched away

your grandmother's mind right in the stuttering
middle of her rage at your bewildered granddad,
the same screeching masquerader my grandmother heard
coughing so helplessly at midnight in my drunken

grandfather's chest—is going to see to it
that we'll never see each other again.
We'd better whisper and make our quiet
peace together while we can.

Nicotine

Is the skeleton flashing
like a heartbeat
through the body.
It's the satisfaction

of knowing that life
like a good meal
will eventually turn to shit.
Your life as well as mine.

Smoke's what we do with our
hands and our mouths to
keep them away from
each other. It's the nipple

we suck instead of fucking. And—when
life suddenly grins—the hot breath
we lick like spun sugar between
screws to savor our scent.

Every twelve year old who tears
the cellophane knows without
reading the warning: Cigarettes
are war, courage, luck. Tobacco,

like fine brown clay wrapped
in white elegance, reminds us
of our place and that flesh
is a candle. Reminds us that

fools have the right to insist
on striking the match themselves.

Jack Foley
(b. 1940)

Born in Neptune, New Jersey, John Wayne "Jack" Foley was the son of John Foley, an Irish American vaudeville singer, dancer, and songwriter who, after his theatrical career, managed a Western Union Office. Foley's mother, Joanna Teriolo, was Italian American, and this mixed heritage, plus his Catholic upbringing in Port Chester, New York, are at the base of the poet's complex identity. "My pattern," he would later write, "in more ways than one, has been that of the shape-shifter." He fell in love with poetry at an early age, and his father's theatrical background assured that he would always understand both its performative aspect and its potential relationship to song. But the path to his own distinctive contribution would be a long one.

Foley attended Cornell University on a scholarship from Western Union. While a student, he met and married Adelle Abramowitz, also a poet. In 1963 they moved to Berkeley, California, where he had a Woodrow Wilson Fellowship for graduate study at the university, and she found a job with the Federal Reserve Bank. Over the next decade, Foley's dissatisfaction with academic life increased as he became more aware of the still-thriving bohemian literary culture in the Bay Area. In 1974 his son, Sean Ezra, was born. His wife kept working at the bank, and Foley stayed at home to look after their son. While making one last effort to research a Ph.D. dissertation on Shakespeare's *Cymbeline*, he came across Charles Olson's *The Maximus Poems*, which redirected his own efforts to write poems and convinced him to drop out of academic life. Immersing himself in the Bay Area poetry scene, Foley soon met most of the major figures of the San Francisco Renaissance, including Allen Ginsberg, Robert Duncan, Lawrence Ferlinghetti, and Michael McClure. His own poetry grew out of their experimental concerns and procedures, but it increasingly emphasized the spoken medium as well as the printed page.

Foley's performance-based aesthetic, which often uses multiple voices, made conventional publication of his work problematic; eventually he would include cassette tapes or CDs with his books. "Performance poetry," he has written, "is an insistence that absence, silence, and whiteness—the page—are not the only conditions in which poetry can be 'heard.'" In 1988 he took charge of poetry programming on Berkeley's listener-sponsored radio station KPFA, where he currently hosts a weekly literary show, *Cover to Cover*. Among his books and cassettes of poetry are *Letters/Lights — Words for Adelle* (1987), *Gershwin* (1991), *Adrift* (1993), and *Exiles* (1996). *Some Songs by Georges Brassens* (2001) includes his translations from the French and an essay on the singer/songwriter.

In 2000, Pantograph Press simultaneously published two large-format collections of Foley's critical prose. Accompanied by a performance CD, these distinctive volumes — *O Powerful Western Star* and *Foley's Books* — consolidated his reputation as one of the most vital literary intelligences on the West Coast. This impression was confirmed when the books received glowing reviews in the *Los Angeles Times*, the *San Francisco Chronicle*, and other periodicals. Here was a poet-critic who refused to accept the usual poetic camps and could write about any kind of poetry with grace, insight, and sympathy. He has also edited *The "Fallen Western Star" Wars: A Debate about Literary California* (2001). Foley served as editor of *Poetry USA*, the periodical of the National Poetry Association, from 1990 to 1995, and he has been a contributing editor to *Poetry Flash*, the Bay Area calendar and review. He also contributes to the online magazine *The Alsop Review*, where his weekly book column, "Foley's Books," has earned a reputation as the most ambitious and comprehensive critical coverage of West Coast poetry currently underway.

Foley's criticism is sharply written, boldly theoretical, and historically informed. One of his most interesting enterprises has been to examine the impact of technology on literary culture. Foley argues that print culture, which has long dominated the art of poetry, now faces a serious challenge from a new kind of orality fostered by the electronic media. This cultural shift, he suggests, has enormous implications for literature.

Prose for Two Voices

> *Though I sleep as much as anyone else,*
> *I am an advocate of being awake.*

It had, he thought, a totemic resonance, that image of the woman suf-
      It had, he thought, a totemic resonance, that image
fering. (This happened later, before I could.) In the dark I thought of

of the woman suffering. (This happened later, before I could.)
her. How can you say that she asked. How can you say that. Undulate,
In the dark I thought of her. How can you say that she asked.
fish. I spoke to her for about fifteen minutes. This is the guarded situ-
How can you say that. Undulate, fish. I spoke to her for about
ation. I am in my thoughts. This is a recollection of last night when we
fifteen minutes. This is the guarded situation. I am in my
all saw a film. I wanted. Children sound and resound. The image of a
thoughts. This is a recollection of last night when we all saw
house, filled with happy children. What more than that. We'll all be in
a film. I wanted. Children sound and resound. The image of a
that house he promised. We'll all be happy. Night darkens. Stains. I am
house, filled with happy children. What more than that. We'll all
in the dream of the happy woman. Terrific! she said. As she crossed her
be in that house he promised. We'll all be happy. Night darkens.
legs I thought: The Renaissance. Her lipstick turned her mouth into a
Stains. I am in the dream of the happy woman. Terrific she said.
scar. I adored him I adored him. Come. Now. I want to play ball. I
As she crossed her legs I thought: The Renaissance. Her lipstick
want you to tell me how I can do it. I don't know. Whenever he opens his
turns her mouth into a scar. I adored him I adored him. Come. Now.
mouth something happens. She was alone so she took off her dress. Now I
I want to play ball. I want you to tell me how I can do it. I don't
am closing the door. I am opening the transit. Folie de doute. What a
know. Whenever he opens his mouth something happens. She was alone
word! I saw you, don't deny it. She had (or so I thought) a totemic reso-
so she took off her dress. Now I am closing the door. I am opening
nance, that image of the tall woman suffering.
the transit. Folie de doute. What a word! I saw you, don't deny it.
She had (or so I thought) a totemic resonance, that image
of the tall woman
suffering.

The Poet's Tango

Nobody reads me
I'm not published enough
My work is magnificent
three steps to the right, turn
Nobody reviews me
Nobody buys my books
If only I were reviewed I could be famous
three steps back, turn
If only I were on the radio
Or on the television
Or if someone would make a movie of my life, THEN
three more steps to the right, turn
Someone would buy my books
Someone would review me
They'd know
three steps back, turn
How magnificent my mind is
What a major poet I am
How my work will be read hundreds of years from now though
three steps to the right, turn
NOW nobody is reading me
There will be books about me
I am great
three steps back, turn
My ex wives will be famous
My children will be famous
My ancestors will light up in their tombs only
three steps to the right, turn
Nobody reads me at the moment
Why can't I be famous while I'm still around
I tell them: Sometimes I publish under the pseudonym, "John Ashbery"
three steps back, turn

Ron Koertge

(b. 1940)

Ron Koertge (pronounced KUR-chee) was born in Olney, Illinois, in 1940. His father, William, opened an ice cream store upon returning from World War II, and later worked as a school janitor. His mother, Bulis, was a homemaker, who nursed him through a frightening case of rheumatic fever, an illness that kept him isolated for long periods of bed rest. With characteristically dark humor, Koertge comments on his illness: "It made me a little more introspective than is good for a twelve-year-old."

After earning a B.A. from the University of Illinois, Koertge went on to the University of Arizona, where he began writing poetry and earned a master's degree. At age twenty-five, he moved to California to teach at Pasadena City College, where he met Bianca Richards, a counselor at the school, whom he married in 1992. He published his first poems in 1970, his first chapbook, *Meat: Cherry's Market Diary*, in 1973, and by 1982 he had published ten more chapbooks. *Making Love to Roget's Wife* (1997) and *Geography of the Forehead* (2000) are his major books. Poet laureate Billy Collins welcomed the latter volume: "Ron Koertge is not only the wisest, most entertaining wise guy in American poetry, he is also a conjurer, a designer of verbal holograms. Step inside any of these poems and you enter the precinct of a uniquely playful imagination."

Koertge continues to teach while writing. He has been awarded a fellowship from the National Endowment for the Arts and a California Arts Council grant, and several of his poems (including "Sidekicks") were selected by Billy Collins for the nationwide "Poetry 180 Project." His poem "1989" was included in *Best American Poetry 1998*.

Koertge's poetry is poignant and humorous, and a deceptively casual narrative line often triggers surprising insights. The same whimsical "sideways seriousness" has made him a favorite of readers of young adult fiction. His first book of this type was *Where the Kissing Never Stops* (1987), and he has since published a handful more, including *Tiger, Tiger, Burning Bright* (1994) and *Confess-O-Rama* (1996). His young adult novels have been lauded for their ingenuity and wisdom, especially *The Brimstone Journals* (2001), a popular novel in verse that generated considerable praise and controversy. His kids' books have been selected for multiple awards, including several from the American Library Association.

Redondo

Beneath my feet the pier shifts
and drools. Above, some gulls carve
out the sturdy air as surfers arrange
themselves like quarter notes across
a distant wave.

It is a relief to stop staring at girls,
to quiet the heart's thick strokes
and calmly pass the man with a truant
officer's soft chest and scowl, a boy
writing a post card — that small hymn —
staring at the pictured sand he is sunk
in, even the great great grandchildren
of Lady Macbeth washing their hands
again and again at the edge
of the unraveling world

What a place to have God rear his
amazing head. Yet here I am, all
the clutter inside made in your image.
The ocean is forever changing its clothes
to be more beautiful for you. There
is the horizon which you have drawn
with a golden rule and outlined, too,
a tiny ship and curl of smoke to make
the scene complete.

Lilith

She did not graze on all fours but
wrapped her arms and legs around Adam
and said, "Oh, Daddy. It feels so good,"
and he promised her a little place of
her own in Manhattan.

God saw that he had made a mistake
and put him to sleep, wiped his brain

smooth as a grape and tried again with
Eve

who lay flat on her back, arms and
legs extended as if she had fallen from
a tree. As Adam tried, she talked out
loud, "So much to do, so many animals
to name, so much adoration to give
Him."

Adam rolled off her, sat up holding his
side, "It hurts," he said.
"What does?"
"Here."
"That's called a rib."
"No. Above that."
"Your heart. I've only been here ten
minutes and already I know ever so much
more than you."
"I think it's broken."
"Oh, pooh. Everything's wonderful and
all you do is complain. You should be
glad you're not an insurance salesman."

Adam had to admit she was right, yet
what was that smell of crushed fern,
such heat disguised as words, a vision:
lovely toes pointing toward the sun.

"Sorrow," he said, "I feel sorrow."
"You eat too fast," said Eve. "It's gas."

Sidekicks

They were never handsome and often came
with a hormone imbalance manifested by corpulence,
a yodel of a voice or ears big as kidneys.

But each was brave. More than once a sidekick
has thrown himself in front of our hero in order
to receive the bullet or blow meant for that
perfect face and body.

Thankfully, heroes never die in movies and leave
the sidekick alone. He would not stand for it.
Gabby or Pat, Pancho or Andy remind us of a part
of ourselves,

the dependent part that can never grow up,
the part that is painfully eager to please,
always wants a hug and never gets enough.

Who could sit in a darkened theatre, listen
to the organ music and watch the best
of ourselves lowered into the ground while
the rest stood up there, tears pouring off
that enormous nose.

Michael Stillman
(b. 1940)

Born in Norfolk, Virginia, Michael Bradford Stillman grew up in the Oceana/Virginia Beach area. Gifted with the ability to play musical instruments by ear, at age sixteen he found himself playing saxophone in local clubs. He spent four years at the University of Virginia, graduating in 1963 in music and English. "I played music everywhere," he remembers of his double life, "in military clubs as well as hotels, nightclubs, and beachfront dance halls with names like The Top Hat, The Peppermint Beach Club, and the Little Casino at Virginia Beach." Stillman took an M.A. at Harvard (1965) and entered the Stanford Ph.D. program on a Danforth Fellowship in 1969. He completed all degree requirements save a dissertation, mainly because he was lured away by the graduate seminars in computer-generated sound at the Artificial Intelligence Laboratory in nearby Palo Alto. Stillman stayed in California to work in the Silicon Valley, pursuing many projects in literature and music, including the development of more than five hundred master tapes of writers reading from their work, done for the Stanford Archive of Recorded Sound. He has since published sound collections of readings by John Hawkes, Janet Lewis, Yvor Winters, and others. Stillman began publishing poetry in 1972, and "In Memoriam John Coltrane," his most successful single work, has appeared in several college texts and anthologies. His chapbooks include *An Eye of Minnows* (1976), a book-length sequence of haiku.

In Memoriam John Coltrane

   Listen to the coal
rolling, rolling through the cold
      steady rain, wheel on

   wheel, listen to the
turning of the wheels this night
      black as coal dust, steel

   on steel, listen to
these cars carry coal, listen
      to the coal train roll.

David Alpaugh
(b. 1941)

David Alpaugh was born in Plainfield, New Jersey, in 1941, to parents who imbued him with a love of music and literature. In the introduction to *The Greatest Hits of David Alpaugh* (2001), he cites the following crisis as turning him to poetry: At age sixteen he read George Orwell's *1984*, and "somehow Orwell and Sputnik got mixed up with religious dogma and adolescent sexual confusion, and I had a nervous breakdown. When I tried to throw my pigeon coop into the sky my family sought professional help and I spent eight weeks in a Cuckoo-Nest-like sanitarium....[The hospitalization] may have saved my life later on by keeping me out of Viet Nam."

When he returned to high school, poetry became his first true "religion." He dabbled with writing a few poems of his own but was drawn more strongly to the theater. He collaborated with his musician brother and a friend on musical adaptations of *The Age of Innocence* and *Tortilla Flat,* and he later had a play produced on the Berkeley public radio station KPFA.

Alpaugh graduated from Rutgers University in English and moved to California to begin graduate school at the University of California, Berkeley. He won both Woodrow Wilson and Ford Foundation Scholarships. He received his M.A. from Berkeley in 1967 and began his doctoral studies, but in 1973, married with a young child and unable to secure a teaching position, Alpaugh accepted a position in marketing. He worked successfully in advertising for many years.

Alpaugh cites a second medical crisis as the event that returned his attention to poetry; in 1982 a supposed ulcer turned out to be colon cancer and, after successful surgery, he bought his first Macintosh computer and "joined the desktop publishing revolution." In 1987 he quit advertising and started Small Poetry Press, a chapbook design and printing service, and several years later, he began writing and publishing his own poems. Although he worried that at near fifty he was too late to establish himself as a poet, he plunged ahead, and his work began appearing regularly in journals such as *Poetry, Exquisite Corpse, The Formalist,* and ZYZZYVA. In 1994 Alpaugh's first book, *Counterpoint,* won the Nicholas Roerich Poetry Prize and was published by Story Line Press. He continues to teach book design and poetry writing in the Bay Area.

The Young

are begging theory
to spare them from experience
politics from history
poetics from the line.

Some sprint, some hobble
to the table—all in time
break bread here
gulp the dead-black wine.

Gerald Locklin
(b. 1941)

Author and editor of ninety books—from chapbooks to novels to anthologies—Gerald Locklin is one of the most widely published authors in the United States. He was born in Rochester, New York, in 1941. His mother, Esther, was an elementary school teacher, and his father, Ivan, did generator maintenance. An only child, Locklin was encouraged to write by his parents, aunts, and Catholic schoolteachers.

He received his B.A. from St. John Fisher College in Rochester in 1961 and his M.A. and Ph.D. from the University of Arizona, Tucson. After finishing graduate work in 1964, he moved to California to teach, spending one year at California State College at Los Angeles (now California State University, Los Angeles), before moving to CSU Long Beach, where he has taught since 1965. Locklin has married three times and has three children with Mary Alice Keefe, two children with Maureen McNicholas, and two children with Barbara Curry.

His first book, *Sunset Beach*, was published in 1967. His next two books, *The Toad Poems* (1970) and *Poop and Other Poems* (1973), are considered to contain his best early work, along with *The Criminal Mentality* (1976). The poems in these books are typical of Locklin's style—playful, anecdotal, and unpretentious. His substantial 1992 collection, *The Firebird Poems*, is a volume of ninety-nine poems that the *Times Literary Supplement* called the "the best introduction to Locklin's variousness." Critic Robert Headley summarized the poet's style in saying earlier poems reveal the poet's struggles and experiments with poetic constructs" while later poems are "characterized by a style that is leaner, more precise, even conversational."

Locklin has been associated with the Long Beach School style of poetry, which he suggests is loosely described as "accessible, conducive to public reading, and often utilizing humor and autobiography and references to public culture. Some have called it populist poetry or vernacular poetry or talk poetry or conversational poetry." If categorization must be done, he prefers to be allied with the Stand Up School, especially with its roots in the Beat movement, "vaudeville, coffeehouses, the oral tradition, American populism…and the new mythology of popular culture."

The Oxford Companion to Twentieth-Century Literature in English says of him, "Like his friend and mentor, Charles Bukowski, Locklin offers candid reports on relations between the sexes, usually (though not always) deflating chauvinism by self-deprecating humor." Many critics have praised the tenderness in his poems, especially toward his children. *The Life Force Poems*, Locklin's most recent collection, was published in 2002.

california

what the hell am i doing anyway?
i mean, my eyes are photo-sensitive,
i'm scared of big waves, and sweating in the sand
bores the knickers off me. furthermore,

i am not exactly mr. abdominal
definition of southern california.
i compensate, however, by being mr.
inarticulate (what do you say

to these blithely dispirited bodies, when
you can't tell whether they're fifteen or
thirty-five and, back home, even the ugly ones
cried rape if you so much as tipped your cap?)

of course, the beach has its moments, like parked
above the phosphorescent scaly tide
at sunset, and the girl will blossom soon,
her nipples gone dusk red, into a young woman.

even here, though, peril. only once i
tried to make it on the shore, and it
was sand up in her crotch, my crevices,
a cold wind howling at my asshole, my

corrugated knees kept sliding out
from under me, and then i lost my glasses
and my credit cards, scuttling like t.s. eliot
in flotsam and jetsam, whichever is which

never again. nor disneyland either,
although it was free and with the girl i love.
the lines are long, the rides aren't scary, people
seem to think they have fun, like

when the whole country jerked off over the moonshot.
no, and i don't want to go to marineland,
let alone busch gardens or universal stupidos.
for all of me, the queen mary could sink.

i do like rooting for the rams though, and
the lakers; i like a big league town.
and the girls don't have legs like farmers,
and it *is* the biggest ocean.

the food is the worst imaginable,
but there are all kinds of movies playing.
there are curiosities like the gay bars;
might as well be where it happens first.

well, the discussion is no doubt academic,
since we're all dying of emphysema.
as grandma always used to say: you made
your oyster bed, now grovel in it.

Robert Hass
(b. 1941)

Robert Hass was born in San Francisco, the son of a businessman, and he was raised a short distance to the north in San Rafael, where he attended Catholic school. In 1962, while still a student at St. Mary's College, he married Earlene Leif. She became a psychotherapist and they raised three children together. After graduating college in 1963, Hass went on to Stanford University, where one of his professors was Yvor Winters. "He bullied, cajoled, ignored, and laid down the law," Hass remembers. "He did everything I now associate with bad pedagogy—and it was the most powerful course I can ever remember." He completed his Ph.D. in 1971, while teaching at the State University of New York at Buffalo, then moved back to California to teach at his alma mater, St. Mary's, from 1971 to 1989, after which he became a professor at the University of California, Berkeley. Among his numerous awards was a MacArthur Foundation "genius grant" in 1984. Serving as U.S. poet laureate from 1995 to 1997, Robert Hass set a high standard of activism for future holders of the position. As the first poet laureate from the West Coast, Hass also signaled that new attention ought to be paid to the literary life of that region. Except for a few years on the East Coast, Hass has lived most of his life in his native state.

Hass's West Coast identity has helped shape much of his work, and the proximity of wilderness and the sea continues to influence his writing about nature and his attention to environmental issues. He also absorbed the complex literary culture of the West Coast—not only the formality of Winters, but also the environmentalism of Robinson Jeffers, the wildness of the Beat poets like Everson and Ginsberg, the bohemian intellectuality of Rexroth, as well as the richness of Asian influences in the area. This West Coast eclecticism has made him a sympathetic reader of diverse poetries. His first collection of poems, *Field Guide* (1973), won the Yale Younger Poets Award. It was followed by *Praise* (1979), the book containing his most often anthologized poem, "Meditation at Lagunitas." In both of these books, Hass's lucid and sensual meditations convey questions about the how of writing. "A word is elegy to what it signifies," he says in his best-known poem, wondering whether the experience of the body can be fully conveyed in language. Sensory and sensual pleasure has been a significant theme for Hass.

He frequently writes about happiness, especially the sheer pleasure of existence in the physical world.

Another enormous influence upon Hass's work has been his collaborative translation of the great Polish émigré poet Czeslaw Milosz. Among the books of Milosz translations to which Hass has contributed are *The Separate Notebooks* (1984), *Unattainable Earth* (1986), *Collected Poems, 1931–1987* (1988), *Road-Side Dog* (1998), and *Treatise on Poetry* (2001). Although his life experience has no doubt been milder and less dramatic than Milosz's flight from totalitarianism, Hass could see that the elder poet's combination of breadth and simplicity dwarfed most contemporary American poetry. Milosz's example may have contributed to the social and political concerns of poems in Hass's fourth collection, *Human Wishes* (1989). His most recent book of poems, *Sun Under Wood* (1996), which explored painful confessional themes like his mother's alcoholism and the poet's own divorce, won the National Book Critics Circle Award. Hass has also published editions of Robinson Jeffers, Tomaz Salamun, and Tomas Tranströmer. His primary collection of criticism to date, *Twentieth Century Pleasures* (1984), is characterized by the breadth of his interests and the informality of his prose. In 1995 Hass married a second time—to the poet Brenda Hillman. He currently lives in Marin County.

Meditation at Lagunitas

All the new thinking is about loss.
In this it resembles all the old thinking.
The idea, for example, that each particular erases
the luminous clarity of a general idea. That the clown-
faced woodpecker probing the dead sculpted trunk
of that black birch is, by his presence,
some tragic falling off from a first world
of undivided light. Or the other notion that,
because there is in this world no one thing
to which the bramble of *blackberry* corresponds,
a word is elegy to what it signifies.
We talked about it late last night and in the voice
of my friend, there was a thin wire of grief, a tone
almost querulous. After a while I understood that,

talking this way, everything dissolves: *justice,*
pine, hair, woman, you and *I.* There was a woman
I made love to and I remembered how, holding
her small shoulders in my hands sometimes,
I felt a violent wonder at her presence
like a thirst for salt, for my childhood river
with its island willows, silly music from the pleasure boat,
muddy places where we caught the little orange-silver fish
called *pumpkinseed.* It hardly had to do with her.
Longing, we say, because desire is full
of endless distances. I must have been the same to her.
But I remember so much, the way her hands dismantled bread,
the thing her father said that hurt her, what
she dreamed. There are moments when the body is as numinous
as words, days that are the good flesh continuing.
Such tenderness, those afternoons and evenings,
saying *blackberry, blackberry, blackberry.*

Tahoe in August

What summer proposes is simply happiness:
heat early in the morning, jays
raucous in the pines. Frank and Ellen have a tennis game
at nine, Bill and Cheryl sleep on the deck
to watch a shower of summer stars. Nick and Sharon
stayed in, sat and talked the dark on,
drinking tea, and Jeanne walked into the meadow
in a white smock to write in her journal
by a grazing horse who seemed to want the company.
Some of them will swim in the afternoon.
Someone will drive to the hardware store to fetch
new latches for the kitchen door. Four o'clock;
the joggers jogging—it is one of them who sees
down the flowering slope the woman with her notebook
in her hand beside the white horse, gesturing, her hair
from a distance the copper color of the hummingbirds
the slant light catches on the slope; the hikers
switchback down the canyon from the waterfall;

the readers are reading, Anna is about to meet Vronsky,
that nice M. Swann is dining in Combray
with the aunts, and Carrie has come to Chicago.
What they want is happiness: someone to love them,
children, a summer by the lake. The woman who sets aside
her book blinks against the fuzzy dark,
re-entering the house. Her daughter drifts downstairs;
out late the night before, she has been napping,
and she's cross. Her mother tells her David telephoned.
"He's such a dear," the mother says, "I think
I make him nervous." The girl tosses her head as the horse
had done in the meadow while Jeanne read it her dream.
"You can call him now, if you want," the mother says,
"I've got to get the chicken started,
I won't listen." "Did I say you would?"
the girl says quickly. The mother who has been slapped
this way before and done the same herself another summer
on a different lake says, "Ouch." The girl shrugs
sulkily. "I'm sorry." Looking down: "Something
about the way you said that pissed me off."
"Hannibal has wandered off," the mother says,
wryness in her voice, she is thinking it is August,
"why don't you see if he's at the Finleys' house
again." The girl says, "God." The mother: "He loves
small children. It's livelier for him there."
The daughter, awake now, flounces out the door,
which slams. It is for all of them the sound of summer.
The mother she looks like stands at the counter snapping beans.

Lyn Hejinian
(b. 1941)

Poet, essayist, and translator Lyn Hejinian was born as Lyn Hall in Alameda in 1941. The daughter of Carolyn Erskine Hall and Chaffee Earl Hall Jr., an academic administrator and painter, Hejinian grew up in the northern California towns of Felton and Willits. In 1955 she left California for thirteen years, during which time she attended college at Radcliffe. She returned in 1968 and has remained in the state since. Hejinian has been the editor of Tuumba Press since 1976, and from 1981 to 1999 she was co-editor (with Barrett Watten) of *Poetics Journal*. Currently, she and Travis Ortiz share the direction of Atelos, a literary project commissioning and publishing cross-genre works by poets. She has traveled widely, giving readings and workshops in Sweden, Finland, France, and the former USSR. She is the recipient of many honors and fellowships, including two Pushcart Prizes, a James D. Phelan award in literature, an Award for Independent Literature from the Soviet literary organization Poetic Function (1989), a writing fellowship from the California Arts Council, a grant from the Poetry Fund, and a translation fellowship from the National Endowment for the Arts.

Rooted in the aesthetic of Language Poetry, Hejinian's work is anti-confessional and anti-realistic, and it is distinctly concerned with how radical innovations in diction, syntax, and poetic line can reveal the hidden social and political subtexts of all forms of writing, including biography and autobiography. From her first full collection, *Writing Is an Aid to Memory* (1978), she has explored the "disjunctions of memory" through interrupted lines and fractured syntax. Her prose poem, *My Life* (1980), continues these explorations as Hejinian offers multiple versions of her childhood self, insists on the subjective nature of our recollections of childhood, and, by deleting transitions between most sentences, requires the reader to be a co-author in the construction of meaning in her narrative.

She took alternating subjectivity even further when, in 1987, she published a revised and expanded edition of *My Life*, which effectively gave two versions of the text for the reader to consider. Since *My Life*, Hejinian has continued to emphasize what she terms "a flow of contexts," the "transitions, transmutations, the endless radiating of denotation into relation" that constitute the core of language, a series of challenging concepts best introduced in her recent collection of essays, *The Language of Inquiry* (2000). Hejinian has published a number of self-reflexive long poems that explore the roles of language, consciousness, and unconsciousness.

Her other works include *Oxoto: A Short Russian Novel* (1991), *The Cell* (1992), *The Cold of Poetry* (1994), and *Sight* (1999), the last being one of a number of collaborative books and projects in which Hejinian has participated. Most recently, she has published *A Border Comedy* (2001) and *Slowly* (2002). In the fall of 2002, she was elected the sixty-sixth fellow of the Academy of American Poets. She is currently a professor in the English Department at the University of California, Berkeley.

from *Redo*

Nostalgia is the elixir drained
from guilt—I've been writing
—with the fingers of my non-writing hand
I patted the dashboard. "Hi, car."
It responded "Hello, Mommy."

The city is uncarlike. She who had lived
all her life in the city and absorbed
all its laws in her blood—madness, really
—she waited for the light
to change and stepped into the traffic

on red. Objects always flicker.
Rain threatens but what can it do?
Knocking, buzzing, sloshing—
somewhere between empty and full—
the excitement is mental, internal

as they remain urgently still.
We have stayed in the city
over which it really is raining.
Reflections water the gardens.
The fields that pressed in the passing

landscapes were immobilized by trees.
Uneven individual glowing.
The photograph craves history.
The automobile drove to the photograph.
It faces me as I awake.

It was only a coincidence

It was only a
coincidence

The tree rows in orchards are capable of patterns. What were Caesar's battles but Caesar's prose. A name trimmed with colored ribbons. We "took" a trip as if that were part of the baggage we carried. In other words, we "took our time." The experience of a great passion, a great love, would remove me, elevate me, enable me at last to be both special and ignorant of the other people around me, so that I would be free at last from the necessity of appealing to them, responding to them. That is, to be nearly useless but at rest. There were cut flowers in vases and some arrangements of artificial flowers and ceramic bouquets, but in those days they did not keep any living houseplants. The old fragmentary texts, early Egyptian and Persian writings, say, or the works of Sappho, were intriguing and lovely, a mystery adhering to the lost lines. At the time, the perpetual Latin of love kept things hidden. It was not his fate to be as famous as Segovia. Nonetheless, I wrote my name in every one of his books. Language is the history that gave me shape and hypochondria. And followed it with a date, as if by my name I took the book and by the date, historically, contextualized its contents, affixed to them a reading. And memory a wall. My grandmother had been a great beauty and she always won at cards. As for we who "love to be astonished," the ear is less active than the eye. The artichoke has done its best, armored, with scales, barbed, and hiding in its interior the soft hairs so aptly called the choke. I suppose I had always hoped that, through an act of will and the effort of practice, I might be someone else, might alter my personality and even my appearance, that I might in fact create myself, but instead I found myself trapped in the very character which made such a thought possible and such a wish mine. Any work dealing with questions of possibility must lead to new work. In between pieces, they shuffled their feet. The white legs of the pear trees, protected from the sun. Imagine, please: morbid myopia. The puppy is perplexed by the lizard which moves but has no smell. We were like plump birds along the shore, unable to run from the water. Could there be swans in the swamp. Of course, one continues to write, and thus to "be a writer," because one has not yet written that "ultimate" work. Exercise will do it. I insert a description: of agonizing spring morning freshness, when through the open window a smell of cold dust and buds of broken early grass, of schoolbooks and rotting apples, trails the distant sound of an airplane and a flock of crows. I thought that for a woman health and comfort must come after love. Any photographer will tell you the same. So I wouldn't wear boots in the snow, nor socks in the cold. Shufflers scuff. That sense of responsibility was merely the context of the search for a lover, or, rather, for a love. Let someone from the other lane in. Each boat leaned toward us as it turned and we, pretending to know more than we did, identified each class as it was blown by. Politics get wider as one gets older. I was learning a certain geometry of purely decorative shapes. One could base a model for form on a crystal or the lungs. She showed the left profile, the good one. What she felt, she had heard as a girl. The point of the foghorns is that you can't see them, need to hear them. More by hive than by heart the mathematics of droves makes it noticeable. It was May, 1958 and reading was anti-anonymous. She disapproved of background music.

Eloise Klein Healy
(b. 1943)

Poet, radio host, and founder of Antioch College's popular low-residency M.F.A. program in Los Angeles, Eloise Klein Healy was born in El Paso, Texas. In 1953 her family moved to Hollywood, where her father worked as a special effects designer for television shows such as *Mission Impossible* and *Policewoman* and films like *Raging Bull* and *Close Encounters of the Third Kind.* Life in North Hollywood was an exotic urban experience for Healy, who felt herself a farm girl at heart. She attended Providence High School in Burbank (a private Catholic girls' school) and went on to earn bachelor's and master's degrees in English and a teaching credential from Immaculate Heart College in Los Angeles. She taught at Immaculate Heart High School for five years. In 1972, she married Matthew Healy, a therapist.

Healy's first book, *Building Some Changes,* won the Beyond Baroque Foundation's New Book Award in 1976. An eclectic collection of early poems, it was distributed free across the country in an edition of eight thousand. By 1980, she had divorced and begun to explore lesbian identity, a theme that characterizes her subsequent work. She became part of the core faculty at the Woman's Building, a pioneering feminist arts center in Los Angeles founded by artist Judy Chicago. She also taught poetry and women's studies at California State University, Northridge.

Healy was an artist in residence at the MacDowell Colony in 1986, and two years later completed an M.F.A. in writing at Vermont College. She joined Antioch University Los Angeles in 1992 and was the founding chairwoman of the M.F.A. creative writing program there. She has been a tireless activist in the service of southern California poetry, and her work is available on several CDs. *Passing* (2002) is Healy's fifth collection. Alice Ostriker praised the volume in writing, "Healy is at the top of her form in this book. Check out 'Louganis,' a powerful sestina about beauty and HIV. You'd say the woman is all heart, except that her 'craft' is so good. The poet's elegies are filled with joy's memory and power, her lust insists on the rights and rites of the body—and her anger is aflame."

Artemis in Echo Park

I turn out the driveway, point down the street,
bend where the road bends and tip down the hill.
This is a trail, even under asphalt.
Every street downtown cuts through adobe
and the concrete wears like the curve
of a bowl baking on a patio or the sway of a brick wall
drying in the sun.
The life before cement is ghosting up
through roadways that hooves and water
have worn into existence forever.
Out to Pasadena, the freeway still behaves
like a ravine, snaking through little valleys.
The newer roads exist in air, drifting skyward,
lifting off the landscape like dreams of the future.
We've named these roads for where they end—
Harbor Freeway, Ventura Freeway, Hollywood Freeway—
but now they all end in the sky.

Moon On The Porch

Moon on the porch thumps his tail when I climb
the stairs. He's got a rock in his mouth, old dog,
and will I play? Old teeth worn into stubs
from carrying rocks. Old Moon who limps
as far as we'll walk him. Drinks from the hot
tub when you're not looking, when the moon slides
over the edge of the roof and naked into the water.
I didn't know then this would be a poem to all
my lovers, planted by you in the full moon,
the water running off your breasts, falling
like silver coins into a pool. I didn't know then
how many women I was learning to love.

Michael Palmer
(b. 1943)

Michael Palmer was born in New York City into an Italian American family. His immigrant father, Giuseppe Palmerini, worked as a hotel manager, and the young poet grew up in Manhattan hotels. Determined that his son receive the finest education possible, his father sent him to the Choate Academy, an exclusive boarding school in Wallingford, Connecticut. Palmer then attended Harvard, where he majored in French history and literature. After graduation in 1965, he spent a year in Europe, mostly in Florence, where he learned Italian, before returning to Harvard to earn an M.A. in comparative literature in 1968. At Harvard he attended courses by the famous Russian linguist Roman Jakobson, who proved influential on Palmer's ideas of language, poetry, and prosody.

In 1969 Palmer moved to San Francisco to escape "the institutional weight" of the Boston literary world. For several years he taught at California State University, San Jose. He also worked as a gardener and landscaper, a trade he had learned from his maternal grandfather. In 1972 he married Cathy Simon, an architect, and the couple has one daughter. Although he has taught at the New College of California, the University of California, Berkeley, and San Francisco State University, Palmer has avoided a full-time academic career. A prolific poet, he published sixteen books and chapbooks—as well as many translations and essays—between his debut volume, *Plan of the City of O* (1971) and *The Promises of Glass* (2000). He served as a contributing editor to *Sulfur*, a literary journal committed to experimental writing. Palmer has also worked for thirty years writing words and narration for San Francisco's Margaret Jenkins Dance Company.

Of the many writers associated with Language Poetry, Palmer has often seemed the one who most successfully merges the movement's restlessly deconstructive urge with its more familiar modernist roots. Clayton Eshleman, editor of *Sulfur*, has concisely summarized Palmer's approach: "Relative to traditional and conventional poetry, Palmer might be said to practice a counter-poetics, based on resistance to meaning in the simplest sense but not resistant to signification in a larger sense." Palmer's poems often seem deliberately obscure or elusive, but they are also lyrical and powerfully evocative. Part of Palmer's expressive force comes from his carefully shaped and highly compressed poetic language—a concision that stands in sharp contrast to the loosely expansive style of much Language Poetry. Although distinctively personal, his poetic style clearly announces its allegiance to modernist models like George Oppen, Louis Zukofsky, Wallace Stevens, and Ezra Pound, as well as earlier European masters like Arthur Rimbaud and Charles Baudelaire, the latter of whose prose poetry seems to have been a special touchstone for Palmer's work).

Palmer's poetic concerns are primarily philosophical, even epistemological. He eschews the autobiographical mode as well as all linear narrative strategies of writing. His characteristic method is suggestive and elliptical. "The problem is that poetry, at least my poetry and much that interests me," he has written, "tends to concentrate on primary functions and qualities of language such as naming and the arbitrary structuring of a code." Such concerns place Palmer among post-modernists in general and Language Poets in particular, but his work rarely seems abstract or generically ideological. For him, the fundamental issues of language and meaning are genuine and personal concerns. However dense and difficult Palmer's poetry can be, it is above all playful in its approach to puzzling questions of meaning. It is this notion of poetry as a verbal game played for both pleasure and insight that makes his potentially intimidating work both attractive and engaging.

Untitled

All those words we once used for things but have now discarded in order to come to know things. There in the mountains I discovered the last tree or the letter A. What it said to me was brief, "I am surrounded by the uselessness of blue falling away on all sides into fields of bitter wormwood, all-heal and centaury. If you crush one of these herbs between your fingers the scent will cling to your hand but its particles will be quite invisible. This is a language you cannot understand." Dismantling the beams of the letter tree I carried them one by one down the slope to our house and added them to the fire. Later over the coals we grilled red mullets flavored with oil, pepper, salt and wild oregano.

Autobiography

for Poul Borum

All clocks are clouds.
Parts are greater than the whole.
A philosopher is starving in a rooming house, while it rains outside.
He regards the self as just another sign.
Winter roses are invisible.
Late ice sometimes sings.

A and *Not-A* are the same.
My dog does not know me.
Violins, like dreams, are suspect.
I come from Kolophon, or perhaps some small island.
The strait has frozen, and people are walking—a few skating—across it.
On the crescent beach, a drowned deer.

A woman with one hand, her thighs around your neck.
The world is all that is displaced.
Apples in a stall at the streetcorner by the Bahnhof, pale yellow to
    blackish red.
Memory does not speak.
Shortness of breath, accompanied by tinnitus.
The poet's stutter and the philosopher's.

The self is assigned to others.
A room from which, at all times, the moon remains visible.
Leningrad cafe: a man missing the left side of his face.
Disappearance of the sun from the sky above Odessa.
True description of that sun.
A philosopher lies in a doorway, discussing the theory of colors

with himself
the theory of self with himself, the concept of number, eternal return,
    the sidereal pulse
logic of types, Buridan sentences, the *lekton*.
Why now that smoke off the lake?
Word and thing are the same.
Many times white ravens have I seen.

That all planes are infinite, by extension.
She asks, Is there a map of these gates?
She asks, Is this the one called Passages, or is it that one to the west?
Thus released, the dark angels converse with the angels of light.
They are not angels.
Something else.

Joseph Stroud
(b. 1943)

Joseph Stroud and his twin brother were born in Glendale in 1943. Stroud's father, Donald, was a safety engineer for an insurance company. Just after World War II, the family lived in Roger Young Village, a temporary community of Quonset huts that was built to house returning servicemen and that was later demolished to make room for a freeway. Stroud wrote of his childhood, "Summers were spent in a cabin in a remote wilderness area where the Tehachapi Mountains and southern Sierra Nevada come together and plunge into the Mojave-Paiute country, high desert and chaparral, river canyons with cottonwood and oak, rising into pine forests; a country of black bear, coyote, mountain lion, abandoned mines, a few scattered ranches."

Stroud started college in 1961, briefly attending the University of San Francisco and California State University, Los Angeles, before settling at San Francisco State University, where he earned his B.A. in English literature and philosophy in 1966 and his M.A. in creative writing two years later. While living in San Francisco, he studied with Kenneth Rexroth, John Logan, William Dickey, and George Hitchcock. He also met Robert Duncan, Jack Gilbert, and George Oppen, who influenced his work. In 1968, he began teaching classes and workshops at Cabrillo College in Santa Cruz County, where he continues teaching today. An avid traveler who has lived in Spain and Greece, spent time in Mexico and the British Isles, and journeyed through Central and South America, the Caribbean, the South Pacific, Australia, and Asia, he divides the rest of his time between Santa Cruz and a cabin at Shay Creek on the east side of the Sierra Nevada.

His first book, *In the Sleep of Rivers*, was published in 1974 by Noel Young at his Capra Press. His second book, *Signatures*, was published in 1982. *Below Cold Mountain* is his most recent book, published in 1998 by Copper Canyon Press. The title is borrowed from classic Chinese poet Han Shan, and the sixty-six poems therein owe their sharpness and compression to such Chinese masters. Poet Jane Hirshfield called *Below Cold Mountain* "one of the finest collections of poems I've read in years—intelligent, sensuous, moving, full of human insight." He also has a chapbook, *Unzen* (2001), and won a Pushcart Prize in 2000.

Missing

I keep looking for my face to appear on a milk carton,
a photo of little me, missing since '52 or '53, who left home
without saying goodbye, left his brothers playing baseball,
left his parents glancing up from breakfast, wondering at this
solitary son who sets out every morning, and returns slightly
more lost, each time less of the child he left home with.

Hear That Phone Ringing? Sounds Like a Long Distance Call

Death is talking on the phone, long distance to somebody,
I'm outside the booth, waiting to call home, impatient,
trying not to be obvious about it, while Death yammers on,
now and then looking over in my direction, his empty gaze
not meant for me, I hope, as I think of that poor guy
on the other end, clutching his phone, not ready to hang up.

Manna

Everywhere, *everywhere*, snow sifting down,
a world becoming white, no more sounds,
no longer possible to find the heart of the day,
the sun is gone, the sky is nowhere, and of all
I wanted in life—so be it—whatever it is
that brought me here, chance, fortune, whatever
blessing each flake of snow is the hint of, I am
grateful, I bear witness, I hold out my arms,
palms up, I know it is impossible to hold
for long what we love of the world, but look
at me, is it foolish, shameful, arrogant to say this,
see how the snow drifts down, look how happy
I am.

Gina Valdés
(b. 1943)

Georgina Valdés was delivered in Los Angeles's segregated California Hospital in 1943, the third daughter of Mary, a seamstress, and George, a professor and musician. She experienced what she calls "double migration" by the time she was eight, moving from Los Angeles to Ensenada, Mexico, and then back to the United States. She grew up in a home with four generations of women who instilled a love of reading, learning, poetry, and storytelling. The first books Valdés read were those of classic Mexican poets from her grandmother's library. She survived two life-threatening illnesses by the time she was fourteen, which led her to practice holistic healing and mysticism, especially in native Mexican and Japanese Zen forms. Exposed to many ethnic traditions in Los Angeles, she developed an affinity for Japanese culture and is also married to artist Tadashi Hayakawa, with whom she has one daughter. In her twenties she traveled extensively as a flight attendant for Western and Japan Airlines. In her thirties she began classes at Los Angeles City College and then attended Palomar College in San Diego before finally transferring to the University of California, San Diego, where she completed her B.A in creative writing in 1980. She earned her M.A. in Spanish literature in 1981.

She published her first book, *There Are No Madmen Here*, with a small press in 1981. Her second book, *Puentes y Fronteras: Coplas Chicanas* (1982), received serious critical attention for the way in which she adapted traditional Mexican *coplas* (four-line stanzas) to a feminist point of view. *Comiendo Lumbre/Eating Fire* (1986) and *Puentes y Fronteras/Bridges and Borders* (reissued 1996) were published in bilingual editions. Valdés's prose and poetry may be characterized as fully multilingual and multicultural with an interest in exploring aesthetic, social, and healing issues from a feminist perspective. She has taught at University of California branches at Los Angeles, Davis, and San Diego, and at the eastern University of Washington and Colorado College. She lives in rural eastern San Diego County near her mother and sister.

English con Salsa

Welcome to ESL 100, English Surely Latinized,
inglés con chile y cilantro, English as American
as Benito Juárez. Welcome, muchachos from Xochicalco,
learn the language of dólares and dolores, of kings
and queens, of Donald Duck and Batman. Holy Toluca!
In four months you'll be speaking like George Washington,
in four weeks you can ask, More coffee? in two months
you can say, May I take your order? In one year you
can ask for a raise, cool as the Tuxpan river.

Welcome, muchachas from Teocaltiche, in this class
we speak English refrito, English con sal y limón,
English thick as mango juice, English poured from
a clay jug, English tuned like a requinto from Uruapan,
English lighted by Oaxacan dawns, English spiked
with mezcal from Mitla, English with a red cactus
flower blooming in its heart.

Welcome, welcome, amigos del sur, bring your Zapotec
tongues, your Nahuatl tones, your patience of pyramids,
your red suns and golden moons, your guardian angels,
your duendes, your patron saints, Santa Tristeza,
Santa Alegría, Santo Todolopuede. We will sprinkle
holy water on pronouns, make the sign of the cross
on past participles, jump like fish from Lake Pátzcuaro
on gerunds, pour tequila from Jalisco on future perfects,
say shoes and shit, grab a cool verb and a pollo loco
and dance on the walls like chapulines.

When a teacher from La Jolla or a cowboy from Santee
asks you, Do you speak English? You'll answer, Sí,
yes, simón, of course. I love English!

                              And you'll hum
a Mixtec chant that touches la tierra and the heavens.

Taylor Graham
(b. 1944)

Born Judith Ann Taylor in 1944 in Pasadena, Taylor Graham grew up in a part of the Los Angeles Basin known as Sierra Madre, when it was still an undeveloped area of sprawling orange groves and grassland perfect for grazing her pony. Her family moved to Newhall ("the fringes of civilization") when she was fourteen. Only thirty miles from Los Angeles, Newhall was mainly alfalfa fields and similar open space back then, but it has since been developed into housing and golf courses. At California Lutheran College (now University) she studied German, French, and Spanish, later receiving her master's degree in comparative literature from the University of Southern California. She worked for a year as a reporter and photographer before marrying Hatch Graham, a forester and wildlife biologist, and moving to pre-pipeline Alaska in 1972.

While in Alaska she began working with search-and-rescue dogs, discovering a lifelong passion while training her own. Her fieldwork in search and rescue has strongly influenced her poetry, and her work reflects such disasters as the 1985 Mexico City earthquake and the 1992 Los Angeles riots. She now lives in a home she and her husband built by hand on twenty acres in El Dorado County, California, where the couple has become active in protecting bluebird nesting areas. According to Graham, "What with search and rescue, bird conservation, and poetry, I figure my life is basically nonprofit."

A late bloomer as a published poet, Graham did not publish her first book, *Looking for Lost*, until 1991, but she has since published five other books of poems, including *Casualties: Search and Rescue Poems* (1995) and *Greatest Hits* (2002). She has also attracted a sizeable audience for a body of recently published tales of horror and traumatic fantasy. One critic describes her as "an acute observer of nature and human nature, and her style, while seemingly chiseled and laconic, allows for a surprising wealth of humor and lyricism."

Chances

These are the birds who nest
in our chimneys,
bundling combustibles
where the draft
sucks flame. Or,
in a ramshackle weave
of sticks and string,
hang their breakable young
on a high thin twig
over nothing.
And if the birdlings grow
to any weight and feather,
they show them, by flapping
of parent wings,
one has only to outstep the edge
to fly.

Pieces of Henry

I. The Borrow Pit Trial

Hanks hasn't spoken since the trial began.
Neither have the seven girls dead in the pit.
Neither do our women behind bolted doors
at midday. "Murder will out." Here,
only the newspapers talk. Column morals,
skirting speculations, a lot of pennies' worth
of words. A short sharp knife is Exhibit A,
and Hanks carries what he knows
wherever he goes.

II. Words of Love

When Ellie wrote me how she loved me,
"Dearest Henry," she wrote
in her garlanded penstroke (a sort
of promissory daisy-chain across the page

as if she meant
hearts and moons instead of good straight-
forward letters) and continued how she
loved me...And I know
a captain had her dancing
just the other night,
her small feet slurring the tempo
and her blue eyes as blind,
she never saw me.

Maybe Hanks was right.

III. He Translates Heinrich Schliemann
"Gold is the flame that polished the walls
of Troy. Gold is the sun that turned
as the flames burned Troy. Gold the gleam
of Helen's hair in the memory of men
after Troy.
Gold the glint of his eye who follows
the sun to dig for gold where it shines.
Gold is the grass of California. Gold
his hand who shovels the soil, gold
to shut the eyes of ashygray ghosts
turning out of their graves for the gold
of Troy and the gold of California."

IV. Corpus canis
...is a marvel, as (in greater degree)
the body of man, the body politic,
the system of earth, water and air;

...to be had for the asking. They bring
the old, ugly and unpedigreed,
the supernumerary: a world full
of dogs.
The marvel is to find
how the foreleg twitches when we uncover

this, the jaw drops, the pupil ignites
when we touch that.

Scalpels
sculpt our knowledge of the universe,
the heart and fibre of man, the body
of the dog.

V. Games Henry Played

Henry drops sizzling
wax in water: it forms
old men, embryos, dancing ladies immobilized
in glass jars. Henry biting his lip
in concentration
finds names
expressive of his yellow blobs: Lark
and Schlupper, Rox-Elena.
But the super-heated extra-special try, the one
that shattered its glass, the spiny
wax crust that thunked when it hit
the floor—that one
he would have called Hanks.

Sherley Anne Williams

(1944–1999)

Novelist, poet, and playwright Sherley Anne Williams was born in 1944 in Bakersfield, the third of four daughters. She grew up in the housing projects in Fresno, where her parents, Lena-Leila Marie Siler and Jesse Winson Williams, picked cotton and fruit, often receiving welfare to make ends meet. Her father died of tuberculosis when Williams was just eight years old, and after her mother died eight years later, Williams found herself back in the cotton fields, struggling to eke out subsistence at age sixteen. Her older sister was left to raise her, and Williams found refuge from the rough neighborhood in reading books, especially history and biography.

Williams attended California State University, Fresno, where she studied with Philip Levine. She graduated in 1966 with a bachelor's degree in history, and began writing seriously. She went on to graduate study at Howard University, and her first story, "Tell Martha Not to Moan," was published in 1967. She transferred to Brown University to continue her graduate studies and earned a master's degree there in 1972, the same year in which she published *Give Birth to Brightness,* a critical study that established her academic reputation. In 1973 she became the first black literature professor at the University of California, San Diego. By the time she died of cancer in 1999, Sherley Anne Williams was regarded as a major African American scholar and writer who drew on her own humble origins to examine major moments and motifs in black life and literature in America.

The work on *Give Birth to Brightness* encouraged Williams to turn to her own literary endeavors, initially as a poet. Her first book of poetry, *The Peacock Poems* (1975), was a blues-influenced collection about childhood, her life as a single mother, and her son. Her second book of poetry, *Some One Sweet Angel Chile* (1982), garnered even more attention, and critic Lillie Howard commented on her style of "blues poetry," in which "Williams fingers the 'jagged edges' of pain that is both hers and ours." That collection became the basis for an Emmy-winning television production.

Williams also found prominence as a fiction writer. She published a novel, *Dessa Rose* (1986), and two children's books, *Working Cotton* (1992) and *Girls Together* (1999). She also wrote a full-length one-woman drama, *Letters from a New England Negro,* produced in 1982.

california light

I have come in my own time
to the age at which she bore
me, rooted among memories
made phantom by my thoughts

say...She was a weaver, born
in an age of ready-made
cloth studying over threads
and colors while some machine
stamped her man's health, Nourishment
for the Kids, the dreams of her
youth, Two Bedrooms in the Project—
But these are symbols of
memory, not memories
themselves, the meat of vision
unfolding. The past does not
always come when you call it:

we are herded through hard clear
light, across a graveled lot;
I see the deep shadows of
cream-colored houses and white
men in brown suits as one is
jerked to the ground. That ball of
flesh and dress is mamma, her
roar precedes her; this is the
time the County declared her
'unfit,' called in the Sheriff.

Emblem of Project-County,
the face of the woman who
fought so is memoried in the
flesh of Miss Le'a's daughter.

Kay Ryan
(b. 1945)

Kay Ryan was born Kay Petersen in San Jose, California, and was raised mostly in the small working-class towns of the San Joaquin Valley and Mojave Desert. Her father, the son of Danish immigrants, was a well-driller and farmhand. Her mother had taught elementary school briefly before marriage but stayed at home to raise Ryan and her brother. The poet grew up in the hot, rural landscape of interior California, an irrigated desert transformed into farmland, and something of Ryan's harsh and hard-worked native terrain is reflected in her carefully cultivated minimalist aesthetic. She completed her B.A. and M.A. in English literature at the University of California, Los Angeles, but she never took a creative writing course. She has lived in Marin County, north of San Francisco, since 1971, and she teaches basic English skills at the College of Marin, a public two-year college, and occasionally at San Quentin Prison.

An outsider to literary circles, Ryan was slow in establishing her literary career. Her first book, *Dragon Acts to Dragon Ends* (1983), was privately published by a subscription of friends and attracted no critical attention. *Strangely Marked Metal* (1985), a more mature and distinctive volume, followed from Copper Beech Press of Rhode Island—a small publisher from America's smallest state with a knack for discovering literary talent—but it too gained little notice. When *Flamingo Watching* (1994) appeared nine years later, Ryan had fully emerged as a poet of unmistakable originality and expressive power. Slowly and steadily her literary reputation has risen, supported by frequent appearances in *The New Yorker*. Her recent volumes, *Elephant Rocks* (1996) and *Say Uncle* (2000), have confirmed her position as one of the finest poets of her generation.

Ryan's poems characteristically take the shape of an observation or idea in the process of clarifying itself. Although the poems are brightly sensual and imagistic, there is often a strongly didactic sense at work; as Andrew Frisardi observed in *Poetry*, Ryan's poems usually say "something useful and important." But the didactic impulse inevitably takes a surprisingly lyric form. The language reflects the shaping hand of a quick and skeptical intelligence often pulling some general notion from the arresting particulars—a process sometimes prefigured in the poem's title. In "Paired Things" from *Flamingo Watching*, for example, image and abstraction dance so consummate a *pas de deux* that one wonders why modern poetics ever considered the two imaginative impulses at odds.

Ryan's characteristic style usually employs dense figurative language, varied diction, internal rhyme, the interrogative mode, and playful free verse, which elusively alternates between iambic and unmetered lines. One of Ryan's signature devices is the counterpoint of sight and sound in the placement of her poetic language; her hidden rhymes and metrical passages only become fully apparent when the poem is spoken aloud. The central images become emblematic of a larger truth, but they usually slip away before the interpretation becomes fixed. Ryan's style is zestfully contemporary, but there is something almost eighteenth-century about her sensibility. She is a *moraliste* in the expansive and exemplary sense of the French philosophes—a theorist of human conduct. In this way, as in several others, Ryan resembles Emily Dickinson, who is surely the presiding *genius loci* of her poetry. Like Dickinson, Ryan has found a way of exploring ideas without losing either the musical impulse or imaginative intensity necessary to lyric poetry. She is one of the genuinely original talents in contemporary American poetry.

Chemise

What would the self
disrobed look like,
the form undraped?
There is a flimsy cloth
we can't take off—
some last chemise
we can't escape—
a hope more intimate
than paint
to please.

Blandeur

If it please God,
let less happen.
Even out Earth's
rondure, flatten
Eiger, blanden
the Grand Canyon.
Make valleys
slightly higher,
widen fissures
to arable land,
remand your
terrible glaciers
and silence
their calving,
halving or doubling
all geographical features
toward the mean.
Unlean against our hearts.
Withdraw your grandeur
from these parts.

Paired Things

Who, who had only seen wings,
could extrapolate the
skinny sticks of things
birds use for land,
the backward way they bend,
the silly way they stand?
And who, only studying
birdtracks in the sand,
could think those little forks
had decamped on the wind?
So many paired things seem odd.
Who ever would have dreamed
the broad winged raven of despair

would quit the air and go
bandylegged upon the ground,
a common crow?

Turtle

Who would be a turtle who could help it?
A barely mobile hard roll, a four-oared helmet,
she can ill afford the chances she must take
in rowing toward the grasses that she eats.
Her track is graceless, like dragging
a packing-case places, and almost any slope
defeats her modest hopes. Even being practical,
she's often stuck up to the axle on her way
to something edible. With everything optimal,
she skirts the ditch which would convert
her shell into a serving dish. She lives
below luck-level, never imagining some lottery
will change her load of pottery to wings.
Her only levity is patience,
the sport of truly chastened things.

Wanda Coleman
(b. 1946)

Born and raised in Watts, California, Wanda Coleman was a bookish and private child. She published her first poems at age thirteen in a local newspaper, but found public education "dehumanizing." By twenty, she was a college dropout (California State University, Los Angeles, and L.A. City College), an outspoken community activist, and a mother of two. She was strongly influenced by the Black Power movement in southern California during the 1960s, specifically the thought and example of cultural nationalist Maulana Ron Karenga and his Organization US, a group working toward cultural and social change. Angry and engaged, this former welfare mother decided to wage her own war against racism as a writer, and by 1970, with the publication of "Watching the Sunset," her first story, she was on her own controversial path.

Although Coleman won an Emmy as a writer for the 1975–76 season of the soap opera *Days of Our Lives*, she worked mainly menial jobs to support her family. She saw poetry as a tool to transform the condition of urban black misery, and she was a natural and electrifying performer herself, strongly influenced by Charles Bukowski and his take-no-prisoners personal and literary style. She sent Bukowski and his Black Sparrow editor John Martin her first poetry manuscript, *Art in the Court of the Blue Fag*, and it was published in 1977. More than ten major collections have followed.

Coleman has been a productive writer and literary figure. Mainly a poet, she has also published prose and edited collections of the work of others, co-hosted a weekly poetry show for KPFK, a local PBS radio affiliate, and energized the Los Angeles poetry scene in giving more than five hundred readings. She is an eloquent and often contentious voice not only for oppressed black women but also for broader cultural freedom for everyone.

Larger-than-life, often inflected with a dark humor, and L.A. to the bone, she has been a major presence in the development of the city's contemporary literary culture. "I've been thrown out of Hollywood night spots for being too rowdy," she wrote recently, "have picked cotton from the roadside in Fresno, and was once pulled over by the CHP for swilling apple juice on the roads of King City....Allen Ginsberg hugged me in Oakland. I've seen L.A. riot twice. I've been blessed out at Mt. Shasta, stoned at Wolfgang's, and nauseated in Palm Springs. My heart lives in Lancaster and my grief dwells in the Russian River. I am a Black Californian, but I am forever married to a New York Jew. I was born here. I intend to die here. At home."

Voices

be quiet. go away

i hear voices. i hear them often. i've heard them
since childhood. soft persistences
shapeless. they come unexpected. hover on my sleep
pierce and distract my study
speaking in rainbow they discuss me as if i'm
the ghost. say wrong things about me. tell me
i'm different i don't belong
i hear them. the voices. the noise of lies & analyses
threatening to follow me into life

Prisoner of Los Angeles (2)

in cold grey morning
comes the forlorn honk of workbound traffic
i wake to the video news report

the world is going off

rising, i struggle free of the quilt
& wet dreams of my lover dispel
leave me moist and wanting

in the bathroom
i rinse away illusions, brush my teeth and
unbraid my hair
there're the children to wake
breakfast to conjure

the job
the day laid out before me
the cold corpse of an endless grind

so this is it, i say to the enigma in the mirror
this is your lot/assignment/relegation
this is your city

i find my way to the picture window
my eyes capture the purple reach of hollywood's hills
the gold eye of sun mounting the east
the gray anguished arms of avenue

i will never leave here

Larry Levis
(1946–1996)

A native Californian, Larry Levis grew up in the San Joaquin Valley near Selma, where his family owned a ranch. He attended California State University, Fresno, where he came under the tutelage of Philip Levine, developing as the most acknowledged participant in the Fresno School after Levine himself. Levis acknowledged his mentor's influence: "Whenever I try to imagine the life I might have had if I hadn't met Phil Levine, if he had never been my teacher, if we had not become friends and exchanged poems and hundreds of letters over the past twenty-five years, I can't imagine it. That is, nothing at all appears when I try to do this." Levine returned the compliment after his student's untimely death, pronouncing him "the most gifted and determined young poet I have ever had the good fortune to have in one of my classes....What he left is a major achievement that will last as long as poetry matters."

At Levine's urging, Levis left Fresno for the Universities of Syracuse and later Iowa. At the age of twenty-five, the precocious poet published *Wrecking Crew* (1972), which won him the United States Award from the International Poetry Forum, the first of many awards, which would include the Lamont Poetry Prize and fellowships from the National Endowment for the Arts and the Fulbright and Guggenheim Foundations.

His four subsequent collections of poetry (the last, *The Widening Spell of the Leaves*, in 1991) cemented his reputation as a poet of singular and moving talent. *Elegy* (1997) and *The Selected Levis: Poems 1972–1992* (2000) were published posthumously. He taught at universities in Iowa, Missouri, and Utah prior to taking his last position at Virginia Commonwealth University, but he often returned to the San Joaquin Valley, and the area was a constant shadow in his poetry, as in one of his most often reprinted poems, "Photograph: Migrant Worker, Parlier, California, 1967." Fellow poet David St. John writes that from "its endless rows of vineyards, its groves of fig and almond orchards, Larry Levis brought to his poetry John Steinbeck's dramatic sweep of the landscape. Although Levis came of age in the late sixties, it was his upbringing on his family farm that helped to provide the sense of social conscience that resonates in all of his work."

Larry Levis died suddenly of heart failure at age forty-nine. Rooted in California, he was in no sense merely regional or provincial and did not use poetry as a convenient vehicle for social commentary. He limned sharp vignettes from his home territory, but drew them out into large themes of ironic conflict, death, and the tragedies of daily life in lines so strong and variable that few poets drew such praise from their fellows in so short a life. On the publication of *The Selected Levis*, poet and scholar Ray Gonzales concluded, "If I could select one book of poetry from the past year to read and read again, this is it. If I could teach only one poet to younger poets, it would be Larry Levis....If I could describe everything poets want their poets to do, regardless of their style and intentions, I would turn to Levis's poetry once again, and not say a word."

The Poem You Asked For

My poem would eat nothing.
I tried giving it water
but it said no,

worrying me.
Day after day,
I held it up to the light,

turning it over,
but it only pressed its lips
more tightly together.

It grew sullen, like a toad
through with being teased.
I offered it all my money,

my clothes, my car with a full tank.
But the poem stared at the floor.
Finally I cupped it in

my hands, and carried it gently
out into the soft air, into the
evening traffic, wondering how

to end things between us.
For now it had begun breathing,
putting on more and

more hard rings of flesh.
And the poem demanded the food,
it drank up all the water,

beat me and took my money,
tore the faded clothes
off my back,

said Shit,
and walked slowly away,
slicking its hair down.

Said it was going
over to your place.

Photograph: Migrant Worker, Parlier, California, 1967

I'm going to put Johnny Dominguez right here
In front of you on this page so that
You won't mistake him for something else,
An idea, for example, of how oppressed
He was, rising with his pan of Thompson Seedless
Grapes from a row of vines. The band
On his white straw hat darkened by sweat, is,
He would remind you, just a hatband.
His hatband. He would remind you of that.
As for the other use, this unforeseen
Labor you have subjected him to, the little
Snacks & white wine of the opening he must
Bear witness to, he would remind you
That he was not put on this earth
To be an example of something else,
Johnny Dominguez, he would hasten to
Remind you, in his chaste way of saying things,

Is not to be used as an example of anything
At all, not even, he would add after
A second or so, that greatest of all
Impossibilities, that unfinishable agenda
Of the stars, that fact, Johnny Dominguez.

David Oliveira
(b. 1946)

David Oliveira was born in the Central Valley town of Hanford in 1946, and was raised in Armona, thirty-five miles south of Fresno. His parents were first-generation Americans, and Oliveira and his six younger siblings were raised "partly European [Portuguese] and partly American." His father, Frank, was a businessman, and his mother, Mary Alice Souza, was a homemaker. Oliveira attended California State University, Fresno, where he received a B.A. in social science and English. He was introduced to poetry via a Fresno poetry reading by English Department faculty, including Philip Levine. "Levine was my teacher for a class called Poetry Writing, in which I had just enrolled with the ill-conceived belief that it would be an easy three units," Oliveira recounts in *How Much Earth: The Fresno Poets* (2001), an anthology he co-edited with Christopher Buckley and M. L. Williams. That class included many talented students, including Larry Levis, Bruce Boston, and Greg Pape, and it introduced Oliveira to Fresno's thriving poetry community.

After graduation, Oliveira continued to write while he taught middle school in Armona. He became intrigued with computers after acquiring one for his classroom and developed considerable skill in digital technology. At about the same time, he grew frustrated by feelings that he was losing his creativity under the pressure of hiding his gay orientation in the conservative Central Valley. When friends suggested he move to Santa Barbara to take a computer job and start afresh, he did so in 1981.

After Oliveira won an Individual Artists Award from the Santa Barbara Arts Council, he and another awardee, Cynthia Anderson, used the money to cofound Mille Grazie Press in 1992. He is also a founding editor of *Solo*, a journal of poetry, and is the creator of Poet Cards, a series of trading cards which feature portraits of poets painted by Oliveira. He was selected to be Santa Barbara's first poet laureate in 2000. He has published a chapbook, *In the Presence of Snakes* (2000), and collaborated with Glenna Luschei and Jackson Wheeler in *A Near Country: Poems of Loss* (1999).

In 2002 he moved to Phnom Penh, Cambodia, where he currently lives with his partner, Vichheka Thong.

Paso Robles, San Luis Obispo, San Luis Obispo

All our lives we've been told how things work.
Yet we persist in believing we barely age,
until some warm afternoon, we catch, by surprise,
a reflection in a store window,

hardly recognizing who we have become.
We take our turn at this, as if following
one another up a mountain without a clear trail,
our steps heavy from the need we carry

to be somewhere else,
some place we have never been,
and will not know when we arrive.
I think of a child's game played in the car

with my brothers and sisters as Dad drives
to the coast on Highway 41. Beverly
reads aloud a road sign, *Paso Robles 45 miles,*
and a hubcap falls off. At the next sign,

it's my turn. I say *Paso Robles,* then before
anything bad happens, Robert starts repeating
the line below, *San Luis Obispo, San Luis Obispo,*
and the hubcaps stay on. Never again

will any of us say *Paso Robles* without
adding two charms of *San Luis Obispo;*
towns we drive through on the way
to somewhere else, linked

in a small arsenal of protections
with Latin spells from mass.
We take it as our mission to say
the dangerous words at odd moments,

quickly adding the incantation that saves
someone from bad luck, a preemptive strike
to rid the world of another reason for sadness,
to let us be happy more often than we are.

The way a photograph of a picnic,
kept for years on the dresser, loses
subtle grays in the lawn, and the spread
of the blanket fades into dim folds

of someone's dress until only dark lines
marking the kindness of a smile, or
shadows proving the curve of an eye,
rise from yellowing distance into a face

beautiful beyond the burden of detail;
so small moments of glad luck
stand out in the picture I have become.
In the picture I dream of becoming,

on a beach, the smallest grain of sand visible
between my toes, watching the expanse of ocean
turn to the enormity of sky, there isn't
enough room for all the brown flights of sparrows

I want to remember. I want so much.
Desire hangs from my cheeks in the morning,
pulls with the weight of years; speaks my name
in the music of coffee, the traffic of work;

whispers at me in public places to let my eyes
call to passing faces which don't stop.
Today want follows me as I'm driving
along those same highways of childhood.

Each road sign now points to a place
where I'm missing a friend; and
I want to be like these hills, which are just hills,
skins of straw blades mining August light

for their splendor—no thoughts of travelers
or the roads where every turn is a sadness for someone.
I say I want to go first, but in truth,
I don't want any of us to go at all.

Foolish wants of a person no smarter than myself.
Like magic words, the few tricks I've learned
that charm the universe to my side
to keep pain at bay, only work when they work,

and there remain unavoidable moments
in the elegance of days passing between
light and dark, when hurt is all I can do.

Lucille Lang Day
(b. 1947)

Scientist, poet, and publisher Lucille Lang Day was born in Oakland
in 1947. She was the only child of Richard, a bookkeeper and loan
officer, and Evelyn, a homemaker. She wrote her first poem at age six,
but, painfully shy "when my teacher, Miss Clydesdale, asked me to read
it to the class, I looked down and mumbled," she wrote. "It would be
another twenty years before I could enjoy giving a poetry reading."
A blithe young spirit (self-described as a "juvenile delinquent"), she
dropped out of school at age fourteen to marry Frank Day, and their
daughter was born the following year. She divorced her husband when
she was sixteen, remarried him at seventeen, and returned to school.
She divorced him again at eighteen, received her high school diploma,
and went on to the University of California, Berkeley. Though she still
thought of herself as a poet, she wanted to be a scientist, and she
graduated in 1971 with a B.A. in biology. She continued graduate studies
at Berkeley and received an M.A. in zoology and a Ph.D. in science
and mathematics education, which she completed in 1979.

Day began writing poetry again during graduate school, took a class
with the legendary Bay Area poet and teacher Josephine Miles, and
completed the M.A. program in creative writing at San Francisco State
University. In 1972, she joined the Berkeley Poets' Cooperative, and in
1974 she married Theodore Fleischman, one of the founders of the
cooperative, with whom she had a daughter. They divorced in 1985.
She has worked as a teacher, journalist, and technical writer, and she is
currently director of the Hall of Health, a small museum in Berkeley.
She is a lecturer in education at St. Mary's College of California and the
editor/publisher of Scarlet Tanager Books, which she founded in 1999.

She has published four full-length collections of poetry: *Self-Portrait
with Hand Microscope* (1982), *Fire in the Garden* (1997), *Wild One*
(2000), and *Infinities* (2002). *Fire in the Garden* was selected by Robert
Pinsky for the Joseph Henry Jackson Award. She also wrote the libretto
for *Eighteen Months to Earth* (1998), a science-fiction opera with music
by John Niec, which was performed at two California State Universities.

Reject Jell-O

The man I married twice—
at fourteen in Reno, again in Oakland
the month before I turned eighteen—
had a night maintenance job at General Foods.
He mopped the tiled floors and scrubbed
the wheels and teeth of the Jell-O machines.
I see him bending in green light,
a rag in one hand,
a pail of foamy solution at his feet.
He would come home at seven a.m.
with a box of damaged Jell-O packages,
including the day's first run,
routinely rejected, and go to sleep.
I made salad with that reject Jell-O—
lemon, lime, strawberry, orange, peach—
in a kitchen where I could almost touch
opposing walls at the same time
and kept a pie pan under the leaking sink.
We ate hamburgers and Jell-O
almost every night
and when the baby went to sleep,
we loved, snug in the darkness pierced
by passing headlights and a streetlamp's gleam,
listening to the Drifters and the Platters.
Their songs wrapped around me
like coats of fur, I hummed in the long shadows
while the man I married twice
dressed and left for work.

Stephen Kessler
(b. 1947)

Countercultural poet, translator, journalist, and editor Stephen James Kessler was born in Los Angeles in 1947, the son of Jack and Nina Kessler. He grew up in exclusive Beverly Hills and resented his privileges. "I was really outraged that I'd grown up so protected and then discovered as I went out in the world that not everyone had such comfort to back them up. To me this was just an unbelievable injustice," he writes in "Initiate," one of several published essays about his youthful drug use.

Kessler received a bachelor's degree from the University of California, Los Angeles, in 1968, and in 1969 when he went to the University of California, Santa Cruz, to attend graduate school, he became a true flower child, experimenting often with LSD, the use of which finally triggered a transformative six-month psychotic episode. He spent time in jail and mental hospitals and, after extensive therapy and soul-searching, he emerged feeling he had experienced a breakthrough rather than a breakdown. "All I really lost in the process was the desire to have a respectable occupation, to fit in and conform, and to do something my mother could be proud to tell her friends about," he remembers. He also emerged sure of his creative path. He finished a master's degree at Santa Cruz. He soon began publishing chapbooks and working as an editor at Green Horse Press (1973 to 1979) and Alcatraz Editions (1978 to 1989). For several years, Kessler also edited *Alcatraz*, an irregularly published literary journal. In his introduction to *Alcatraz 2*, Kessler criticized the light escapism of commercial entertainment and proclaimed works of truth-telling as "the only escape worth making." *Alcatraz* was critically acclaimed as a serious alternative journal and featured breakthrough writers ranging from Charles Bukowski to Julio Cortazar and Sharon Olds.

Nostalgia of the Fortuneteller, his first collection of poems, was released by Kayak Books in 1975, and he has since published over a dozen books of poetry and translations. His translations include *Save Twilight* (by Julio Cortazar), *Widows* (by Ariel Dorfman), and *The Funhouse* (by Fernando Alegría). His most recent collections are *After Modigliani* (2000) and *Tell It to the Rabbis and Other Poems 1977–2000* (2001). Poet Juan Felipe Herrera describes the irreverent Kessler as "a language rogue, a bard of solitude, and singer for a greater harmony. He delivers the breakdown, the soulmix of a civilization on the edge, a word runner cutting through Phenomena into the grave pleasures of the Real."

Kessler lives in Gualala, on the Mendocino coast, where he is the editor of the *Redwood Coast Review*.

Cigarette Case

When you come to smoke
with me in the mountains
I like the spark in your eyes
when we light up

the mist over the river reminds me
of the drift our friendship follows
through years of dinners in town
at Chinese restaurants where the beer
in our frosted mugs cooled and seduced
our tongues as we talked

in the pavilion of moonlit religion
tobacco was our sacrament
and the taste of gossip
left us reckless
with useless and beautiful
bad habits

Amy Uyematsu
(b. 1947)

Amy Uyematsu was born in Pasadena, California, in 1947. Her father owned a nursery with her grandfather. Writing was a family tradition; her paternal grandmother wrote haiku and tanka in Japanese and her mother wrote a newspaper column. Before Uyematsu was born, her parents and grandparents were interned in the Japanese relocation camps during World War II, an experience that gave her a powerful sense of her ethnic identity. A member of the *sansei*, the third generation of Japanese Americans, Uyematsu was raised in Sierra Madre, an attractive suburban community where she lived directly behind the public library, which she would walk to through her own backyard. Although living in a mostly white southern California suburb, the family often drove to Los Angeles's thriving Little Tokyo section, and the distance between Sierra Madre and Little Tokyo provided the title for Uyematsu's first collection, *30 Miles from J-Town* (1992). Growing up, Uyematsu sought to reconcile her Japanese identity with the "bleached blond culture of Los Angeles." How did one "stay Japanese and cool?" she and her friends wondered.

She attended the University of California, Los Angeles, where she took an M.S. in mathematics in 1969 and an M.Ed. in 1972. While at UCLA she also helped pioneer the Asian American Studies program, an experience that shaped her literary achievement. "My poetry roots," she has remarked, "can be traced back to my 'yellow power' period of political activism." Uyematsu teaches mathematics at Grant High School in Van Nuys, California, and lives with her son in Culver City.

Uyematsu's *30 Miles from J-Town*, won the Nicholas Roerich "first book" competition from Story Line Press in 1992. Incorporating both Japanese and Japanese American slang, the book chronicles the poet's emotional and intellectual coming-of-age amid the complex and contradictory cultural forces of contemporary California. Uyematsu's second collection, *Nights of Fire, Nights of Rain* (1998) portrays a darker vision of California with the use of fire—the flames of the Watts riots, the inferno of Western wildfires, the emotional fires of violence—as its central metaphor and symbol.

Deliberate

So by sixteen we move in packs
learn to strut and slide
in deliberate lowdown rhythm
talk in a syn/co/pa/ted beat
because we want so bad
to be cool, never to be mistaken
for white, even when we leave
these rowdier L.A. streets —
remember how we paint our eyes
like gangsters
flash our legs in nylons
sassy black high heels
or two inch zippered boots
stack them by the door at night
next to Daddys' muddy gardening shoes.

The Ten Million Flames of Los Angeles

a New Year's poem, 1994

I've always been afraid of death by fire,
I am eight or nine when I see the remnants of a cross
burning on the Jacobs' front lawn,
seventeen when Watts explodes in '65,
forty-four when Watts blazes again in 1992.
For days the sky scatters soot and ash which cling to my skin,
the smell of burning metal everywhere. And I recall
James Baldwin's warning about the fire next time.

> *Fires keep burning in my city of the angels,*
> *from South Central to Hollywood,*
> *burn, baby, burn.*

In '93 LA's Santana winds incinerate Laguna and Malibu.
Once the firestorm begins, wind and heat regenerate
on their own, unleashing a fury so unforgiving
it must be a warning from the gods.

Fires keep burning in my city of the angels,
how many does it take,
burn, LA burn.

Everybody says we're all going to hell.
No home safe
from any tagger, gangster, carjacker, neighbor.
LA gets meaner by the minute
as we turn our backs
on another generation of young men,
become too used to this condition
of children killing children.
I wonder who to fear more.

Fires keep burning in my city of angels,
but I hear someone whisper,
"Mi angelita, come closer."

Though I ready myself for the next conflagration,
I feel myself giving in to something I can't name.
I smile more at strangers, leave big tips to waitresses,
laugh when I'm stuck on the freeway, content
just listening to B.B. King's "Why I Sing the Blues."

"Mi angelita, mi angelita."

I'm starting to believe in a flame
which tries to breathe in each of us.
I see young Chicanos fasting one more day
in a hunger strike for education,
read about gang members preaching peace in the 'hood
hear Reginald Denny forgiving the men
who nearly beat him to death.
I look at people I know, as if for the first time,
sure that some are angels. I like the unlikeliness
of this unhandsome crew—the men losing their hair,
needing a shave, those with dark shining
eyes, and the grey-haired women, rage

and grace in each sturdy step.
What is this fire I feel, this fire which breathes freely
inside without burning them alive?

> Fires keep burning in my city of angels,
> but someone calls to me,
> "Angelita, do not run from the flame."

Christopher Buckley
(b. 1948)

One of the central West Coast's best known poets, Christopher
Buckley was born in Arcata, where his father, William, was studying
communication at Humboldt State College. For several years, the
family followed his radio jobs to Missouri, Ohio, and Kentucky before
returning to California, where his father found work at a local station.
They bought a home in Montecito, an affluent suburb of Santa Barbara,
and Buckley was enrolled in Catholic school. He remembers growing
up in an idyllic atmosphere, spending his time surfing, riding bikes
along the oak-lined streets, and listening to pop music records;
this classic childhood continues to inform his poetry and nonfiction.
A competitive tennis player of high regional ranking, Buckley earned
a mention in *World Tennis* magazine when he was just thirteen.

Buckley enrolled in St. Mary's College of California to study business
but found classes in the English department more interesting. After
seeing poet William Stafford at a reading, he was inspired to become a
poet himself. A casual artist at first, he wrote privately while he taught
junior high, finally deciding to study poetry in graduate school. He went
to San Diego State University, where he worked with Glover Davis,
a student of Philip Levine, and soon after attended the University of
California, Irvine, to get his M.F.A. When he graduated in 1976, he
taught at a series of colleges including Fresno State; the University
of California, Santa Barbara; Murray State (in Kentucky); and West
Chester University in Pennsylvania, where he taught for nine years. In
1998 he moved back to California with his wife (painter Nadya Brown)
and children to take a position as a professor and chairman of the
creative writing program at the University of California, Riverside.
Although he had hoped to return to Santa Barbara, he writes in the
preface to *Closer to Home*, "I can only afford to live an hour north in
Lompoc, in the wind and fog, but it's close to home. I still want to live
forever in this light."

Buckley published his first chapbook, *6 Poems*, in 1975. His first
full-length collection, Last Rites, came out in 1980. Since then he has
published eleven more full-length books, including *Camino Cielo*
(1997), *Fall from Grace* (1998), *Star Apocrypha* (2001), and *Closer to
Home: Poems of Santa Barbara 1975–1995* (2002). Buckley is also the

author of widely read nonfiction, including a memoir, *Cruising State: Growing Up in Southern California* (1994), and *Appreciations: Selected Reviews, Views, and Interviews—1975–2000* (2001). A champion of his native state's literature, he has edited four books, including an important collection of contemporary California poets, *The Geography of Home: California's Poetry of Place* (with Gary Young, 1999) and a major collection of Fresno poets, *How Much Earth* (with David Oliveira and M. L. Williams, 2001). His awards include two grants from the National Endowment for the Arts (1984 and 2001), a Fulbright award to study creative writing in Yugoslavia (1989), and four Pushcart Prizes.

Sparrows

for Gary Soto

Like the poor, they are with us always…
what they lack in beauty is theirs
in good cheer—tails like pump handles
lifting them first among songsters, chiding
citylight or roadside to evening's praise.
Gristmills, hardy gleaners, but for them
the weeds and thorns would find us wanting.
Ragmen to the wind, Sophists of the twig,
they pause to bathe in the ample dust,
and accept the insect as relish to the seed.
So it is becoming to not be too fastidious
when you are rapidly inheriting the earth.

Leaving the West Coast

(after Cavafy)

When suddenly you wake to shouts and music
rising from the street—someone's convertible
top down, quad stereo up all the way—
it is too late to mourn for plans gone
wrong, the life that is abandoning you.
Just as there are always the unaccountable

clouds, dull silverware of the moon, shunting
over the hills, so too there is something
tuneless in sun-burned eucalyptus leaves,
in stars salted obliquely over the sea.
For now, looking out to stars, it takes little
to say they've failed you, to fault your luck
turned black—or there, in that one thick
cluster to the north, to point out the dogs
of academe, the bright tossing of the bones.

And in the drive, a rented truck gleams
like the promise of riches in the east—
two more hours and you cross the desert
by night as if carrying something stolen,
as if the gods ever slept. Isn't it useless
to plead before the moon, to wish things
otherwise? Instead, as one who has seen
this coming all along, nod with emotion
to the dry rose canes and amaryllis,
to every illusion likewise laid bare.

Take your courage out on the balcony while
the star jasmine still breathes for you
into this dream-deep sky. But above all,
don't fool yourself, don't say it was a dream—
not the Spanish villas and red tile roofs,
not the violet air of jacarandas above the streets,
nor lemon blossoms riding a salt breeze
like some lost afternoon of love.
                            It was good
to have been given such a city, this city
you're losing now, for truly you were not
deceived unless you let yourself believe
that bromide about the inheritance of the meek.
You made a living. You were worthy
of sun-stropped days, the azurite bay
calm with the slowed motion of sailing boats
as you drank white wine on Wednesdays

from the deck of the restaurant—palm fronds
going blue, the street lamps pearl-like
in a string beyond the breakwater and the pier.

Look out now on the extravagant procession
of the night—a two-toned '59 Bel Air idling
at the light, at the wheel someone you once knew—
say goodbye as his tail lights dissolve into the dark.
Goodbye as well to streets full of European cars
the colors of money or champagne, to red and white
umbrellas, the Mexican beach cafes—goodbye
even to the generally drunken noise downstairs—
the young waiters, the speculators in land, none
of whom will remember a thing, come morning.

Santa Barbara, 1987

Juan Felipe Herrera
(b. 1948)

The son of migrant farmworkers, Juan Felipe Herrera was born in Fowler, California, in 1948. His father, Felipe Emilio Herrera, and mother, Maria de la Luz Quintana de Herrera, had both come from Mexico as teenagers. An only child, Herrera lived a life of constant movement as his parents followed crops northward as the seasons changed. The family finally settled in Barrio Logan, a Chicano suburb of San Diego, where Herrera began third grade, the first time he had attended school regularly. When he was about to begin junior high school, his family moved from Barrio Logan to downtown San Diego, where Herrera first experienced living in an urban setting. He attended Roosevelt Junior High School, adjacent to museum-rich Balboa Park and, although he had a passion for art and theater, he later chose to major in social anthropology at the University of California, Los Angeles. While earning his degree, he paused for a year to study indigenous theater in Mexico, a journey into his bicultural past and present which "changed [his] life entirely." After graduation, he returned to San Diego to work for the Centro Cultural Toltecas en Aztlan and began what would become his first book of poems, *Rebozos of Love/We Have Woven/Sudor de Pueblos/On Our Back*. Published in 1974, the book is a series of Spanish and English chants to be read aloud, interweaving literature and performance with pre-Columbus myths that celebrate the roots of Chicano heritage. He worked at the Center for Cultural Pluralism at San Diego State University before going to graduate school at Stanford, where he earned his M.A. in anthropology in 1980. By the publication of his second book, *Exiles of Desire* (1983), his work was garnering critical attention. His collection *Facegames* (1987) won an American Book Award, and he enrolled in the Iowa Writer's Workshop. He earned his M.F.A. in 1990 and accepted a position in the Department of Chicano and Latin American Studies at Fresno State University.

Married to the poet Margarita Luna Robles in 1985, he is the father of five children and recently began writing successfully for younger audiences; his work ranges from picturebook memoirs like *Calling the Doves: El canto de las palomas* (2001) to young adult fiction like *CrashBoomLove* (1999). As with his poems, his children's writing is strongly oral and musical, exploring issues of Chicano history, identity, and culture.

Herrera's recent works are mixed media compositions of graphics, found poetry, folk art, performance pieces, and original verse. Projects such as *Loteria Cards and Fortune Poems: A Book of Lives* (2001), a series of incantatory poems based on Mexican *la loteria* and illustrated with linocuts by Artemio Rodríguez, have established him as one of the most original Chicano poets in the United States. *Notebooks of a Chile Verde Smuggler* (2002) was hailed as "a veritable smorgasbord of originality," and critics acknowledge Herrera's ability to concoct a complex recipe from many arts fused by a voice and vision that "show us a writer at the height of creative powers."

Exiles

> *and I heard an unending scream piercing nature.*
> —from the diary of Edvard Munch, 1892

At the greyhound bus stations, at airports, at silent wharfs
the bodies exit the crafts. Women, men, children; cast out
from the new paradise.

They are not there in the homeland, in Argentina, not there
in Santiago, Chile; never there no more in Montevideo, Uruguay
and they are not here

in *America*

They are in exile: a slow scream across a yellow bridge
the jaws stretched, widening, the eyes multiplied into blood
orbits, torn, whirling, spilling between two slopes; the sea, black,
swallowing all prayers, shadeless. Only tall faceless figures
of pain flutter across the bridge. They pace in charred suits,
the hands lift, point and ache and fly at sunset as cold dark
birds. They will hover over the dead ones: a family shattered
by military, buried by hunger, asleep now with the eyes burning
echoes calling *Joaquín, María, Andrea, Joaquín, Joaquín, Andrea,*

en exilio

From here we see them, we the ones from here, not there or across,
only here, without the bridge, without the arms as blue liquid
quenching the secret thirst of unmarked graves, without
our flesh journeying refuge or pilgrimage; not passengers
on imaginary ships sailing between reef and sky, we that die
here awake on Harrison Street, on Excelsior Avenue clutching
the tenderness of chrome radios, whispering to the saints
in supermarkets, motionless in the chasms of playgrounds,
searching at 9 a.m. from our third floor cells, bowing mute,
shoving the curtains with trembling speckled brown hands. Alone,
we look out to the wires, the summer, to the newspapers wound
in knots as matches for tenements. We that look out from
our miniature vestibules, peering out from our old clothes,
the father's well sewn plaid shirt pocket, an old woman's
oversized wool sweater peering out from the make-shift kitchen.
We peer out to the streets, to the parades, we the ones from here
not there or across, from here, only here. Where is our exile?
Who has taken it?

Rachel Loden
(b. 1948)

A self-described "agoraphobic housewife," Rachel Loden was born Rachel Edelson in 1948 in Washington, D.C. Her father, an actor and radio announcer, was blacklisted by Richard Nixon and the House Committee on Un-American Activities in the same month as her birth, events that influenced *The Last Campaign* (1998), her first chapbook, and *Hotel Imperium* (1999), her first full-length collection. "My parents paid an unimaginable price for organizing unions and integrating radio stations," she said in an interview with *Jacket* magazine in 2003. The beleaguered family moved to Berkeley in 1954 and, by the time she was twelve, the family had collapsed. With her mother in and out of hospitals, Loden and her brother were separated by different foster families. Reading became a refuge, especially the alternative poetry she discovered in *The New American Poetry 1945–1960*, edited by Donald Allen. "That was the mother lode," she said. "Here was this group of wildmen and bohemians and rebels and outsiders and people, conceivably, a little like me. It was like coming home when I found that book....By the time I got to the Berkeley Poetry Conference in 1965 and saw Ted Berrigan read and bought a mimeo copy of *The Sonnets*, something like a poetics was well underway."

During high school in Connecticut, she wrote privately, filling small black and white composition books with her poems and journal entries, but she stopped attending school when her mother suffered a breakdown. In the mid-sixties, she moved to New York City's Lower East Side, where she enjoyed "a ragged teenage street life with a cast of anarchists, saints, and oddballs."

Loden eventually returned to Berkeley, where she joined a poets' commune, gave readings, co-edited a magazine, and met many more prominent poets. Without finishing high school or attending college, she was inspired to publish by learning that her grandmother's sister, Rebecca Harding Davis (1831–1910), and her son, Richard Harding Davis (1864–1916), had both been prominent writers in their day. Seeing their books on the bookshelf was a revelation: "Those books were so important because they said that even somebody from a family like mine could write a book. Even a girl. That was liberating." She married a logician and moved to Palo Alto in 1977 when he began working at Stanford University. She has one daughter.

Loden has placed many poems in journals and small presses, but she did not publish a full-length collection until 1999. *Hotel Imperium* garnered strong reviews and won the Contemporary Poetry Series competition from the University of Georgia. It was also selected as one of the ten best poetry books of 2000 by the *San Francisco Chronicle Book Review*, was a finalist for the Bay Area Book Reviewers Award, and is a selection of the Poetry Book Club of the Academy of American Poets. Her chapbook *The Last Campaign* won an award from the Hudson Valley Writers' Center.

My Test Market

Let's fly off to Finland, far
from the long arm of Olestra. There

in bog, arctic fen, and sand
are others who may understand

our epic innocence. Oh, how many
names for snow! and none

with growing market share. Where
are the snows that make no sense

so early in the morning, when the snow
is blue and blowing on the steppes?

Where is the *qanisqineq*,
the 'snow floating on water'?

We may ask Vigdís Finnbogadóttir,
who's not a Finn. She may not know,

but she may point us toward
the northern lights. Her aim is true,

her snowshoes always full of snow.
We won't come back. You come too.

The Gospel According to Clairol

If I have but one life, let me live it.
As a blonde, knowing what I know,
counting among my friends both Kennedys
and diamonds. But darling,
I was waiting in a negligée
beneath a pink and vacant sky
when God demanded Mansfield's ditsy head.
I dreamed I brought it to him
in my Maidenform bra, and woke up
in a cold sweat. James Brown sings
this is a man's world, and any magazine
can tell a girl the way to clean him, mount
him, and give him that last wish in bed.

Leslie Monsour

(b. 1948)

Born in Hollywood, Leslie Monsour moved to Mexico City with her family when she was four. Her father ran a Packard Bell factory there, and Monsour remembers the days fondly. "I had a charmed life in Mexico," she told the *Lummox Journal*. "The capital was a beautiful city in those days....I attended an English school modeled after Eton.... I took ballet lessons from the Royal Academy. I was instructed in Olympic horse jumping by the Mexican cavalry. I formed the Canis Major Club, a fund-raising group to help vaccinate Mexico's stray dogs."

Things changed abruptly when Monsour contracted polio and her mother was diagnosed with cancer. When she was twelve, the family moved to Chicago briefly before returning to California. Then, in the middle of her senior year at Palisades High School, her mother died. When her father took a position at the State Department and was assigned to Panama, Monsour and her younger sister stayed in the United States with a housekeeper. After graduating high school in 1965, she spent a summer in Monterey, Mexico, where she sang folk songs on the local television station. In the fall, she began classes at Scripps College, where she studied for a year before joining her father in Panama and enrolling in Canal Zone College. She spent her free time enjoying the native wildlife, taking horseback rides into the jungle, and performing as a singer and go-go dancer; "I was a little wild!" she admits. After a year in Panama, she moved to Boulder, Colorado, where she earned her B.A. in English from the University of Colorado in 1969.

Monsour eventually returned to California, working as a reference librarian at the Huntington Library, as a news reporter, and as a book critic for the *Los Angeles Herald Examiner*. After her two sons were born, she began writing poetry. "I always thought I would write fiction," she says, "but when I was at home with two small children, I found the interruptions were so many, I was better off struggling with a line of poetry than the chapter of a novel or the opening paragraph of a short story."

In 1987, through a poetry class with Timothy Steele at the University of California, Los Angeles Extension, Monsour was introduced to formal poetry. "I never went back to free verse," she says. Her first chapbook, *Earth's Beauty, Desire, and Loss*, was published in 1998. Her other chapbooks are *Indelibility* (1999) and *Travel Plans* (2001).

She teaches at UCLA Extension and lives in the Hollywood Hills with her husband and children.

Parking Lot

It's true that billboard silhouettes and power
Lines rebuke dusk's fair and fragile fire,
As those who go on living have to prowl
And watch for someone leaving down each aisle.
While this takes place, a tender moon dips toward
The peach and blood horizon, pale, ignored.

I try to memorize impermanence:
The strange, alarming beauty of the sky,
The white moon's path, the twilight's deep, blue eye.
I want to stay till everything makes sense.
But oily-footed pigeons flap and chase—
A red Camaro flushes them apart,
Pulling up and waiting for my space;
It glistens, mean and earthly, like a heart.

Nimis Compos Mentis

The paper table cloth was tastefully bleak,
The misty morning light shone on his cheek,
And made him look alone and masculine.

He talked of Seneca and bad translations,
Of modern critics' lightweight observations;
A bread crumb rested sweetly on his chin.

Behind him, through the glass, the ocean's heave
Uncurled against the sand, beside his sleeve,
As Eros aimed his toxic javelin.

I ducked out of the way to no avail;
It glanced my flesh, injecting quite a cocktail
That blurred my sight and gave my head a spin—

Never mind the coffee we were drinking,
Whatever I said was not what I was thinking:
I wanted to become his mandolin,

And lie across his lap, a dainty lute,
And sing to him and feed him ripened fruit,
While light upon the sea turned opaline.

Instead, this conversation about art
And formal education—God, he's smart!
Such rationality should be a sin.

The hour was up, he had to run, of course;
A handshake and a peck of shy remorse—
Outside, the sea was gray and dull as tin;
It ruled the shore with tedious discipline.

Wendy Rose
(b. 1948)

Wendy Rose was born Bronwen Elizabeth Edwards in Oakland, California, in 1948. Her father was a full-blooded Hopi Indian from Arizona, her mother was of mixed Scottish, Irish, and Miwok Indian blood. "The Hopi side of my family is more sympathetic to my situation," Rose said in an interview with writer Laura Coltelli, "but our lineage is through the mother, and because of that, having a Hopi father means that I have no real legitimate place in Hopi society." This feeling of alienation was increased by the fact that she grew up in an urban environment. Much of her life and work have involved the recovery of identity and coming to terms with what she has called "halfbreedness"— both themes that appeal to many Americans of diverse backgrounds.

Rose studied at several colleges before completing her B.A. in 1976 at the University of California, Berkeley—the same year in which she married magician and judo instructor Arthur Murata. Both while an undergrad and a graduate student working toward her M.A., she managed the bookstore of the Robert Lowie Museum of Anthropology on campus. From 1979 to 1983 she lectured in Native American studies at Berkeley, and she has since held similar positions at California State University, Fresno, and Fresno City College. While teaching, she continues to work as a painter, book illustrator, anthropologist, and poet. With regard to her poetry, Rose clearly wishes to be considered in literary rather than anthropological terms, and she has objected strenuously to having her work categorized in bookstores under non-literary headings.

A prolific writer, Rose has published many literary books in addition to her works of history and anthropology. Her collections of poetry include *Hopi Roadrunner, Dancing* (1973), *Lost Copper* (1980), *The Halfbreed Chronicles and Other Poems* (1985), *Going to War with All My Relations: New and Selected Poems* (1993), *Bone Dance: New and Selected Poems, 1965–1993* (1994), and *Itch Like Crazy* (2002). She has also published a book of prose ruminations, *Academic Squaw: Reports to the World from the Ivory Tower* (1977). In both prose and verse she has been critical of what she calls "white shamanism," a term referring to whites who romanticize and adopt Native American rituals and beliefs to which they have no birthright. A social advocate, academic, and artist, Rose is deeply concerned with intersections of the personal and political.

For the White Poets Who Would Be Indian

just once
just long enough
to snap up the words
fish-hooked
from our tongues.
You think of us now
when you kneel
on the earth,
turn holy
in a temporary tourism
of our souls.
With words
you paint your faces.
chew your doeskin,
touch breast to tree
as if sharing a mother
were all it takes,
could bring
instant and primal
knowledge.
You think of us only
when your voice
wants for roots,
when you have sat back
on your heels
and become primitive.
You finish your poem
and go back.

Timothy Steele
(b. 1948)

Timothy Reid Steele was born in Burlington, Vermont, in 1948. His father was a teacher, his mother a nurse, and his grandparents worked a farm in New England, a subject that surfaces in several of Steele's poems. Since 1966, however, when he entered Stanford University, his life and work have been rooted in California. He took his B.A. at Stanford in 1970, when the English department was still very much under the influence of the formalist poet-critic Yvor Winters and his disciples, and he also did graduate work with one of Winters's strongest advocates, J. V. Cunningham, at Brandeis University, where he earned his Ph.D. in 1977. Steele returned to Stanford twice—first as a Stegner Fellow (1972–1973) and later as a lecturer (1975–1977). He has taught at California State University, Los Angeles, since 1987. Steele's first marriage soon ended in divorce, and in 1979 he married Victoria Erpelding, with whom he lives in Los Angeles.

The mark of strong teachers like Winters and Cunningham reveals itself in Steele's skill with meter, lucid style, and tendency toward rationalism. He has even published epigrammatic verse, but unlike Cunningham's epigrams, his poems tend not to reflect bitter personal difficulties. Rather, like another mentor, Richard Wilbur, Steele often conveys a sense of the joy and awe of living. This is not to say that there is no sadness in his poems but only that Steele's emotions are usually hidden beneath burnished verbal surfaces. He has a knack for displacing the confessional.

The title of Steele's first book, *Uncertainties and Rest* (1979), suggests something of his dual vision, in which the poet's formal poise becomes a stay against undeniable transience. Though the book was respectfully reviewed, it seemed to many an anomaly in a world where most poets had abandoned rhyme and meter. At about this time, the term New Formalism began to enter critical parlance, and Steele has since been associated with that movement. Like many other poets given this distinction, Steele has found the term misleading: "Meter's always been around for anyone wishing to explore it," he remarked; "the only true New Formalist in English is Geoffrey Chaucer." His next small book, *The Prudent Heart* (1983), was followed by more chapbooks, and then a successful full-length volume, *Sapphics Against Anger and Other Poems*

(1986), in which form is again perceived as a way of living with one's human passions. Steele has written admiringly of eighteenth-century writers for their wit and love of reason, dualities displayed in his verse as well, yet in his subjects he is very clearly a man of his own time. *The Color Wheel* (1994) was followed by *Sapphics and Uncertainties: Poems 1970–1986* (1995), which reprinted and slightly corrected his first two volumes.

As a critic, Timothy Steele has made a major impact on his generation, first with his scholarly treatise *Missing Measures: Modern Poetry and the Revolt Against Meter* (1990), a careful argument for the viability of meter that places his subject in the context of the modernist revolution. Steele has also published one of the most substantial textbooks on poetic technique, *All the Fun's in How You Say a Thing: An Explanation of Meter and Versification* (1999), which takes its title from Robert Frost. In these books, as well as in his edition of *The Poems of J. V. Cunningham* (1997), Steele's methodical scholarship makes him an indispensable literary historian.

An Aubade

As she is showering, I wake to see
A shine of earrings on the bedside stand,
A single yellow sheet which, over me,
Has folds as intricate as drapery
In paintings from some fine old master's hand.

The pillow which, in dozing, I embraced
Retains the salty sweetness of her skin;
I sense her smooth back, buttocks, belly, waist,
The leggy warmth which spread and gently laced
Around my legs and loins, and drew me in.

I stretch and curl about a bit and hear her
Singing among the water's hiss and race.
Gradually the early light makes clearer
The perfume bottles by the dresser's mirror,
The silver flashlight, standing on its face,

Which shares the corner of the dresser with
An ivy spilling tendrils from a cup.
And so content am I, I can forgive
Pleasure for being brief and fugitive.
I'll stretch some more, but postpone getting up

Until she finishes her shower and dries
(Now this and now that foot placed on a chair)
Her fineboned ankles, and her calves and thighs,
The pink full nipples of her breasts, and ties
Her towel up, turban-style, about her hair.

Sapphics Against Anger

Angered, may I be near a glass of water;
May my first impulse be to think of Silence,
Its deities (who are they? do, in fact, they
        Exist? etc.).

May I recall what Aristotle says of
The subject: to give vent to rage is not to
Release it but to be increasingly prone
        To its incursions.

May I imagine being in the *Inferno*,
Hearing it asked: "Virgilio mio, who's
That sulking with Achilles there?" and hearing
        Virgil say: "Dante,

That fellow, at the slightest provocation,
Slammed phone receivers down, and waved his arms like
A madman. What Attila did to Europe,
        What Genghis Khan did

To Asia, that poor dope did to his marriage."
May I, that is, put learning to good purpose,
Mindful that melancholy is a sin, though
        Stylish at present.

Better than rage is the post-dinner quiet,
The sink's warm turbulence, the streaming platters,
The suds rehearsing down the drain in spirals
      In the last rinsing.

For what is, after all, the good life save that
Conducted thoughtfully, and what is passion
If not the holiest of powers, sustaining
      Only if mastered.

David St. John
(b. 1949)

David St. John was born in Fresno, a flat and dry landscape that turned California's coastline into "places of profound relief and release." An only child, he followed the example of a tennis pro uncle and played in competitive tournaments until his teenage years. At thirteen, St.John became involved with the Fresno Folk Music Society, and by fifteen he had extended his passion for music by playing in rock and roll bands. St. John came of age when California pop music and singer/songwriters like Joni Mitchell and Jackson Browne dominated the national scene, and music remains an essential literal and metaphorical component of his poetry. As he put it in a 1999 interview, he is especially concerned with "the music of the language, the music of what the poems say."

St. John completed his B.A. at California State University, Fresno, an unlikely place for poetry and an especially unlikely locus for the group that would be known as the Fresno School of poets, of which St. John was a member. He moved from California for the first time to attend the Iowa Writers' Workshop, receiving his M.F.A. in English and creative writing in 1974. He continued at Iowa for two more years as a teaching/writing fellow, and it was not until 1975, when he was offered a job as an assistant professor of English at Oberlin College, that he dedicated himself to an academic career. After two years at Oberlin, St. John moved to Johns Hopkins University and remained there for a decade. In 1987, he returned to his home state, taking a position at the University of Southern California, where he continues to teach.

St. John emerged early as a poet. His first book of poetry, *Hush*, was published in 1976. Numerous collections followed, including *The Shore* (1980), *No Heaven* (1985), *Terraces of Rain: An Italian Sketchbook* (1991), *Study for the World's Body: New and Selected Poems* (1994), *In the Pines: Lost Poems, 1972–1997* (1999), *The Red Leaves of Night* (1999), and *Prism* (2002). He has also published a book of prose, *Where The Angels Come Toward Us: Selected Essays, Reviews, and Interviews* (1995), and has edited and translated other volumes. Among his many awards are the Prix de Rome Fellowship in literature, the O. B. Hardison Poetry Prize, fellowships from the Getty Research Institute, grants from the Guggenheim Foundation and the National Endowment for the

Humanities, the James D. Phelan Award, and the Academy Award for Literature from the American Academy of Arts and Letters.

Influenced by both his youthful days as a folk rocker and his later training in art, David St. John writes poetry that is highly imagistic and richly visual, often imbued with sensual colors and textures. Some have termed it fin de siécle poetry, an acknowledgment of his affinity with late nineteenth- and early twentieth-century French symbolists and surrealists. St. John himself feels a West Coast sensibility in the freedom he has to work outside of the literary pressure so often felt on the East Coast. Having spent more than a decade in the East, he marvels at his good fortune of having been born in California, living and writing near the Pacific Ocean in a region he acknowledges as powerfully paradisiacal. "What could be more glorious?" he asks.

Hush

for my son

The way a tired Chippewa woman
Who's lost a child gathers up black feathers,
Black quills & leaves
That she wraps & swaddles in a little bale, a shag
Cocoon she carries with her & speaks to always
As if it were the child,
Until she knows the soul has grown fat & clever,
That the child can find its own way at last;
Well, I go everywhere
Picking the dust out of the dust, scraping the breezes
Up off the floor, & gather them into a doll
Of you, to touch at the nape of the neck, to slip
Under my shirt like a rag—the way
Another man's wallet rides above his heart. As you
Cry out, as if calling to a father you conjure
In the paling light, the voice rises, instead, in me.
Nothing stops it, the crying. Not the clove of moon,
Not the woman raking my back with her words. Our letters
Close. Sometimes, you ask
About the world; sometimes, I answer back. Nights

Return you to me for a while, as sleep returns sleep
To a landscape ravaged
& familiar. The dark watermark of your absence, a hush.

I Know

> *The definition of beauty is easy;*
> *it is what leads to desperation.*
> —Valéry

I know the moon is troubling;

Its pale eloquence is always such a meddling,
Intrusive lie. I know the pearl sheen of the sheets
Remains the screen I'll draw back against the night;

I know all of those silences invented for me approximate
Those real silences I cannot lose to daylight...
I know the orchid smell of your skin

The way I know the blackened path to the marina,
When gathering clouds obscure the summer moon—
Just as I know the chambered heart where I begin.

I know too the lacquered jewel box, its obsidian patina;
The sexual trumpeting of the diving, sweeping loons...
I know the slow combinations of the night, & the glow

Of fireflies, deepening the shadows of all I do not know.

Laurel Ann Bogen
(b. 1950)

Poet, artist, and lifelong Los Angeles resident Laurel Ann Bogen was born in 1950. Her father, Max, a native New Yorker, was a prizefighter during the 1930s and a New York Yankee farm team baseball player. He met Helen Marguerite Ramsay in 1945, when he was stationed in Los Angeles after World War II, and after the two wed, he took a job as a physical education teacher at Hamilton High School in Los Angeles. Laurel Anne Bogen was the middle of three children and attended the Marlborough School for Girls.

She went on to the University of Southern California, where she became the first freshman to receive the top college award from the Academy of American Poets in 1968 (she won the prize a second time as a graduate student in 1999). She graduated in 1971 with a major in English and minors in speech, anthropology, and cinema, and she returned to the University of Southern California for her M.A. in professional writing, which she completed in 2001. She began writing in 1976 as the book review editor for *BookWest Magazine*. She has worked as a journalist and copywriter and was, from 1998 to 2000, the editor of *Southern California Anthology*, the literary magazine of USC's professional writing program.

Bogen is a well-known teacher of writing in the Los Angeles area, working at the University of California, Los Angeles Extension, the University of Southern California, the Beyond Baroque literary arts center, and Whittier College. She has also led private master's-level workshops for over twenty years. An energetic and witty stage presence known for many years as "the hat lady," she was selected by the *L.A. Weekly* as the "Best Female Poet/Performer" of 1989. She also performs regularly as a member of the poetry performance troupe Nearly Fatal Women, along with Linda Albertano and Suzanne Lummis.

The Disappearing Act, her first book, was published in 1978. Other books of poetry include *The Burning: New and Selected Poems, 1970–1990* (1991), *The Last Girl in the Land of the Butterflies* (1996), and *Washing a Language* (2003). She has also published two books of short fiction and three limited-edition chapbooks.

Pygmy Headhunters and Killer Apes, My Lover and Me

Pigmy headhunters and killer apes play basketball at the Y. The killer apes win but the pigmy headhunters are not sore losers. They take the basketball home and boil it in your cast iron pot.

Hair. Lots of hair. Hairy devils those pigmy headhunters and killer apes. Vidal Sassoon chewed on this dilemma for awhile.

Pigmy headhunters and killer apes had flannel cakes at Musso and Franks. They were very hungry and ate three helpings each. But they wondered about the flesh beneath my flannel.

Pigmy headhunters and killer apes were homesick for Africa. They watched Make Mine Maltomeal on TV. They especially liked the part where John saved the world with gruel. It reminded everyone of home and they all had a good cry.

A cup of coffee is an honest thing. More honest than I am now. Its velocity in my veins throbs with need. I need to tell you this. You make my head hurt like sutures. You make this silly fist a killer.

Bone, hair, water, food. It is morning again. Last night the jungle used my fractured jaws to spear a message. Pigmy headhunters dance while killer apes beat their chest forget about you forget about you forget about you.

Dana Gioia
(b. 1950)

Michael Dana Gioia (pronounced JOY-a) was born in Los Angeles, the oldest child in a working-class family of Italian, Mexican, and Native American heritage. His father, Michael Gioia, was a cab driver who later owned a shoe store. His mother, Dorothy Ortiz, was a telephone operator. "I was raised in a tightly-knit Sicilian family," he once told an interviewer. "We lived in a triplex next to another triplex. Five of these six apartments were occupied by relatives. Conversations among adults were usually in their Sicilian dialect." In the same interview, Gioia recalled his Catholic education: "I was in the last generation that experienced Latin as a living language." Although he was expelled for bad conduct three times from his all-boys Catholic high school, Gioia graduated in 1969 as valedictorian.

Receiving a scholarship to Stanford University, Gioia became the first person in his family to attend college. At Stanford he wrote music and book reviews for the *Stanford Daily*, and later edited the school's literary magazine, *Sequoia*. He spent his sophomore year in Vienna, Austria, studying German and music. After taking his B.A. with highest honors in 1973, he went to Harvard, where he received an M.A. in comparative literature in 1975, having studied with two influential poet-teachers, Robert Fitzgerald and Elizabeth Bishop, as well as the critic Northrop Frye. At Harvard, Gioia decided his ambitions to be a writer had little to do with an academic career. Leaving the doctoral program, he returned to Stanford to earn an M.B.A. "I am probably the only person in history," he has remarked, "who went to Stanford Business School to be a poet." Moving to New York City after graduation in 1977, Gioia worked for the next fifteen years as an executive for General Foods, eventually becoming a vice president. In 1980 he married Mary Hiecke, whom he had met at business school.

During his years in business, Gioia devoted several hours a night to writing. His poems, essays, reviews, and memoirs gradually appeared in such magazines as the *Hudson Review, Poetry,* and *The New Yorker*. His first full-length collection of poems, *Daily Horoscope*, appeared in 1986. Although the book contained poems in both free verse and metrical forms, it was Gioia's formal work that caught the attention of critics, who began debating the merits of what they termed the "New

Formalism." The volume was widely reviewed, winning both high praise and bitter condemnation from different poetic camps.

In 1987 the sudden death in infancy of his first son compelled Gioia to stop writing for nearly a year. When he resumed, he composed the darkly personal lyrics and narratives that made up his second collection, *The Gods of Winter* (1991), which was also published in England, where it was chosen as the main selection by the Poetry Book Society. A decade passed before the publication of his third book of poems, *Interrogations at Noon* (2001), which won the American Book Award. That same year saw his verse libretto for *Nosferatu* (2001), an opera by neo-romantic composer Alva Henderson. To many readers Gioia is best known as an iconoclastic literary critic. When his essay "Can Poetry Matter?" first appeared in the *Atlantic Monthly* in 1991, it ignited an international debate on poetry's place in contemporary culture. The essay became the title piece of his collection *Can Poetry Matter?: Essays on Poetry and American Culture* (1992), which was a finalist for the National Book Critics Circle Award.

In 1992 Gioia left business to become a full-time writer. Although he has occasionally taught as a visiting poet at universities and colleges, including Johns Hopkins, Wesleyan, Sarah Lawrence, Mercer, and Colorado College, he has never taken a permanent academic appointment. Instead, he has modeled his new life after the careers of public intellectuals of an earlier era—writing, reviewing, editing, and lecturing. In 1996 he returned to California to live in Santa Rosa. Since leaving the business world, Gioia has published many other books, including numerous anthologies and translations from Italian, German, and Latin. A second collection of essays, *Barrier of a Common Language: An American Looks at Contemporary British Poetry* was published in 2003. He also served as the music critic for *San Francisco* magazine and as a commentator on American culture for BBC Radio. In 2003, he was unanimously confirmed by the U.S. Senate as the Chairman of the National Endowment for the Arts. He currently divides his time between Washington, D.C., and California.

California Hills in August

I can imagine someone who found
these fields unbearable, who climbed
the hillside in the heat, cursing the dust,
cracking the brittle weeds underfoot,
wishing a few more trees for shade.

An Easterner especially, who would scorn
the meagerness of summer, the dry
twisted shapes of black elm,
scrub oak, and chaparral, a landscape
August has already drained of green.

One who would hurry over the clinging
thistle, foxtail, golden poppy,
knowing everything was just a weed,
unable to conceive that these trees
and sparse brown bushes were alive.

And hate the bright stillness of the noon
without wind, without motion,
the only other living thing
a hawk, hungry for prey, suspended
in the blinding, sunlit blue.

And yet how gentle it seems to someone
raised in a landscape short of rain –
the skyline of a hill broken by no more
trees than one can count, the grass,
the empty sky, the wish for water.

Planting a Sequoia

All afternoon my brothers and I have worked in the orchard,
Digging this hole, laying you into it, carefully packing the soil.
Rain blackened the horizon, but cold winds kept it over the Pacific,
And the sky above us stayed the dull gray
Of an old year coming to an end.

In Sicily a father plants a tree to celebrate his first son's birth—
An olive or a fig tree—a sign that the earth has one more life to bear.
I would have done the same, proudly laying new stock into my
    father's orchard,
A green sapling rising among the twisted apple boughs,
A promise of new fruit in other autumns.

But today we kneel in the cold planting you, our native giant,
Defying the practical custom of our fathers,
Wrapping in your roots a lock of hair, a piece of an infant's birth cord,
All that remains above earth of a first-born son,
A few stray atoms brought back to the elements.

We will give you what we can—our labor and our soil,
Water drawn from the earth when the skies fail,
Nights scented with the ocean fog, days softened by the circuit of bees.
We plant you in the corner of the grove, bathed in western light,
A slender shoot against the sunset.

And when our family is no more, all of his unborn brothers dead,
Every niece and nephew scattered, the house torn down,
His mother's beauty ashes in the air,
I want you to stand among strangers, all young and ephemeral to you,
Silently keeping the secret of your birth.

Garry Gay
(b. 1951)

Photographer and haiku master Garry Gay was born in Glendale, California, in 1951. He attended Moorpark College and earned a B.P.A. degree from the Brooks Institute of Photography in 1974, and he has worked as a commercial and fine art photographer since graduation. He currently lives in Windsor, California, with his wife, Melinda, and their daughter, Alissa.

His earliest poems, written in high school and college, were a variety of blank verse, free verse, rhyme, and meter work. Inspired by Basho's *Narrow Road to the Deep North*, he began writing haiku in 1975. He now writes almost exclusively in haiku, tanka, renku, senryu, and rengay. Rengay is an Americanized version of Japanese linked verse (renku) that Gay created and popularized in the early nineties. The six-stanza rengay follows one theme, and each stanza may be written by a different author, creating a series of haiku-like images that build toward a central idea from varied angles.

Gay's haiku first began appearing in anthologies in 1979, and three years later he published his first two collections, *The Billboard Cowboy* and *The Silent Garden*. His other collections are *Wings of Moonlight* (1993) and *River Stones* (1999). As a photographer and poet, he often pairs his poems with photographs, as he did in *The Long Way Home*, a "visual haiku reading" currently available online that he created in 1998 and presented to the Haiku Society of America.

Gay has been extraordinarily active in forming haiku organizations; he was a cofounder of the Haiku Poets of Northern California, the American Haiku Archives in Sacramento, and Haiku North America (for which he has also served as president). He has also edited several anthologies of haiku.

Haiku

New snow
   the path you made last night
      has gone with you

Slowly…
   the scarecrow
     becomes the snowman

Hole in the ozone
my bald spot…
sunburned

Bald tire
still getting good mileage…
as a tree swing

Family reunion—
again explaining
what a haiku is

Brenda Hillman
(b. 1951)

Brenda Hillman was born in Tucson, Arizona, in 1951 and spent most
of her young life in a desert clime. She recalls early years with parents
Jimmye Standard and Helen (Smith) Hillman in a recent interview:
"My mother, an intense person with a brilliantly fervent and
philosophically inward nature, married something of an opposite: a
large, cheerful dreamer, a handsome caretaker with a purely American
imagination." Young life near the Sonora desert has since influenced
her poetry, not so much in subject matter as a vision of powerful magic
alive in the material world. She remembers a desert "community of
oddities: the horned toad with its collar of spikes. Plants talked back.
Dust waved. Ordinary things were inhabited by a liquid fire that was
simultaneously viscous and particulate, not an easy thing to manage, for
a substance." An extended childhood stay in Brazil reinforced Hillman's
sense of the powers of natural place, and she came to see topographies
of every sort as evidence of a buried spiritual realm.

Graduating from Pomona College in 1973, she spent the next few
years in the poetry program at the University of Iowa, completing her
M.F.A. in 1975. Hillman married the late Leonard Michaels (a former
Iowa Workshop teacher) in 1976, and they had a daughter, Louisa.
They moved to Kensington, California, shortly thereafter, and Hillman
worked as a bookseller in Berkeley while her husband taught at the
University of California. The couple divorced in 1985.

Brenda Hillman's first published book, *Coffee, 3 A.M.*, was published
by Penumbra Press, a small press in Iowa. Including *White Dress* (1985),
she has published six additional volumes to date, most recently,
Cascadia (2001). Widely published and frequently anthologized,
Hillman also edited a volume of Emily Dickinson's poetry in 1985. "My
girlhood poets were Millay, Dickinson and Plath," she writes in a recent
article, and she links them in a shared "longing for the ineffable mystery
of existence, by a confusion about the senses and sensual nature, and by
a passion for the beauty of language and what it feared to approach."

Hillman's poetry is demanding of her readers, dense and frequently
fractured in syntax and shifts of voice, and she is strongly reliant on a
strain of mysticism "from Heraclitus on: first and second century
Gnostics, neo-Platonists, medieval alchemists and Protestants of all

inner light varieties." She has been especially influenced by Gnosticism
and captivated by a long fascination for magic as it flickers forth in the
natural landscape. In *Cascadia* (2001) she explores the formative
geology of California and the Pacific Northwest as evidence of a deeper
spiritual world. Named for one of numerous major tectonic plates that
continue to shape and reshape the region, the volume explores the
many registrations of "the idea of mind-as-earth."

Hillman is married to former U.S. Poet Laureate Robert Hass and has
been on the poetry faculty at St. Mary's College in Moraga since 1984.

Recycling Center

The labeled bins on the California hillside
catch the glint and quarter-glint of passing cars.
Families pull up with their interesting trash
and start unloading: Here, sweetheart,
this goes over in Newspaper. The bundle
hits with a thud. Diet soda cans
spin almost noiselessly down, and the sun-
permitting bottles from a day's pleasure
are tossed into Mixed Glass by the children
who like to hear the smash, unknowable, chaotic,
as matter greets itself and starts to change.

What mystery is inside a thing! If we peered
into the bin, we could see it waiting there,
could believe everything is alive and specific
and personal, could tell by the tilt of one
bottle against the next that it's difficult
to be singular, to have identity, to keep
an outline safe in the terrors of space.
Even the child knows this. Bye, bottle! she shouts,
tossing it in; and the bottle lies there
in the two o'clock position, temporarily itself,
before being swept into the destiny of mixture…

And what if some don't want to. What if some items
in the piles of paper, the orange and blue

envelopes from a magazine sweepstakes, numbers
pressing through the cloudy windows
with our names, some among those pale sheets curled
with moisture, would rather stay as they are.
It's spring; we've thrown away mistakes—
tax forms, recipes, tennis-ball-sized
drafts of poems—that which was blank
shall be made blank again—but what if

that failed letter wants to be a failure,
not go back to pulp, and thought…
Or across the parking lot, where light insists
on changing the dull cans, a few cans don't want
to be changed, though they should want to,
shouldn't they, should want to be changed
by light, light which is called sweet reason,
honeyed, spectra, magnitude, light that goes
from the parking lot looking helpless
though it is matter that has been betrayed…

All afternoon the bins are carried off
by those who know about where things should go,
who are used to the clatter the cans make,
pouring out; and the families, who believed change
would heal them are pulling away in their vans,
slightly embarrassed by that which refused…
The bins fill again with hard substances,
the hills bear down with their fugitive gold,
the pampas grass bending low to protect
what was briefly certain and alive with hope.

Suzanne Lummis
(b. 1951)

One of the central figures in the contemporary Los Angeles poetry world, Suzanne Lummis was born in 1951 and grew up far from the city in which she is so familiar. Descended from a long line of educators, artists, adventurers, and newspapermen, including prominent Los Angeles author, historian, and cultural booster Charles Lummis, she reminds people "I was not born in Los Angeles." She was born in Oakland "by accident" while her parents were living in San Francisco. Both parents worked for the U.S. Secret Service, and her mother, Hazel McCausland, was the third woman ever to be hired by the agency. When her father transferred to the Foreign Service, the family moved to Palermo, Sicily, where they lived until just before Lummis's fifth birthday. When they returned to California, her father, Keith, managed the Clair Tappaan lodge near Donner Summit in the Sierra Nevada.

Lummis spent a year in London when she was twenty-one, then completed her B.A. at Fresno State University in 1974. While at Fresno State, she wrote for both campus papers and co-edited the school's literary journal, *Backwash*. She earned her M.A. in English with a creative writing emphasis in 1978.

Lummis's first published book of poems, *Idiosyncrasies*, appeared in 1984, followed by *Falling Short of Heaven* (1990) and *In Danger* (1999). Central to all three volumes are pop culture, pulp fiction, and the underbelly of Hollywood—what one commentator called "Los Angeles noir life and dog days." Lummis has edited several poetry anthologies, including *Grand Passion: The Poets of Los Angeles and Beyond* (with Charles Harper Webb, 1995). She has also written award-winning plays, including *Night Owls* and *October 22, 4004 B.C., Saturday*, both produced initially in 1989. Strongly influenced by her experiences with performance and theater, she occasionally appears in local theater productions and is a leading figure in Nearly Fatal Women, a poetry-based performance group. She is also a teacher of writing with the University of California, Los Angeles Extension, and she directs the annual L.A. Poetry Festival.

Shangri-la

*In New York they think all of California is like
L.A. And they think everyone in L.A. has a
maid. And they don't believe you if you try
to tell them.*
   — Radio talk show caller

It's true, here we are all blonde,
even in the dark, on Mondays
or in slow traffic.

Even in our off-guard moments,
startled by a passer-by,
we are young.

Here we are all privileged,
even in our sleep. At night
the maids hover like sweetly

tranquilized angels over
the glazed or enameled surface
of things, purring *clean clean*...

It's all true. We girls sip lemon-lime through a straw,
make love, Revlon our nails.
We take our long sleek legs out for a walk,
let them catch light.

When someone snaps, "Get real!"
it hurts us, real pain like we've seen
in the news. So we throw beach robes
over our tans, and cruise down the boulevard
tossing Lifesavers into our mouths,
car radios singing *am*.

New York, is it true
that in the rest of the world it is winter?

Our state is a mosaic of blue pools,
even the Mojave, and the palm trees

line up straight to the Sierra Nevadas,
And the surf comes down slow like
delirious laundry, even near Fresno.

New York, is it true that great cold
makes the bones ache as if broken?

We're sorry we can't be reached
by plane or bus, sorry one can't pull
even the tiniest thing out of a dream.
We're like the landscape inside
a plastic dome filled with water.

But turn us over, then upright.
See?
No snow falls.

Sea Chanty

San Francisco

What winds around your feet
is the shade of tarnished
armor, cold. A cramp
shoots up your bones, drives
you out, like tacks. Out
there, the bulky mass sounds
along its floor. Over
you head, deep, cold. If
you wade out your heart
might crack, you
think. It's smell is salt,
feral, both cold and hot.
You let it burn you white,
sole of foot, of palm, your
heart will snap. It goes like
this: we love the sea, it
doesn't love us back.

Jim Powell
(b. 1951)

Poet, translator, and classicist Jim Powell was born in Berkeley, California, and grew up in the Santa Clara Valley, where both sides of his family settled in the early twentieth century. He studied poetry in classical and modern languages while attending graduate school at the University of California, Berkeley, and he published two chapters of his unfiled dissertation in Northwestern University's literary journal, *TriQuarterly*. From 1988 to 1990, he was poet in residence at Reed College, in Portland, Oregon, where he taught as an assistant professor of English during his second year. His tenure at Reed along with ten months spent in Manhattan during 1976 and 1977 constitute the only time Powell has lived outside of California. He currently resides in Berkeley, where he has taught privately on a limited basis and published poetry for over twenty-five years.

Powell's first published book, *It Was Fever That Made the World*, impressed the poetic scene when it was published in 1989. A collection of original verse and translations, the book brought him acclaim for its precision of image and rhythm as well as its mature understanding of the passion and power of the ancients. Powell is an accomplished and original translator, and he reads Latin, ancient Greek, French, Italian, and German, the last three of which he taught himself. Noting Powell's ability to capture in translation the fluidity, ease, grace, and melodic variety of the Sapphic measure, *The New Republic* termed his book *Sappho: A Garland: The Poems and Fragments of Sappho* (1993) "a brilliant success." His translation won a Bay Area Book Reviewers Association Award in 1993 and a Fred Cody Special Recognition Award in 1994, and it continues to be praised for its depth and beauty.

As a reader and translator of classical poetry, Powell notices similarities between the San Francisco Bay Area lifestyle and the Mediterranean landscape, ecology, and cultures of the ancient Greeks and Romans. His awareness of the history that informs the work of these poets makes him more attentive to the youth and fragility of contemporary culture and of the slow sedimentary accretion of historical depth, fissure, nuance, accommodation.

In addition to his two books, he has also published three chapbooks, *A Victorian Connoisseur of Sunsets* (1999), *California Blue Indian Ghost*

Dance (2000), and *Catullan Revenants* (2001). His work appears in a
number of anthologies, including the *Norton Introduction to Literature*
and the *Oxford Book of Classical Verse in Translation*. He won a
Coordinating Council of Literary Magazines Younger Poets Prize in
1986 and a MacArthur Fellowship in 1993 for his work as poet,
translator, and critic.

from *Time and Light*

Now in the tight trench you go
down beyond shadow at noonday, footsteps
        lost where the long slope
quickens you downward, shouldered on
through the swarming dank and mute trampling
        down where the bloodless press close,
bone white dice in the massive cold and formal hysteria
where forgetfulness rules the Death Lord's gaze,
his sunken island and iron horns,
        his eyeless bride,
you go down
to be lost in a waste of burning cities,
        Dresden, Gomorrah, Dis:
there, haze gnaws at the rust air and communion ends—
there, still pools cast no light back to be lost.

Doxology

Praise monsters if you mean to rise.
Praise them that fatten on their neighbors' hunger
dividing each from each and all from all to make weak prey.
They are above the law because they own the law.
Praise monsters.

Praise clear-cutters and strip-miners,
praise marketeers of poison and delusion,
manufacturers of scarcity and profiteers of famine.
The earth is their inheritance to desecrate.
Praise monsters.

Praise the single eye that blazes
atop the pyramid where we keep our places
by keeping down those underneath and rise by the betrayal
of those who stand beside us. Praise servitude. Praise fear.
Praise monsters.

Last praise the dust thrown in your eyes.
Throw another fistful for yourself!
Can't you see a brighter future glinting in the grime?
Praise your gag and praise your blinders.
Praise monsters.

Gary Soto
(b. 1952)

A prolific poet, playwright, essayist, and children's writer, Gary Soto was born in Fresno in 1952 to Manuel and Angie Trevino Soto. Most of his writing reflects his vivid memories of the sensations and voices of the San Joaquin Valley. Soto's parents were born in the United States, but the culture in their home was Mexican American. His family held jobs in the fields (where Soto worked side by side with them) and at the Sun Maid Raisin packing plant. His father was killed in a work-related accident when Soto was five years old, leaving his mother and grandparents to raise three children. They struggled to make ends meet, and there were few books around. "I don't think I had any literary aspirations when I was kid," he recalls. "In fact we were a pretty illiterate family. We didn't have books, and no one encouraged us to read. So my wanting to write poetry was pretty much a fluke."

He did not plan to become a writer, but he knew he didn't want to spend life as a field worker. After graduating from high school in 1970, Soto went to Fresno City College, where he planned to study geography, that is until he discovered poetry in the college library. He chanced on "Unwanted," by Edward Field, and was immediately struck by poetry's ability to capture his feelings of alienation. He transferred to California State University, Fresno, where he studied with Philip Levine before graduating magna cum laude in 1974. That same year, he married Carolyn Sadako Oda, with whom he has one daughter. They currently live in the Bay Area.

Soto went on to earn a master's degree in creative writing from the University of California, Irvine. In 1977 he took a teaching position at UC Berkeley and published his first book of poems, *The Elements of San Joaquin*. His next collection, *The Tale of Sunlight* (1978), was nominated for a Pulitzer Prize and National Book Award.

Drawn by a desire to reach a young audience, he began writing for children in the 1990s. Since the publication of his first collection, *Baseball in April and Other Stories* (1990), the majority of his numerous publications have been written for children and teens. While many of his characters struggle with racism and poverty, Soto is less interested in political struggles than personal ones. It is estimated that he has sold more than one million books directed at juvenile and adolescent audiences.

He has also written two novels for adults—*Poetry Lover* (2001) and *Nickel and Dime* (2000)—and biographies of United Farm Worker organizers Jessie De La Cruz (2002) and Cesar Chavez (2003). The former field worker has earned fellowships from the Guggenheim Foundation, the National Endowment for the Arts, and the California Arts Council, as well as an Andrew Carnegie Medal and dozens of other awards and honors. His *New and Selected Poems* (1995) was a finalist for the *Los Angeles Times* Book Award and the National Book Award.

One of the reasons for his success is his willingness to, in his words, "take [his] show on the road." He estimates that over a nine-year period he has spoken to over 300,000 teachers and students. As he explains: "My business is to make readers out of non-readers."

A Red Palm

You're in this dream of cotton plants.
You raise a hoe, swing, and the first weeds
Fall with a sigh. You take another step,
Chop, and the sigh comes again,
Until you yourself are breathing that way
With each step, a sigh that will follow you into town.

That's hours later. The sun is a red blister
Coming up in your palm. Your back is strong,
Young, not yet the broken chair
In an abandoned school of dry spiders.
Dust settles on your forehead, dirt
Smiles under each fingernail.
You chop, step, and by the end of the first row,
You can buy one splendid fish for wife
And three sons. Another row, another fish,
Until you have enough and move on to milk,
Bread, meat. Ten hours and the cupboards creak.
You can rest in the back yard under a tree.
Your hands twitch on your lap,
Not unlike the fish on a pier or the bottom
Of a boat. You drink iced tea. The minutes jerk
Like flies.

It's dusk, now night,
And the lights in your home are on.
That costs money, yellow light
In the kitchen. That's thirty steps,
You say to your hands,
Now shaped into binoculars.
You could raise them to your eyes:
You were a fool in school, now look at you.
You're a giant among cotton plants.
Now you see your oldest boy, also running.
Papa, he says, it's time to come in.

You pull him into your lap
And ask, What's forty times nine?
He knows as well as you, and you smile.
The wind makes peace with the trees,
The stars strike themselves in the dark.
You get up and walk with the sigh of cotton plants.
You go to sleep with a red sun on your palm,
The sore light you see when you first stir in bed.

Suzanne J. Doyle
(b. 1953)

Born in Missouri in 1953, Suzanne J. Doyle was a Marine Corps child, and as her father was re-stationed, she moved from her home state to Hawaii (before it was a state) to North Carolina and finally to southern California. Her father was positioned at El Toro and then Point Mugu, just south of Oxnard. When he transferred back to North Carolina in 1974, Doyle stayed in California with a friend and her extended family to complete her education. She attended the University of California, Los Angeles, for one year before transferring to UC Santa Barbara. "There," she says, "I met Edgar Bowers and my education finally began."

Doyle graduated from UC Santa Barbara with honors in English in 1975 and was accepted into the creative writing program at Stanford University, where she studied with Kenneth Fields and Helen Pinkerton Trimpi. She completed her M.A. in 1977 and worked as an English teacher at Castilleja School in Palo Alto from 1976 to 1981. Her first book, *Sweeter for the Dark*, was published in 1982. Her other books are *Domestic Passions* (1984), *Dangerous Beauties* (1990), and an e-book, *Wild Lightning* (2002), produced by *The Formalist* magazine. In a note for *Wild Lightning*, poet Timothy Murphy wrote, "Her forceful rhythms and rhymes are admirably suited to the high seriousness and sorrow that she brings to her themes of loss and love." She was anthologized in *A Formal Feeling Comes: Poems in Form by Contemporary Women* (1994). *Calypso*, a new chapbook, is expected in 2003.

For over twenty years, Doyle has been successful in the business sphere, writing marketing materials for high-tech clients in the Silicon Valley and founding her own company, High/Low Communications, in 1990. In "You Learn to Steal as Much Time as You Can," a 1998 interview with *Poets and Writers*, she talked at length and with wit about the unlikely but surprisingly compatible marriage between poetry and the corporate world. She currently lives in Palo Alto.

Some Girls
for Andrea Vargas

The risk is moral death each time we act,
And every act is whittled by the blade

Of history, pared down to brutal fact,
The fact: we only want what we degrade.
No beauty in the glass makes our loss good,
No hero in the wings can take the stage,
The clash of blood at war with its own blood
Intoxicates us with colossal rage.
A cold beer and the young moon's tender horns
Are shining on the table where we spar
Like women gladiators, bred and born
To wear our father's breastplates, greaves and scars.
There's something not quite right here. We can't talk
Like some girls, who'd say, "Hell, the bastards broke our hearts."
We are a different kind of tough; we hawk
Our epic violence in bleak bars, in bed, in art.

Hell to Pay

When the children are asleep and our old bed
Fills with the drama of your dreams, I head
Downstairs to double check the locks and pour
Neat bourbon down, just like I did before
I ever locked a door, back when I blazed by night
Through danger in a yellow whiskey light.
I am again the wildhearted and lonely,
To whom the angel will appear, the only
Angel I have known, who drags her wings
On dance hall floors while some bright jukebox sings
Of sadness gone too sweet, and I am caught
Up in the arms of all the feeling I have fought.
Against that torn mouth no kiss comes to bless,
I answer to the shame I can't confess,
The old wound coiled up bitterly in me,
The one your love relieves but cannot free.
Hers is the power of darkness, fierce, defiled,
To which fate led me willing as a child,
And though I kneel to Love to serve each day,
I know in time there will be hell to pay.

Jane Hirshfield
(b. 1953)

Born in 1953 and raised in the Lower East Side of New York City, Jane Hirshfield has been influenced by Asian culture and spiritual study since childhood. "The first book I bought for myself was a haiku collection from Peter Pauper Press, so I was drawn to Japanese poetry and ideas from the time I was nine or so." Educated at Princeton University, she was a member of the first class to include women, receiving her A.B. (Phi Beta Kappa) in 1973. Her undergraduate poems won a contest sponsored by *The Nation*, and she worked on a farm for a year before heading to California in a "red Dodge van hung with tie-dyed curtains."

The central event in Hirshfield's life so far was an almost eight-year period of study at the San Francisco Zen Center, which included three years at their rural Tassajara retreat. The spiritual path of Zen Buddhism and the study of Japanese art and literature are still major chords in her work. *Alaya,* her first book, was published shortly after she left formal study, in 1982.

Since that time, she has published four full-length collections of poetry: *Of Gravity and Angels* (1988), *The October Palace* (1994), *The Lives of the Heart* (1997), and *Given Sugar, Given Salt* (2002). She is also the editor of three widely read and cited volumes of translations and essays. The translations in *The Ink Dark Moon: Love Poems by Ono no Komachi and Izumi Shikibu, Women of the Ancient Court of Japan* (1990) focused her more tightly on classic Asian poets and their spiritual path and poetry. *Women in Praise of the Sacred: 43 Centuries of Spiritual Poetry by Women* (1994), one of her most popular collections, broadened her scope and deepened her study.

Hirshfield is also an occasional freelance editor, a visiting writer to many academic institutions, a familiar figure on national reading and lecture circuits, and a presence at summer writing conferences (her *Nine Gates: Entering the Mind of Poetry* (1997) is a collection of essays composed for such occasions). Her many awards include Guggenheim and Rockefeller fellowships and the Commonwealth Club of California Poetry Medal.

While Jane Hirshfield's life has been steeped in Zen practice, she rarely refers to it specifically in her poetry, She is, however, influenced by the discipline it taught her, as it has shaped her "unobtrusive awareness" of instants of life on the planet. She is concerned with the relationship between humans and nature, almost always grounding her poetry in a concrete image of the moment that triggers wide-ranging observations. *Given Sugar, Given Salt,* her most recent collection, was praised for what W. S. Merwin described as having "some of the calligraphic plainness of Chinese painting: a few strokes and a new landscape appears, with a life not seen in it before but at once recognized." Central to the collection is the poem "Tree," a brief lyric of disarmingly direct address, a work that dwells at once on the great power of living things, the unexpected consequence of religious practice, and how a good poet's gaze can elicit a shock of recognition that resounds from a simple instant.

Tree

It is foolish
to let a young redwood
grow next to a house.

Even in this
one lifetime,
you will have to choose.

That great calm being,
this clutter of soup pots and books—

Already the first branch-tips brush at the window.
Softly, calmly, immensity taps at your life.

Leaving the October Palace

In ancient Japan, *to travel*
meant always away—
toward the capital, one spoke only of return.
As these falling needles and leaves speak of return,
their long labors of green tired finally into gold,

the desire that remembered them into place
prepared at last to let go.
Though not for want of faithfulness—
all that once followed the sun still follows it now,
as it turns away.
The courtiers assemble their carriages, fold up their robes.
By daybreak, the soundless mountains bow under snow.

Robert McDowell

(b. 1953)

"Read with your eyes, read with your heart, or slash-slash!" So writes the
Reaper, the editorial persona of poet and critic Robert McDowell. Born
in Alhambra ("in the shadow of the San Gabriel mission") in 1953, he
attended public schools before entering the University of California,
Santa Cruz, where he received his B.A. in writing and literature in 1974.
At UC Santa Cruz he studied with short-story master Raymond Carver
and poet George Hitchcock, editor of *Kayak* magazine and press. After
earning his M.F.A. at Columbia University in 1976, McDowell returned
to the West to teach briefly at Antelope Valley College in Los Angeles
County. It was while living nearby in the Mojave Desert outside
Palmdale that his poetry began to manifest its distinct and then
unfashionable interest in narrative. He moved from California to teach
at the University of Southern Indiana as an assistant professor and writer
in residence, but despite his success in academia, he quit after six years
to write and edit full time, basing his new life back in Santa Cruz.

In 1980, while still in Indiana, McDowell launched *The Reaper*,
an outspoken critical journal that espoused a return to the expansive
culture of storytelling and traditional form in American poetry.
Co-edited with fellow poet Mark Jarman, whom he met as an undergrad
at UC Santa Cruz, *The Reaper* was outspoken, argumentative, and
occasionally outrageous. Frustrated by the prevalence of confessional
self-indulgence and formlessness in contemporary American poetry,
the Reaper (an editorial persona created by McDowell and Jarman)
demanded a return to formal principles and the ruthless excision of the
solipsistic. The Reaper was not always grim, however, and contemporary
readers will do well to read the ten delightful "non-negotiable demands"
reprinted in *The Reaper Essays* (1996), which collects the journal's most
influential essays.

McDowell extended these poetic principles in founding Story Line
Press in Santa Cruz in 1985—the original mission of which was to
advance poetry that tells a story, a return to the poetic lineage of Edwin
Arlington Robinson, Robert Frost, and Robinson Jeffers. McDowell
and Story Line Press have championed the revival of formal poetry and
verse narrative while also publishing a variety of work in other styles.
Two decades and over two hundred volumes of serious literature later,

Story Line has, on their notably multicultural list, published Pulitzer Prize winners, discovered important new authors, and sustained significant writers in mid-career. Now located in Ashland, Oregon, it remains one of the West Coast's leading literary presses.

McDowell's first full-length collection was *Quiet Money* (1987), which revealed his penchant for quirky subjects, dark comedy, and psychological realism. His most ambitious work to date has been *The Diviners* (1991), a book-length narrative poem that chronicles a family saga set in a middle-class Los Angeles suburb, tracing the characters from the 1950s through the 1990s. One prominent scholar praised it as a work that "unabashedly reappropriates the basic privilege of the novelist—to tell the human stories of his time and place. Yet for all its narrative thrust, *The Diviners* remains palpably poetic even if its lyric turns as often come in the evocative juxtapositions between scenes as in the scenes themselves….[It] is one of the most absorbing and original long poems of recent years." McDowell's third collection, *On Foot, in Flames*, which combines short lyrics with mid-length narrative poems, appeared in 2002.

McDowell has also been vigorous in advancing his inclusive populist agenda, editing and co-authoring critical works and anthologies including *Poetry After Modernism* (1991, revised and expanded in 1998) and *Sound and Form in Modern Poetry* (with Harvey Gross, 1996). His wide-ranging interests have also taken him into territory untrod by conventional contemporary poetics, one obvious example being *Cowboy Poetry Matters* (2000), an intelligent and informed survey of cowboy poetry, tales, and essays. Robert McDowell currently lives with his family on a small farm in the Willamette Valley of Oregon.

Where and what you are

I see you in a hundred places. Now
You've gone into the writing where anything
Can happen, and nothing is still. If you know
A short-cut to the flesh, a sweet sighing
From the souls of trees that we might make our own
Just say it, so. At least tonight the moon
Is confident. The riverbed is wet
From a summer squall. Tonight I'll make a bet

With you. I'll wager that the hands that tear
The living from the writing disappear,
As will the distance that is like too many
Clothes between us. Naked in my fear,
You are a light that calms and covers me.
You own me now that you are everywhere.

The Origin of Fear

The Death Month, August, wears a driver out,
But he is almost home, speeding over
A residential street with his windows down.
A woman on a corner screams or laughs,
Her disembodied cackle crashing in.
He turns. He sees a blur of toothy face

And breaks into the sweat of an eight-year-old.
Melting down his hands run off the wheel.
He squirms against an ice chest in the back.
He fixes on the back of his mother's head,
And sticking to the seat he thinks it's beautiful.
An hour goes, an hour of gas and heat,
And he is moaning now, pleading for his
Angel of the Douglas Fir to take him home.
But no Angel appears. "Mother," he wants to say,
But she is driving to the radio.
There is barely room in the car for parent and child,
Barely room for the ice chest, and winter coats
They'll need up north, barely room for breath.
One window, broken, swallows spanking heat.
"Hang on," his mother says. "Hang on
Until we climb out of L.A." To the child
The drive seems longer than a long, long day.
He tries to think of heroes who hang on,
But soon he retches out the broken window.
Empty then he falls back in his seat
And offers up his spirit to the sun.
He thinks he knows Extermination now.

About the time the nausea returns
The Edsel starts up 99, crossing the Grapevine.
There is nothing to the boy but Death hills, Death sun,
Then, miracle of miracles, Death
In images he cannot stand to look at.
Fascinated, he stares at a giant billboard
Where a woman like his mother, dressed
In black, weeps above an open casket.
A gray man in a gray suit lies inside.
Their two small grieving children flank the box
While a black oak highway trails off behind.
And over a hill, in the upper left-hand corner,
A black-cowled, risen Death's Head smiles.
Now the boy can feel his own death near,
Though a merciful distraction might dismiss it.
Instead, a second billboard offers up
A scene so dark the boy stares hard to see it.
A sickly moon. A stormy hill of tombstones.
A mother-woman stands before a grave.
The boy looks at her back and feels her tears.
The chill he feels keeps growing as they come
Up on a third billboard, a fourth, a fifth,
All images of Grieving After Death.
In one a suited shadow-man walks off
With Death, his children's faces wailing as
The veiled mother-woman holds them back;
In another a white cross dwarfs the highway;
In the last the smiling Death's Head waits for traffic
Like a parent willing children home.

The boy will never sleep the same again,
Feeling kinship with the broken billboard
Boy and girl, agonizing over
How his mother and the billboard lady looked
So much alike, how the father left
The billboard family, too.
                          But that was years ago.
Today, at thirty-two, he's driving home
While the billboard painter pours himself a drink

Down south in a hillside home, warming up
His voice for the evening air of the Coliseum.
     ✦   ✦   ✦

The team from *People* magazine, paid
To feel this way, nod and act enthralled.
"Tell us how his word first came to you,"
The writer says. "Tell us how the artist
Turned to God."
               Their subject squirms and swallows,
Crunching on an ice cube while he thinks.

"You ever drive up north on 99?
Ever see my work before the Commission
Tore it down?"
             The *People* people stare,
All natives of the East. Their subject shrugs.

"You know I studied art in Hollywood,
Even shared a studio with Pollock.
I was in a gallery on Melrose then,
And sold a painting every three or four months.
Much good it did! Jackson hit New York
And made it big but I…I was stuck.
It got so I was lucky just to eat,
And then I saw the ad in the L.A. *Times:*

CALL FOR ARTISTS: OPEN COMPETITION!

The State Highway Commission had a plan
To gag the outcry over traffic deaths
By putting up a string of nightmare billboards
Along the most fatal stretch of road in the system.
I heard a thousand artists sent in slides.
A month went by, another week. I sagged,
And for the first time in my life I prayed.
Then I was called.

             I had a week to sketch
A winning series based on traffic death.

The day of the interview my competition
Laid out gory scenes of mangled steel,
Bodies missing arms, legs, eyes—even heads!
His colors were red, autopsy blue-and-white.
Now me, I kept my colors somber—
Blacks and grays—and focused on survivors,
The grieving Left Behind, women and children
Victimized by witnessing. I focused
On their agony and fear and on
Their grinning master, Death. I'd slow cars down
Through paralyzing shock alone! I said
'Suggestion is more awful than the crash.'

"My argument paid off. They hired me.
I had six months, a massive studio,
A vision I believed was worth my skill.
Day and night I sketched and painted Death—
And not Death you might reason out in time.
I sketched and painted Death, and then I prayed.
Michelangelo knew what I'm talking about.
My girlfriend didn't. She said she wouldn't come
To the studio anymore—*couldn't* come—
Because she woke up sweating, dreaming of Death.
One day as I was working on a child
It came to me I hadn't heard from her
In more than a week. And that, my friends, was that.
You wonder did it bother me? Not much.
When the Commission toured my studio
I felt as John the Baptist must have felt
To see the waders changing as they came.
I knew then what my life was all about.
My signs went up.

　　　　　I laid my brushes by.
Often I would drive up north and park
Just close enough to see the Series whole.
Exulting I observed the drivers flinch,
Their cars slow, swerve, then pick up speed.
Face to face they'd seen what God could do!

Fatalities declined because The End
Was there on giant boards for all to see.

"I had seen. I read the Scriptures and
At night I took an elocution class.
I perceived that I must master words.
I'd done the visual, which only reached
The few who drove that way. I dropped my friends
And spoke in bars and unemployment lines.
I pestered the press, pressuring for space,
And one fine Letter to the Editor
Led to my first call to address a church.

"The pastor introduced me as a painter
Who had given up a lie for Him.
As he pointed toward the ceiling I looked up,
Then took the pulpit to correct his gaffe.
Paint was the avenue He took to me;
My failed life was all I had denied.
That little talk was good. Afterward
The congregation greeted me with a found look.
From there the invitations multiplied,
As did my following, and then my friends
From local business clubs made clear to me
The need for one sane voice to make a church.
I guess you know the TV part of it.
Today so many hide out in their homes!
I have to get to them in God's New Way."
                    ✦   ✦   ✦
Nearing ten, the tired man up north
Pours three fingers neat and pulls a downstairs
Chair before the color console screen.
Sitting in the dark, his left hand strokes
The neutral body of remote control,
And thinking of that disembodied scream
He presses. The screen glows,
Then hums and focuses like prophecy.
Feeling a little better, he punches through
The major network news, a canceled show

From nervous boyhood, a horror film.
He doesn't feel enough to stay with these
And turns to cable just in time to see
The L.A. Coliseum from the air.
The next shot is a close-up of a man
Whose manner seems to open like a psalm.
The viewer straightens, leaning into it.
He tries to create distance with a curse,
But turning to other channels he comes back
To that accusing, urgent voice of calm.
The viewer grips his stomach, feeling sick,
And wonders why he just can't go to bed.
He curses the sleep, for him, that lies ahead
And thinks of words he said above a casket,
His hollow mother, rigid, facing him.
He rubs his eyes then drops his hands and stares.
Unbeliever! I know I'll pay for it.
He witnesses, he moans, he fears his bed.

Aleida Rodríguez
(b. 1953)

Now living on "the steepest hill in Los Angeles," Aleida Rodríguez was born on a kitchen table in Güines, Cuba, a small town south of Havana, in 1953. She was the youngest of three children, and her father was a butcher, her mother a cook and factory worker. Shortly after Fidel Castro took control of Cuba in 1959, schools were closed and many children were sent to collective farms in the Soviet Union for "re-education." In a desperate response, the U.S. State Department and the Catholic Church devised Operation Pedro Pan, and Cuban parents sent almost fifteen thousand children unaccompanied to the United States to live temporarily. Rodríguez was airlifted out of Cuba at age nine and placed with a foster family in Springfield, Illinois. While there, she learned English and became a voracious reader. Five years later, she was reunited with her Cuban family and they moved to Los Angeles.

After high school, Rodríguez left L.A. briefly in 1972 to attend the Boston Conservatory of Music, but she later returned to take classes at California State University, Los Angeles, and the University of California, Los Angeles. Rather than pursue a degree, she took classes that interested her, "preferring to follow my own desire line," she says, "which, at that time, included founding and editing my own literary magazine and press." In 1978 she cofounded *rara avis* magazine and Books of a Feather press, the latter the first women-run literary venture of its kind in Los Angeles. Both the magazine and the press focused on underrepresented minority poets and writers, culminating in a 1984 anthology titled Southern California Women Writers and Artists. In that same year, Rodríguez received a Vesta Award from the Woman's Building and a Mayor's Certificate of Appreciation from Tom Bradley for her contributions to the literary arts for women of color.

Rodríguez is a study in patient commitment: she began publishing poems in 1973, received a poetry fellowship from the National Endowment for the Arts in 1982, but did not publish her first collection until 1999. *Garden of Exile* won a PEN-USA West 2000 Award, was selected for a Kathryn A. Morton Prize, and was chosen by the *San Francisco Chronicle* as one of the best books of 2000. She has also published fiction pieces and has had many poems and essays included in anthologies. An arts activist in Los Angeles's lesbian and Latina circles, she writes with a bilingual lexicon. In her own words, "The earth's language is a continuous current, translating the early voices of my trees along the ground. I can't afford not to listen."

Rodríguez is self-employed as an editor and translator and lives in the Elysian Heights area of Los Angeles with a twenty-five-year-old Amazon parrot she raised from a chick.

Lexicon of Exile

> Animals seem to fill their skins, trees their bark, rivers
> their banks, so beautifully, that we cannot help but see in
> their wildness a perfect at-homeness.
> —Scott Russell Sanders

There is no way I can crank a dial,
scroll back the scenery,
perch *sinsontes* outside my windows
instead of scrub jays and mockingbirds and linnets.

There is no way the brightly lit film
of childhood's cerulean sky, fat with meringue clouds,
can play out its reel unbroken by the hypnotist's snap:
You will not remember this.

There is no way I can make that Pan American plane
fly backward, halt the tanks of the Cuban revolution,
grow old in Güines, smelling the sour blend of rice and milk
fermenting in a pan by the chicken coop.

There is no way I can pull the harsh tongue
from my mouth, replace it with lambent
turquoise on a white sand palate,
the cluck of coconuts high in the arc of palm trees.

The trees fingering their dresses outside my windows now
are live oak, mock orange, pine, eucalyptus.
Gone are the *ciruelas, naranjas agrias,*

the *mamoncillos* with their crisp green shells
concealing the pink tenderness of lips.

Earth's language is a continuous current,
translating the voices of my early trees along the ground.
I can't afford not to listen.
They find me islanded in Los Angeles,
surrounded by a moat filled with glare,
and deliver a lost dictionary of delight.

A lingual bridge lowers into my backyard,
were the Fuju persimmon beams in late summer
and the fig's gnarled silver limbs become conduits
for all the ants of the world; where the downy woodpecker teletypes
a greeting on the lightpost and the overripe sapotes fall
with a squishy thud; where the lemon, pointillistically studded
with fruit, glows like a celebration; where the loquat drops
yellow vowels and the scrub jays nesting in the lime
chisel them noisily with their hard black beaks
high in the branches, and the red-throated hummingbird—
mistaking me for a flower—suspends just inches from my face,
deciding whether or not to dip into the nectar of my eyes
until I blink, and it sweeps all my questions into the single sky

Kim Addonizio
(b. 1954)

Kim Addonizio was born in Washington, D.C., the daughter of Bob Addie, a sports writer, and Pauline Betz, a tennis champion. When she was seventeen she learned that her surname had been shortened after her paternal grandparents had emigrated from Italy, and she would later change it back to its original form. She grew up Catholic and Italian American in Bethesda, Maryland. "I got straight As in school and felt superior and alienated," she remembers. After a brief flirtation with undergraduate studies at Georgetown University, she spent a few years leading a rambling and disconnected life, experimenting with drugs and sex in ways that would later inform her poetry. By the late seventies she had made her way to the San Francisco Bay Area, where she has lived ever since. She earned her B.A. summa cum laude at San Francisco State University in 1982 and an M.A. four years later. Addonizio has taught at several colleges and universities.

Addonizio's poetry is characterized by its energy, humor, and utter refusal of gentility. *The Philosopher's Club* (1994), her first full-length collection, is notable for its range of subjects, sexual frankness, and lively use of traditional forms such as the sonnet. She followed that volume with a verse novel, *Jimmy and Rita*, in 1997. Written in lyric bursts, the poem details in raunchy specificity the dissolute life of a Bay Area couple and is one of the boldest experiments in recent verse narrative. Addonizio's third book, *Tell Me* (2000), which was a finalist for the National Book Award, displays less formality in its verse and an even more exuberant attention to sex. Her strict Catholic upbringing is evident not only in her rebellious stance in some poems, but also in her relentless drive toward an honest interrogation of life. In 2003 she received the John Ciardi Award from *Italian Americana*. Among her other works is another novel, *In the Box Called Pleasure* (1999), and, with Dorianne Laux, a textbook titled *The Poet's Companion: A Guide to the Pleasures of Writing Poetry* (1997).

Twice married and divorced, she is the mother of one daughter. She currently lives in Oakland.

First Poem for You

I like to touch your tattoos in complete
darkness, when I can't see them. I'm sure of
where they are, know by heart the neat
lines of lightning pulsing just above
your nipple, can find, as if by instinct, the blue
swirls of water on your shoulder where a serpent
twists, facing a dragon. When I pull you
to me, taking you until we're spent
and quiet on the sheets, I love to kiss
the pictures in your skin. They'll last until
you're seared to ashes; whatever persists
or turns to pain between us, they will still
be there. Such permanence is terrifying.
So I touch them in the dark; but touch them, trying.

Stolen Moments

What happened, happened once. So now it's best
in memory—an orange he sliced: the skin
unbroken, then the knife, the chilled wedge
lifted to my mouth, his mouth, the thin
membrane between us, the exquisite orange,
tongue, orange, my nakedness and his,
the way he pushed me up against the fridge—
Now I get to feel his hands again, the kiss
that didn't last, but sent some neural twin
flashing wildly through the cortex. Love's
merciless, the way it travels in
and keeps emitting light. Beside the stove
we ate an orange. And there were purple flowers
on the table. And we still had hours.

Francisco X. Alarcón
(b. 1954)

Francisco X. Alarcón was born in Wilmington, California, but during his childhood he moved back and forth between Los Angeles and Mexico. Being educated in both English and Spanish, Alarcón developed an early sense of his double identity. "I consider myself bi-national," he says, but that duality has made him both an outsider and insider in each culture; in Mexico he was called "Pancho," an insulting nickname for an Americanized Mexican. Returning to California, he worked briefly as a dishwasher and grape picker before finishing his high school diploma at an adult school. Alarcón eventually earned a B.A. at California State University, Long Beach, and an M.A. at Stanford. He also received a Fulbright Fellowship to study in Mexico City.

In adulthood Alarcón came to terms with another sort of double identity—the alienation of being a gay man in the Latino community. In 1984 he was under public suspicion of a young boy's murder in San Francisco, although he had been giving a poetry reading at the time of the crime. Until the actual murderer was apprehended months later, Alarcón was the subject of prolonged police persecution. This humiliating experience served as the impetus for his first book of poems, *Tattoos* (1985).

Alarcón is a prolific poet. His books include *Body in Flames* (1990), the American Book Award winner *Snake Poems* (1992), *No Golden Gate for Us* (1993), *Sonnets to Madness and Other Misfortunes* (2001), and *From the Other Side of Night* (2002). He has also written numerous bilingual books for children. His poetry is characteristically taut and compressed, the utterance reduced to the fewest words possible, with much being left to implication. The title poem of *Tattoos*, for instance, is only seven words long: "poems / fill up / pages / tattoos / puncture / flesh." Much of his poetry is also written bilingually, with the English and Spanish texts side by side. Alarcón is currently a professor of Spanish and classics at the University of California, Davis.

The X in My Name

the poor
signature
of my illiterate
and peasant
self
giving away
all rights
in a deceiving
contract for life

Frontera

ninguna
frontera
podrá
separarnos

Border

no
border
can ever
separate us

Marilyn Chin
(b. 1955)

Marilyn Mei Ling Chin was born in Hong Kong in 1955. The oldest of four children, she moved with her family to Portland, Oregon, in 1962, where they worked in a variety of restaurants. Her Americanized name reflects her father's fascination with Marilyn Monroe (another sister is named for sex symbol Jayne Mansfield), and her father eventually left the family for a Caucasian woman. As neither her mother nor grandmother knew English, Chin was raised speaking a sub-dialect of Cantonese at home. While growing up, she was encouraged to "have a profession" as a way of achieving the American dream but, she explains, "I guess I became a poet partially out of rebellion...as an oppositional force to my family's practical mindset." The challenge of blending Asian origins and American identity runs throughout her published work, most directly in the poem "How I Got that Name" in *The Phoenix Gone, The Terrace Empty* (1994).

Chin majored in Asian studies and Chinese language and literature at the University of Massachusetts, Amherst, before earning an M.F.A. in poetry from the writing program at the University of Iowa. She came to California in 1982, where she worked as a bilingual counselor and adult-education instructor at a private psychiatric hospital before being awarded a post-graduate Stegner Fellowship at Stanford University. After editing several books of translations, Chin published her first book of original poetry, *Dwarf Bamboo* (1987), for which she was nominated for the Bay Area Book Reviewers Award. *The Phoenix Gone, The Terrace Empty* won the PEN-Josephine Miles Award in 1994, and her third book, *Rhapsody in Plain Yellow*, was published in 2002. She was a Fulbright professor in Taiwan and has been awarded two fellowships from the National Endowment for the Arts and several Pushcart Prizes. She taught at the University of California, Los Angeles, and UC San Diego prior to transferring to San Diego State University in 1989, where she is now a full professor.

As a young poet, Chin was strongly influenced by Adrienne Rich and June Jordan, feminist poets who developed her feeling that poetry should "do something." More recently, throughout her poetry and many essays, she has written about the competing pressures to become completely assimilated into American culture and to maintain her unique Chinese identity. In *Rhapsody in Plain Yellow* she is especially successful in exploring ancient ancestral history and aesthetic traditions, balancing them with a vibrant, erotic, multicultural, and urban spoken-word presence that is uniquely contemporary Western American. Her poems often set images and themes from China against a backdrop of American experience and attitudes, juxtaposing ancient ways with pop culture, heightened formal language with streetwise slang.

Leaving San Francisco

for Weldon Kees

The coldest winter's day I remember
was a summer's night in San Francisco.
An old hoary sage-poet said something like that.
But if you live here you must don a new layer
and let the consequences take over.

No, this is not Xian, where the peasants sold you
Ch'in's tomb for a dollar. No, this is not Kaifeng
where the poets ate cinnabar to become immortals.
The connubial geese have stopped migrating;
they've settled on a stagnant tarn near Anza Terrace.

The Bay swells with winter and waits for reprieve.
This spring the sun will heal the wound on your head
and you'll be famous for a moment. Alone in the motel room
you recite to an audience of one. The crack clambering
the wall deserves a villanelle if not a sestina.

But the Goddess of Mercy is weary; she averts her eyes,
as the demon's dark hand grips us, dragging our regrets
deep into the bay with the bottomfish.
If I float a poem over the Golden Gate Bridge,
Master Weldon, will you answer?

How I Got That Name

an essay on assimilation

I am Marilyn Mei Ling Chin.
Oh, how I love the resoluteness
of that first person singular
followed by that stalwart indicative
of "be," without the uncertain i-n-g
of "becoming." Of course,
the name had been changed
somewhere between Angel Island and the sea,
when my father the paperson
in the late 1950s
obsessed with a bombshell blond
transliterated "Mei Ling" to "Marilyn."
And nobody dared question
his initial impulse—for we all know
lust drove men to greatness,
not goodness, not decency.
And there I was, a wayward pink baby,
named after some tragic white woman
swollen with gin and Nembutal.
My mother couldn't pronounce the "r."
She dubbed me, "Numba one female offshoot"
for brevity: henceforth, she will live and die
in sublime ignorance, flanked
by loving children and the "kitchen deity."
While my father dithers,
a tomcat in Hong Kong trash—
a gambler, a petty thug,
who bought a chain of chopsuey joints
in Piss River, Oregon,
with bootlegged Gucci cash.
Nobody dared question his integrity given
his nice, devout daughters
and his bright, industrious sons
as if filial piety were the standard
by which all earthly men were measured.

+   +   +

Oh, how trustworthy our daughters,
how thrifty our sons!
How we've managed to fool the experts
in education, statistics and demography—
We're not very creative but not adverse to rote-learning.
Indeed, they can *use* us.
But the "Model Minority" is a tease.
We know you are watching now,
so we refuse to give you any!
Oh, bamboo shoots, bamboo shoots!
The further west we go, we'll hit east;
the deeper down we dig, we'll find China.
History has turned its stomach
on a black polluted beach—
where life doesn't hinge
on that red, red wheelbarrow,
but whether or not our new lover
in the final episode of "Santa Barbara"
will lean over a scented candle
and call us a "bitch."
Oh God, where have we gone wrong?
We have no inner resources!

                +   +   +

Then, one redolent spring morning
the Great Patriarch Chin
peered down from his kiosk in heaven
and saw that his descendants were ugly.
One had a squarish head and a nose without a bridge
Another's profile—long and knobbed as a gourd.
A third, the sad, brutish one
may never, never marry.
And I, his least favorite—
"not quite boiled, not quite cooked,"
a plump pomfret simmering in my juices—
too listless to fight for my people's destiny.
"To kill without resistance is not slaughter"
says the proverb. So, I wait for imminent death.
The fact that this death is also metaphorical
is testament to my lethargy.

So here lies Marilyn Mei Ling Chin,
married once, twice to so-and-so, a Lee and a Wong,
granddaughter of Jack "the patriarch"
and the brooding Suilin Fong,
daughter of the virtuous Yuet Kuen Wong
and G.G. Chin the infamous,
sister of a dozen, cousin of a million,
survived by everybody and forgotten by all.
She was neither black nor white,
neither cherished nor vanquished,
just another squatter in her own bamboo grove
minding her poetry—
when one day heaven was unmerciful,
and a chasm opened where she stood.
Like the jowls of a mighty white whale,
or the jaws of a metaphysical Godzilla,
it swallowed her whole.
She did not flinch nor writhe,
nor fret about the afterlife,
but stayed! Solid as wood, happily
a little gnawed, tattered, mesmerized
by all that was lavished upon her
and all that was taken away!

Samuel Maio
(b. 1955)

Samuel Maio (pronounced MY-o) was born in New Mexico in 1955, the second of three children. His father, Ernest, became an educator after working as a coal miner, and his mother, Norma, was an elementary school teacher. Both his parents were born to Italian immigrants but, because the United States curtailed Italian immigration for a short period after World War II, his mother was born in Argentina before her family was eventually admitted into the United States. Maio grew up in southern Colorado, in Aguilar, a small rural town of Italian Americans and Mexican Americans, most of whom worked in the mines and on the railroad. The Italian community was "close-knit and closed," and Maio grew up strongly connected to the ways of the Old Country. His grandparents, with resourcefulness honed by the Depression, gathered mushrooms and greens near Aguilar, reminded of the hillside villages they had left in Italy.

Maio attended the University of Utah, where he earned his bachelor's and master's degrees. He married Kathryn Todd, an elementary school librarian, while still in graduate school. He taught briefly at Trinidad State Junior College in Colorado before moving to California in 1981. It was while earning his Ph.D. in English and modern poetry at the University of Southern California that he was inspired to begin writing poetry for the first time. By the time he completed his Ph.D. in 1986, he had won an award from the Academy of American Poets. After graduation, he lectured at the University of California, Davis, for five years before moving to San Jose State University, where he has taught since 1990. He and his wife have four children and live in Pleasanton.

Moved by the contrasts he witnessed in L.A. between rich and poor, privileged and oppressed, he began reading as widely as he could about Los Angeles and California; he was especially influenced by Nathanael West's novel *The Day of the Locust,* in which West claims that "people come to California to die." The result of Maio's study was the publication of the collection *The Burning of Los Angeles* (1997). The book was named after West's protagonist Todd Hackett's unrealized masterpiece, a vast panorama of the final degradation of 1940s Los Angeles that he hoped (but failed) to paint. Maio's *The Burning of Los Angeles* was nominated for the Pulitzer Prize by the *Los Angeles Times* and was widely acclaimed as a visionary work.

In addition to poetry, Maio has published the critical volume
Creating Another Self: Voice in Modern American Personal Poetry (1995).

Love Song

We have lingered in the chambers of the sea
By sea-girls wreathed with seaweed red and brown
Till human voices wake us...

— "Prufrock"

The new pier is concrete, the streets are paved.
The surfers wear short hair—nothing's been saved
Since you were last here, an epoch ago.
Everyone's faster and thinner than you,
The glassy bodies, ageless, browned, and bleached.

Most stands have changed, but the food still tastes of brine.
And the shore is constant, the day plays on without time.
The games remain, world-class and record-breaking:
A sleek-muscled young man digs and dives and spikes.
The crowd shrieks and shouts his name: "Troy! Troy!"

So once you thought you governed this beach...
Now, twice the age of girls catching you stare.
Surprised to find the sudden urge still there,
You glance away and study partial shells....
And imagine you'd still be received well.

You'd leave your life for the Filipina on skates,
Whose long black hair shines like copper in the sun.
It falls on her back to a perfect "v,"
Pointing to the cleft showing above her bikini.
She circles and smiles past you, smelling of lemons.

Down coast a Latina—or southern European—
Knows you're looking and shifts her hips in the sand.
She slowly smoothes lotion on her almond thighs,

Frowning in a glamorous pose she's gleaned
From the perfumed pages of her magazine.

You'll speak with that blonde, just now parting her legs
To better paint her toenails pink.
She unties her shoulder strings to tan—
What will you say? Your hair matches her zebraskin mat?
You hadn't seen her tall boyfriend playing catch.

Is your stroll over? Is it getting dark?
You've had this afternoon to your old self.
Late boats sail toward port, a family lights a fire and sings.
Your wife is waiting to nurse the baby.
They, too, mock your time and lead back home.

In Memoriam

> *"People come to California to die."*
> —Nathanael West

On this coast where they once arrived destined
To fulfill the now distant promises
Which brought them here, each with a certainty
For success, these young, beautiful women
And thin, handsome men, few tired poets
And many vain prophets—all gathered to die
At last, among the glory and stardom
They created to crown and adore themselves.

Some came with talent enough to remain
Famous just longer than those before them.
Others played to fleeting audiences
Offering rhapsodic applause, when told,
Or unrestrained laughter when needed.
Everyone performed on this shore each night,
The sun benumbing their work by day.

We see them standing like the marble statues
Of the Renaissance they decidedly scorn,
Facing the sea, awaiting their time
To be called forth, impatient to receive
The final praise for their most current words,
Valued less than their attendant manicures.

We know what they will say when asked to speak:
In sands they've buried ancient art and thought,
And the world will end with them, as they've wanted,
Believing their fashion alone of worth.

Counting their gold, numbering their prizes,
They are silenced now and cannot endure.
They fade in the sun with their monuments.

Amy Gerstler
(b. 1956)

Poet, journalist, and creative artist Amy Gerstler was born in San Diego in 1956 and now lives in Los Angeles. She received a B.A. from Pitzer College and has taught at numerous universities, including in the acclaimed creative writing program at the University of California, Irvine, as well as at the California Institute of Technology, the University of Southern California, the University of Utah, Antioch University, Pitzer College, and the California Institute for the Arts. She has been a performance artist and a collaborator with museums including the Los Angeles County Museum of Art, the Santa Monica Museum of Art, and the Whitney Museum. She was also an assistant director at Beyond Baroque, a poetry center in Venice, California. As a journalist, she frequently publishes book and art reviews and is a regular contributor to *Artforum*.

She published her first book of poetry, *Yonder*, in 1981, but it was her sixth collection, *Bitter Angel*, that established her critical reputation. *Bitter Angel* received widespread praise from reviewers and won a prestigious National Book Critics Circle Award in 1990. *The American Book Review*'s Sarah Gorham said the poems in *Bitter Angel* "strip down all basic assumptions about beauty and truth and holiness, and begin to struggle from redemption from the gutter.... Because of this, the drive for ascension in Gerstler's work becomes that much more valiant, and comic." Her other publications include *Crown of Weeds* (1997), which won the California Book Award, and *Medicine* (2000). *Publishers Weekly* describes her work by saying her "best poems are relentless, soul-searching, surreal and wonderfully inexplicable." In addition to nine books of poetry, she has published two books of fiction and the nonfiction text for an edition of artist Darren Waterston's paintings. She received an M.F.A. from Bennington College in 2001, where she now serves on the faculty of the low-residency writing program.

Among her literary influences, Gerstler includes comic books, James Tate, old science textbooks, and popular films. In a recent rumination on classic American film titles she located her interest in pop culture: "[The film titles] often seem to represent an attempt to marry literary and popular culture—'high' and 'low' art interests in a single one to five word phrase....[This] is indicative of a deep, longstanding double urge in the American psyche: to be as learned and rooted in great, historical traditions, as other, older cultures; but also to be original, iconoclastic trailblazers who invent and embrace the new....Americans can be wowed by both princes and gangsters....and by extension, American Poetry reflects this duality of interest and ambition, which gives our language a lot of its personality and punch."

Bitter Angel

You may appear in a tinny, nickel-and-dime light. The light of turned milk and gloved insults. It could be a gray light you're bathed in; at any rate, it isn't quite white. It's possible you show up coated with a finite layer of the dust that rubs off moths' wings onto kids' grubby fingers. Or you arrive cloaked in a toothache's smoldering glow. Or you stand wrapped like a maypole in rumpled streamers of light torn from threadbare bedsheets. Your gaze flickers like a silent film. You make me lose track. Which dim, deluded light did I last see you in? The light of extinction, most likely, where there are no more primitive tribesmen who worship clumps of human hair. No more roads that turn into snakes, or ribbons. There's no nightlife or lion's share, none of the black-and-red roulette wheels of methedrine that would-be seers like me dream of. You alone exist: eyes like locomotives. A terrible succession of images buffets you: human faces pile up in your sight, like heaps of some flunky's smudged, undone paperwork.

Kevin Hearle
(b. 1958)

Kevin Hearle was born in 1958 in Santa Ana, California, to parents who were both elementary school teachers. His mother was a descendant of gold-seeking forty-niners, but his father's family, he explains almost apologetically, "didn't make it to California until either the 1900s or 1910s." Congenital birth anomalies delayed his development, but Hearle—the middle of three sons—went on to serve as student body president, the lead in several school productions, and a member of California's all-state Honor Choir, all while in high school in Irvine.

After briefly attending Claremont Men's College, he transferred to Stanford University, where he graduated with distinction in English in 1980. He earned an M.F.A. from the University of Iowa in 1983, the year he married Elizabeth "Libby" Henderson. In 1991, he earned a Ph.D. in literature from the University of California, Santa Cruz, where he served as poetry co-editor for the literary magazine *Quarry West*. Hearle's first book of poems, *Each Thing We Know Is Changed Because We Know It*, was published in 1994.

Hearle was a founding editor of the Steinbeck Newsletter and is co-editor of *Beyond Boundaries: Rereading John Steinbeck* (2002) and a critical edition of Steinbeck's *The Grapes of Wrath* (1997). He is also an engaged scholar of California literature, especially the work of poet Robinson Jeffers and that of various Native American authors. He has taught in several programs, including at California State University, Los Angeles; UC Santa Cruz Extension; and Santa Clara University. He is currently a lecturer in the English department at Notre Dame de Namur University in Belmont, California.

The Politics of Memory

I was born in a state
where everything had to be named twice
to survive:
where Hangtown became Placerville,
where La Brea couldn't hold its bones
in Spanish, but had to be redundant

and bi-lingual—
The La Brea Tar Pits,
redundant, like the Sierra Nevada Mountains,
in name only;

a state so arid in parts
that what has been forgotten
is blown to dust
in the wind across the alkali flats;
a state where you change the name
and all is forgiven:
where Gospel Swamp
loses both its muck and its religion
to emerge the model suburb.

Fountain Valley forgives the swamp,
but what of Manzanar?
In a state where everything
has to be named twice
or be forgotten,
who will remember Manzanar
(a place in exile
from the maps)? The detention camp is closed,
but I was born into this state,
and, for now, I know the name.

Joshua Clover
(b. 1962)

Joshua Clover was born in 1962 and attended Boston University, where he earned a B.A. in 1987. He then attended the Iowa Writers' Workshop, earning an M.F.A. in 1991. From 1992 to 1993, he was a resident fellow in poetry at the Fine Arts Work Center in Provincetown, Massachusetts, and in 1994 he received a National Endowment for the Arts grant. His first published poems appeared in the *Boston Review* in 1994, and he has since received two Pushcart Prizes and been anthologized in *Best American Poetry 1997*.

Clover achieved recognition when poet Jorie Graham selected *Madonna anno domini*, his first book-length collection, for the coveted Walt Whitman Award in 1996. Graham commented, "With this extraordinary first collection, Joshua Clover has written a poetic manifesto—as well as a prayer-book—for the millennial generation. Part metrical magician, part avant-gardist mathematician, the speaker of this book searches out avenues of belief through a vertigo-ridden array of technical, moral, aesthetic, and imaginative means....A physicist of syllables, a mesmerizing singer of near-apocalyptic lullabies, a rememberer, a forgetter, a reinventer, a destroyer—this poet actually sees the new world we are emerging into."

Clover has been praised as a poet whose work both derives from and quickly goes beyond the traditions of John Ashbery and the Language Poetry movement to create an absolutely original voice. "The Nevada Glassworks," his first published poem and the first selection in *Madonna anno domini*, demonstrates the verbal energy and supersonic vision of his best work as it conflates the creation of the atomic bomb in the Nevada desert with his mother's sexual coming-of-age (and eventually his own conception).

Clover has pursued a parallel career as a journalist of high and low culture, writing on film, music, and poetry in more than 150 articles for *Spin* and the *Village Voice*, where is currently contributing editor. This outlet has both nourished his poetry and brought it to the attention of many readers. Clover has also taught widely, including at the University of California, Berkeley, and St. Mary's College of California, and in 2003 he joined the creative writing faculty at the University of California, Davis.

Bathtub Panopticon

I had a little desert, I kept it in the study,
it was a few inches across, like a hand mirror,
it moved a few inches at a time, like an ice age,
I listened to *Cortez*, the atonal *opéra mécanique*,
you could spend a *siècle* waiting for it to begin,
cancel every date, another *siècle* before the *fin*,
who isn't happy to be a killing machine?,
for 6 years I didn't cut myself shaving, Charlotte,
my razor spoke in the voice of the world historical,
my desert bloomed with thumb sized palms,
had a little Revolution, had a little mirage,
brained me with a calendar, I loved the 2nd act,
"Fear, comma, The Great," the white voice of it,
the score wheeling around like a spinning jenny,
the littlebook smashed like a spinning jenny,
I leaned the bathwater back into your cotton bodice,
oh I knew I was supposed to locate it in the body,
this modest end-of-things, you need the body
to have the phrase "to go to bed," Charlotte,
you need the body to have a place to hang your head,
you send the desert to the Foreign Legion: like the razor says,
"you need the Mountain to have Cortez,"
the razor says "the *avant-garde* is ideologically unsound,
Charlotte, you need the razor to have Marat"

Chryss Yost
(b. 1966)

Chryss Yost was born Christine Elizabeth Anderson in San Diego. After graduating high school, she entered college but soon dropped out and embarked on a series of jobs as a cook, waitress, veterinary assistant, office manager, and pet store employee. She had a child, moved to Santa Barbara, and eventually returned to college, earning a B.A. in English (Phi Beta Kappa) from the University of California, Santa Barbara, in 1997. She won several literary awards in college, and her poems began appearing in literary journals such as the *Hudson Review*, *Quarterly West*, *Solo*, and the *Louisiana Review*.

After graduation, Yost divorced and worked as a marketing communications writer and website designer. She currently works in the Center for Black Studies at the University of California. She is an editor for *Solo: A Journal of Poetry*, and the director of the Santa Barbara Poetry Series. She also co-edited *Poetry Daily* (2003) with Dan Selby and Diane Boller.

Yost's first poetry chapbook, *Escaping from Autopia*, appeared in 1998 and was soon followed by *La Jolla Boys* (2000). Her poems have been widely anthologized, including in the collections *The Geography of Home: California's Poetry of Place* (1999), edited by Christopher Buckley and Gary Young; *Real Living: Poets in Unusual Places* (2002) by Maura Gage; and *The Misread City: New Literary Los Angeles* (2003), edited by Scott Timberg and Dana Gioia. She currently lives in Santa Barbara with her daughter, Cassidy, three dogs, and an enormous tortoise.

Lai with Sounds of Skin

Shall we dress in skin,
our living linen?
bone weft,
pull of masculine
into feminine,
the heft,
the warp, weave and spin
of carded days in

tightly-twisted thin
yarns that we begin—
like wool
like *will,* like *has been,*
spoken to silken—
to spool:
thick bolts of linen,
skin to skein to skin.

Last Night

When the sun sets, and he isn't home, she walks
Not to be waiting, but she leaves a note:
Back soon, her only message, only wish.

After all, she didn't think he'd stay;
No plans, so no surprises when it ends.
The dishes wait unwashed. Bitter stains

Stretch out like shadows on the tablecloth.
Once you believe in finding gods in mortal men
You understand their restlessness as faith;

The way she feels his truth against her skin,
The rough edge of a matchbook, while she grieves
To see her saviors lost, and lost again.

God save the church that she takes refuge in,
The sanctuary given fools and thieves,
This silent girl who loves a man who leaves.

Jenny Factor
(b. 1969)

Jenny Factor was born in New Haven, Connecticut, where her father—
a Los Angeles native—was finishing law school. Her mother grew up in
rural Pennsylvania and instilled in her daughter a love of seasons and
nature, quality reflected in her poetry. Her family returned to California
when she was three and she grew up in Beverly Hills. Myra Cohn
Livingston, working locally as part of California's "Poets in the Schools"
program, was an early influence, nurturing Factor's talent and becoming
a lifelong friend. Factor says, "She taught us that a poet's tools should be
practiced with exercises and repetition, the way a young musician
practices scales." Factor took the advice to heart, writing at least one
poem a day from 1976 to 1988.

Due to a combination of pure talent and careful tutelage, Factor
entered poet Seamus Heaney's master class as a freshman at Harvard
—an unusual honor for an incoming student. She completed a
bachelor's degree in anthropology (summa cum laude) in 1991 and
eventually got her teaching credential. The late nineties were filled
with "crucible events" that would form the core of Factor's first book:
the death of Livingston, the end of her marriage, the birth of her son,
and her coming out as a lesbian. "I had a story to tell," she says. "And
I rediscovered form as a vehicle for doing that."

Factor received her M.F.A. from Bennington College and was awarded
an Astraea Foundation grant in 2000. Her first full-length collection,
Unraveling at the Name, won the 2001 Hayden Carruth Award and was
published shortly after to considerable acclaim. Poet Marilyn Hacker
hailed Factor as a "new voice accomplished both in mind and music.
[She] is a poet with perfect pitch in her mother tongue, its meters
and *mot justes*, a poet who is not afraid to dare the extravagant gesture
(the fifteen-sonnet heroic crown) or to focus on the minuscule event
(a toddler playing trucks in the lamplight)." The poems in Factor's book
use traditional poetic forms and are often strongly autobiographical.
"Battle of Will & Exhaustion, Mother & Child" is often cited as the
poet's work at its strongest. Factor skillfully explores form in combination
with innovative phrasing and striking twenty-first-century issues,
including sensuality, parenting, and self-creation.

Factor lives with her son in San Marino, California.

Scotch and Soda

The front door slipped from its latch and he
came in—the man you're married to and love.
He knows about this "us," this you-and-me,
and it is for his sake that words like "love"
and "tomorrow" don't flow between us easily;
when Ella slips into the groove on the CD
player, your shirt lifts above your head
(my ice settling in my glass, I feel sour beads
of sweat from the summer heat rising
on my skin). Here the truth is surprising
even to me: I don't mind what we *don't*
say, what you *can't* feel. "I love you" is scary.
I mean something lighter. What I want:
Lay with me, wide-eyed, wary.

Rubyfruit

You kissed my mouth as if it were my sex
before you kissed me everywhere, before
that night in Rubyfruit's, my glasses off,
the room elided, darkness stretched, a blur
zip-studded by red pinlights, hemmed and held
a cloth we had no future written on.
Around us, well dressed women stirred the darkness
as they walked. The bar's cold black streak streamed
past willows, necks swayed in to sup and speak.
I learned the map of textures on your cheek.
Benched near the place where others knit limbs, lives,
my body's affirmation—a surprise—
to our established friendship. You confessed—
amazing humming of my flesh's yes.

Permissions

Index

A California Legacy Book

Santa Clara University and Heyday Books are pleased to publish the California Legacy series, vibrant and relevant writings drawn from California's past and present.

Santa Clara University—founded in 1851 on the site of the eighth of California's original twenty-one missions—is the oldest institution of higher learning in the state. A Jesuit institution, it is particularly aware of its contribution to California's cultural heritage and its responsibility to preserve and celebrate that heritage.

Heyday Books, founded in 1974, specializes in critically acclaimed books on California literature, history, natural history, and ethnic studies.

Books in the California Legacy series appear as anthologies, single author collections, reprints of important books, and original works. Taken together, these volumes bring readers a new perspective on California's cultural life, a perspective that honors diversity and finds great pleasure in the eloquence of human expression.

Series editor: Terry Beers
Publisher: Malcolm Margolin
Advisory committee: Stephen Becker, William Deverell, Charles Faulhaber, David Fine, Steven Gilbar, Ron Hansen, Gerald Haslam, Robert Hass, Jack Hicks, Timothy Hodson, James Houston, Jeanne Wakatsuki Houston, Maxine Hong Kingston, Frank LaPena, Ursula K. Le Guin, Jeff Lustig, Tillie Olsen, Ishmael Reed, Alan Rosenus, Robert Senkewicz, Gary Snyder, Dr. Kevin Starr, Richard Walker, Alice Waters, Jennifer Watts, Al Young.

Thanks to the English Department at Santa Clara University and to Regis McKenna for their support of the California Legacy series.

Other California Legacy Books

If you would like to be added to the California Legacy mailing list, please send your name, address, phone number, and email address to:

California Legacy Project
English Department
Santa Clara University
Santa Clara, CA 95053

For more on California Legacy titles, events, or other information, please visit www.californialegacy.org.